PRAISE FOR
MY SON, THE PRIEST

"Kristin Grady Gilger wowed me with an astonishing memoir about her son's joining the Jesuits despite her having high-tailed it out of the Church for the typical reasons—birth control and abortion, the hierarchy and scandals. But over time, his profound faith opened her heart and mind in ways you'll never see coming. I champion this read for reader and cynic alike: it's a page turner. Bravo!" —**Mary Karr**, author of the *New York Times* best-selling memoirs *The Liars' Club*, *Cherry*, and *Lit*

"There is no greater gift than the love of a parent and Kristin Gilger beautifully captures her journey and that of her beloved son Paddy when he makes the decision to become a Jesuit priest. You will be touched." —**Manuel Garcia**, editor-in-chief of *Houston Landing*, and former executive editor, *Austin American-Statesman*

"A generous, insightful, and charismatic young man tells his family he wants to become a Jesuit. What does his loving, fiercely intelligent, lapsed-Catholic mother want? As journalist Kristin Grady Gilger tells us in this gorgeously written account of her son Patrick's journey to the priesthood, 'I wanted it to stop.' Gilger's book is spiritual biography, as much hers as her remarkable son's. If the admirable Paddy Gilger, SJ's example does not incline you more deeply toward the mysteries, demands, and surprises of faith, his mother Kristin's just might." —**Tracy Fessenden**, Steve and Margaret Forster Professor of Religious Studies, Arizona State University

"In this thoughtful and empathetic memoir, Kristin Gilger invites readers to experience the highly unusual journey of a lapsed Catholic mother whose son decides to become a priest. With a journalist's eye for observation and detail, she invites us into the story of how her son's radical life choices have impacted their family. This book asks tough questions about faith and the Catholic Church, but never loses sight of the humanity at the center of all things." —**Kaya Oakes**, author of *The Defiant Middle: How Women Claim Life's In-Betweens to Remake the World*

"Kristin Gilger has written a startlingly intimate and honest book. She doesn't just grapple with her son's decision to become a priest, but with the complex way the institution has impacted her Catholic family over generations, served as a vehicle for social politics she abhors, failed in the most hideous ways in its responsibilities, and yet nonetheless offered the structure and rituals that still help those of us who pray, 'Lord I believe, help my unbelief' to find a pathway to God." —**Phil Klay**, author of *Redeployment*, winner of the National Book Award

"There are many ways to approach a book like *My Son, the Priest*. It's about Paddy [Gilger's son], of course, and the Jesuits. It's about the legions of people who have become disillusioned with the Catholic Church and the many who have stayed despite the Church's obvious problems. It's about parents and the lengths they will go to in to keep their children close. But more important, it's a beautifully written tale of spiritual growth, the kind of growth that happens when you're brave enough or scared enough or inspired enough to open yourself up to the possibility of the life of faith." —**James Martin, SJ**, author of the *New York Times* bestsellers *Jesus: A Pilgrimage* and *Learning to Pray*

"A masterfully told tale about a mother and her son, a readable, relatable book that asks and answers challenging questions about family and spiritual growth. This is not only a story for Christian readers, although they will find special meaning in the compelling exploration of the Jesuit lifestyle and of the rich and often troubled history of Catholicism. It is not just a book for mothers and sons, although the author explores the nature of that relationship with the keen and revealing eye and clear voice of a journalist. It is a book for all who wrestle with questions of faith, who wonder about our paths as we watch our children choose their own." —**Mark Hass**, author of *The Days Before Tomorrow*; Arizona State University professor

MY
SON,
THE
PRIEST

A
MOTHER'S
CRISIS
of
FAITH

KRISTIN GRADY GILGER

FOREWORD *by*
JAMES MARTIN, SJ

MONKFISH
BOOK PUBLISHING COMPANY
RHINEBECK, NEW YORK

Paperback ISBN 9781958972939
eBook ISBN 9781958972946

Library of Congress Cataloging-in-Publication Data

Names: Gilger, Kristin, 1952- author
Title: My son, the priest : a mother's crisis of faith / Kristin Grady
  Gilger ; foreword by James Martin, SJ.
Description: Rhinebeck, New York : Monkfish, Book Publishing Company,
  [2025] | Includes biographical references. | Includes bibliographical
  references.
Identifiers: LCCN 2025024903 (print) | LCCN 2025024904 (ebook) | ISBN
  9781958972939 paperback | ISBN 9781958972946 ebook
Subjects: LCSH: Gilger, Patrick | Catholic Church--United
  States--Clergy--Biography | Jesuits--United States--Biography | LCGFT:
  Biographies
Classification: LCC BX4705.G528 G55 2025 (print) | LCC BX4705.G528
  (ebook)
LC record available at https://lccn.loc.gov/2025024903
LC ebook record available at https://lccn.loc.gov/2025024904

Book and cover design by Colin Rolfe

Monkfish Book Publishing Company
22 East Market Street, Suite 304
Rhinebeck, New York 12572
(845) 876-4861
monkfishpublishing.com

For all seekers, that they may find their way.

CONTENTS

FOREWORD

My Son, the Priest tells the true story of a young man's journey to become a Jesuit priest—written by his mother, a lapsed Catholic who, as you will soon read, must come to terms with her son's decision or risk losing him. It is an intimate, sometimes irreverent, and often searing examination of faith, family, and reconciliation.

Ever since I decided to enter the Jesuit Order almost forty years ago, I've read a lot of books about spiritual formation, the Jesuits, and the experience of being a priest. I'm going to estimate that number somewhere in the dozens, ranging from the very good (like Thomas Merton's *The Seven Storey Mountain*) to the very bad, which I will, as Jesuits say, "pass over in silence." But I've never before encountered one written from the point of view of a woman, a feminist, and a mother. The result is a completely refreshing account of everything from the highly unusual Jesuit formation process (aka training), which includes sending would-be priests off on pilgrimages with $35 in their pockets, what happens when a priest falls in love, and what it's like to share living quarters with a bunch of guys who don't always make perfect housemates.

If you've ever wondered how Pope Francis got to be pope (after all, he was a Jesuit who made a public promise not to "strive for" or "ambition" high offices in the church), why Jesuits may be harder to

spot than other priests, or what the virgin martyrs may still have to
say to us, the answers are here in this captivating memoir.

The book also takes on tough issues, from the church's history of
sexual abuse to its treatment of women, and asks some challenging
questions, such as whether it's possible to be Catholic, liberal, and a
feminist all at the same time. By the way, that's an important question for men and women alike.

As I read, I remembered my own mother's response to my decision to join the Jesuit order in 1988. It was Mother's Day (I know,
bad timing) when I told her that I planned to quit my corporate job
and enter the Jesuit novitiate. She heard me out, then began to cry.

I can't blame her really: I didn't go to a Catholic school, was a
desultory Mass-goer, and had given her no warning. She (and my
dad) eventually came around, particularly once they realized that I
wouldn't be locked away somewhere where they would never see me
again. Another important factor in their change of heart was simply meeting other Jesuits. In time, both my mom and dad became
extremely supportive of my life as a Jesuit and celebrated with me at
my First Vows, my ordination to the priesthood, and my Final Vows.
But I wish I had a copy of this book to give them way back when!

The Jesuit Order (more formally known as the Society of Jesus)
isn't all that big—there are about 2,000 of us in the United States,
so it's no surprise that I should know Kristin Gilger's son Patrick, or
Paddy, as the rest of the world calls him. My good friend Paddy is
just as smart and thoughtful and charismatic as his mother describes
him. Today he's a beloved teacher, an in-demand spiritual director,
a promising scholar, and a compassionate priest: all in all, a great
Jesuit. I'm proud to know him—and his mom. And given his many
talents, Paddy could have done anything with his life. The fact that
he chose to be a Jesuit priest reminds me of how inexplicable, how
countercultural, that choice can seem.

There are many ways to approach a book like *My Son, the Priest*.
It's about Paddy, of course, and the Jesuits. It's about the legions of
people who have become disillusioned with the Catholic Church

and the many who have stayed despite the church's obvious problems. It's about parents and the lengths they will go to in order to keep their children close.

But more important, it's a beautifully written tale of spiritual growth, the kind of growth that happens when you're brave enough or scared enough or inspired enough to open yourself up to the possibility of the life of faith.

James Martin, SJ is a Jesuit priest, editor at large of America Media, consultor to the Vatican's Dicastery for Communication, and the author of many books, including The New York Times *bestsellers* The Jesuit Guide to (Almost) Everything; Jesus: A Pilgrimage; *and* Learning to Pray.

INTRODUCTION

or an institution that has clung for centuries to ritual and tradition, the Catholic Church can still manage to pull off a pretty good surprise now and then. The recent election of the first American pope, Cardinal Robert Francis Prevost, now Leo XIV, was certainly one of them. The election of his predecessor, Pope Francis, was another, but for different reasons altogether.

It started when Francis' predecessor, Pope Benedict, resigned, something no pope had done for 600 years or so. I first got word of the resignation from my son, Patrick, who was writing about it for the website he ran for the Society of Jesus, the order of Catholic priests better known as the Jesuits.

The thought of my son writing a big news story on deadline tickled me. I have been a journalist for a long time, and I was sure I could be of some help, so I jumped in to do a little research for him. The history of popes, it turns out, is pretty entertaining. For instance, did you know there was once a Pope Hilarius? Patrick did not think that was very funny, so I kept digging.

Historians believe there are ten popes who have stepped down since about 200 CE, most of them in the Middle Ages. The reasons for some of their departures are a little murky. Still, it's clear that several were deposed by emperors, one resigned to prevent a schism of the church, and one appears to have been caught in a bribery scandal. But my hands-down favorite is Pope Celestine V, who literally ran away from the Vatican in 1294.

Celestine, a hermit, apparently didn't want to be pope in the first place. But the cardinals, who had been unable to agree on a choice for more than two years, decided Celestine was their man. Several of them climbed up to his mountain retreat to fetch him back to Rome. With no other recourse, Celestine holed up in a hut he had built in the Vatican, dithering over every decision while people pretty much did whatever they wanted. After just three months, one of the cardinals took matters into his own hands. He inserted a reed into the wall of Celestine's hut and, pretending to be the voice of God, ordered him to quit. Celestine, whether convinced by the voice (which one imagines must have been very deep and very scary) or just fed up with the whole thing, agreed, whereupon a new pope was named and promptly locked him up. Celestine managed to escape into the woods but was soon recaptured. He died a prisoner a few months later, and no subsequent pope has ever taken the name Celestine—for understandable reasons.

Patrick gave Celestine only a passing mention in the article he posted on *The Jesuit Post*, saying Celestine "was a hermit and a bit overwhelmed by being asked to be pope." I personally think he missed all the best parts.

A few weeks after the flurry of excitement over Benedict, Patrick texted me with even bigger news: "Holy crap," he wrote. "This is completely surprising."

An Argentinian Jesuit, Jorge Mario Bergoglio, had been elected the new pope, taking the name Francis. It was the first time in the 472-year history of the Society of Jesus that a Jesuit would be the leader of the Roman Catholic Church, which, as Patrick put it, "makes us one for 266 papal elections."

"But wait," I protested. "I thought a Jesuit couldn't be pope."

This, as it turns out, is normally—but not always—the case, for reasons that date back to 1540 when the Society of Jesus was founded by an Italian ex-soldier who read a book about Catholic saints and decided he could be one, too.

It is perhaps a little too revealing of the kind of mother I am that one of my first thoughts upon hearing about this new Pope Francis was that Pope Patrick doesn't have such a bad ring to it. It seemed to me the path had been cleared. Patrick's friends on Facebook had pretty much the same reaction. "Gilger SJ – 2043!" one friend wrote on his wall. "I'm voting Paddy," declared another, using the nickname Patrick acquired in college. Someone else wrote: "I see you liked a comment about your candidacy for pope, Paddy. I think that just got you disqualified."

The Jesuit Post, or TJP as the editors call it, is run by the young, hip, cool Jesuits, who had plenty of fun with what you would think would be pretty serious business for anyone of the Catholic persuasion, especially if the new pope just happens to be your boss. But that didn't stop the editors, who posted articles that included "You Can't Take It With You: Papal Edition," which recalled for readers the last four popes "who have gone to the big Popemobile in the sky," and "Habemus Me, or Twelve Reasons Why I Should Be the Pope," a tongue-in-cheek commentary by James Martin, who is probably the best known Jesuit on the planet due to his stint as the official chaplain of "The Colbert Report" on Comedy Central. "(Ah-ha," I thought when I came across Martin's posting. "I'm not the only one with ambitions!")

The Jesuits had some serious things to say as well. Martin wrote another piece posing the question: "Does the Holy Spirit Choose the Pope?" His answer: "Yes, and no and it depends"—a Jesuit answer if I've ever heard one. Other Jesuits wrote about the sometimes controversial stands the new pope took while he was a cardinal, denouncing same-sex marriage and adoption in Argentina while supporting civil unions for gay couples and passionately decrying the human trafficking of girls and women. They pointed out examples of his simplicity—picking up his own bags, trying to pay his own hotel bill, and calling home to cancel his newspaper subscription when it became apparent that he would be staying in Rome for a while.

In articles and an exuberant video that they made for the TJP website, Patrick and other young Jesuits around the country brimmed over with excitement and hope. Matt Spotts described what it was like when he and four or five other members of his Jesuit community in St. Louis got word that white smoke was wafting from St. Peter's. They rushed from their rooms to the TV, jockeying for position and arguing about which channel to watch, never imagining it would be one of their own who would walk out onto that balcony.

Then they heard the name "Bergoglio," and the place exploded. They began calling, emailing, tweeting, and posting the news when, Spotts wrote, "Pope Francis started to pray. Quietly and simply, he started to pray the prayers we all know. The Our Father. The Hail Mary. And as I looked around our crowded, eclectic, digitally exploded TV room, it was like the new pope had flipped a switch. Those of us locked in our frantic digital cycles stopped—and then calmly lowered our screens, set down our phones and began to pray ... the very first prayers many of us had ever learned."

It's easy for me to imagine them in their frayed living room, bowing their heads and reciting the familiar prayers out loud, matching the new pope word for word. They would not have felt even a little embarrassed by this, and they would have celebrated later with a good bottle of wine over dinner.

In the two decades since my son joined the Jesuits, I have come to know many men like these, but I have never really understood them. They have chosen a life that is as countercultural as you can get in twenty-first century America. They take vows of poverty, chastity, and obedience, and, even then, they must wait a decade or more before they are ordained as priests and are allowed to do the things priests aspire to do: say Mass and administer the other sacraments of the Catholic Church.

They study—endlessly, it seems—and the reward for all their degrees may be nothing more than grinding work in a prison or parish, a school or soup kitchen, a homeless shelter or immigration detention center. They go where they're told to go and do the work they're told to do, and when they're too old to work any longer, they go to a Jesuit retirement home where they live out their days praying with other old men.

They have no cars, no paychecks or homes of their own. They live together in communities that may range from a handful of men to several dozen, and these are the only families they will ever know outside of the ones they were born into because, as long as they are Jesuits, they will never be allowed to marry or have children of their own.

This is the life my son has chosen. It is most certainly not the life I would have chosen for him.

I am not foolish enough to have ever thought I could dictate what my son would do or become—or even what he would believe. No parents get to decide those things for their children, as much as they might like to, but that surely does not prevent many of us from trying. One mother I know uses the word "betrayal" to describe her son's decision to write and perform music instead of going to medical school like she did. My sister cannot fathom the choices her son has made that drive him in and out of rehab for alcohol abuse. The Mormon parents of a friend pray incessantly that their daughter will return to the religion that gives their family identity and meaning.

Like me, these parents wonder how what they did—and who they are—influenced their children, or whether they had any influence at all.

I had been spending a lot of time thinking about this notion of influence when a friend suggested another reason for my son's choice. We were having coffee at an outdoor café and I was telling him that my son, against all reason, had decided to become a Catholic priest. "We didn't even raise him Catholic!" I said, my voice rising. I had expected curiosity and maybe even a little sympathy about the wayward things children will do, but instead he said something that made me sit back hard in my chair.

"God has his hands on your family in such a special way," he told me gently. Something inside of me shifted when he said those words: It was the first time I had considered whether God had anything to do with it.

If my friend was right, I thought, God had something to answer for. I kept trying to picture the kind of life Patrick would lead and where he would end up—no doubt lonely and alone in one of those retired priest homes where no one would come to visit—because who would come?

When I shared these worries with my son, he tried to reassure me. "I'm close to a lot of people," he said. "Everyone on earth is alone or lonely at times. And people want good priests in their lives. I've really felt that. I feel very valued and loved in those moments when people let me in."

"But who will hug you?" I pressed. This was motherly chicanery at its best. Patrick loves hugs. He is a world-class hugger.

He laughed and started telling me about some especially good hugs during last Sunday's Sign of Peace.

"What?" I asked, before remembering the part of the Catholic Mass during which members of the congregation—some of them perfect strangers—shake hands and sometimes hug. It's the part I don't like.

But Patrick wasn't listening. "It's awesome," he said. "One of the best things about being a celibate man is I can be a safe person for women, and where else can they find that today? It seems to me that everyone really, but women especially, sometimes just need to be with someone and feel safe and taken care of and know that there's not an ulterior motive." Besides, he said, if it was hugging I was worried about, there was no need; Jesuits are really good at hugging.

So that's it, I thought. There's no way I'm going to talk him out of this. So, I started in on God. Being out of practice, it was a short conversation.

"Why is it that you have to take my only son?" I began, but that sounded a little too biblical for me, so I tried again. "He's being asked to make a choice no one should have to make. He wants a family—a wife and children. But he also wants to be a priest, and no matter what he chooses, he loses a huge part of what can make him happy. He shouldn't have to make that choice. No one should."

I have the feeling that if God had spoken to me that day, he would have agreed: The world is an imperfect place and some choices are hard—harder than they have a right to be.

I do not know whether the things that happen to us are the consequence of fate or luck or the choices we make or whether they are, as my friend suggested, the result of God's hand in our lives. All I know is that my son's choices have forced me to reconsider a lot of things in my life, including my decision to leave the church he now so loves. I have come up hard against the question of what I believe and what I don't.

And so, I ask: What if my son is right? And what if he is not?

I have no way of knowing where such questions will lead or even whether they have answers. I can only retrace what is certain, fingering the bits of evidence and hoping that in the end I will have built a bridge from what I know to what I don't know—a link from the possible to the impossible.

CHAPTER I

THE RECRUITER

"People who are called tend to violate the rules
in annoying ways."
KATHLEEN NORRIS, *Cloister Walk*

The priest pulled up to the house in a shiny red convertible, my son and a college classmate with him, laughing and tousled. They were running late, and the weather, they said, was entirely to blame: The day was just too pretty not to take the shiny red car out for a spin, top down, music blaring.

I didn't mind. Dinner was a stovetop affair and wouldn't suffer from the wait, and, in any event, I wasn't in a hurry to hear what they had to say.

Patrick, a twenty-year-old college junior, had told us he was considering joining the Jesuits, the Catholic religious order formally known as the Society of Jesus, and that the director of vocations for his province wanted to visit our home. This immediately made me think of child protective services. Would he be inspecting the premises like a caseworker, making sure there were no dangerous objects laying around and the showers were clean? Or would he be more interested in checking our religious credentials? I was reasonably sure the showers were clean, but if it was religious credentials he was interested in, he was almost sure to be disappointed.

It was true that we had sent Patrick to Creighton, a Catholic university in Omaha, Nebraska, and that our daughters were attending a Catholic high school in our new city of Phoenix, Arizona, where I was an editor at the local newspaper. But those decisions had not been for religious reasons; we had just been seeking the best education we could find (and afford) for our children.

It also was true that my husband, Gary, went to our neighborhood Catholic church for Mass on most Sundays, but his primary incentive was to drop off our donation—required in order to get a discount at the girls' high school. But when we all went to services, which wasn't all that often, we headed to an Episcopalian church. I hadn't stepped inside a Catholic church in years.

No, I thought as I watched Warren Sazama, SJ, walk up the driveway. You really couldn't call us Catholic at all.

I had rehearsed each of these points and was ready to insert them into the conversation at the first opportune moment, but Father Saz, as Patrick called him, didn't seem to be in a hurry to bring up religion. Casual in his short-sleeved shirt and khaki pants and oversized glasses, he did his best to put us at ease, chatting about the friend who had loaned him the car and asking our daughters about their classes and the sports they played. Their brother, he told them, had made quite an impression at Creighton, where he had been an undergraduate for almost three years. And it wasn't just in the classroom; it was hard to find anyone on campus who didn't know who he was.

While Father Saz talked, my eyes kept wandering to the place where the white collar of a priest should have been. Had he left it at home because he thought it would put us off? Maybe at this very minute it was laying on the front seat of the sporty car, and he would snap it on as soon as he left. He seemed sincere, charming even, but what about that hair? Wasn't it a shade darker than the brownish mustache? He had to be in his fifties. Was he trying to look younger, more hip, than he really was?

It wasn't until after the plates were cleared and coffee was served that Father Saz got to the point. "So, has Patrick told you of his interest in becoming a Jesuit?" He looked around the table, taking us all in—Patrick, his two younger sisters, my husband, my mother-in-law, and me.

We all nodded tentatively—except for my mother-in-law, who just stared into her coffee. Because she was almost totally deaf, it was hard to tell whether she was making a statement ("I don't like your question, so I'm going to ignore you.") or whether she had heard the question at all.

"I'm sure there's a lot you want to talk about, but first let me tell you what I see in Patrick," Father Saz said. "I think he may have a genuine vocation. It's early, of course, and we think he should finish college first, but this seems to be a calling from God."

He's a *recruiter*, I thought. He could be representing a college football team or the United States Army. He's got Patrick all but signed, sealed, and delivered, and he's here to make sure mom, dad, grandma, and the kids don't screw it up. I wondered if he got a bonus for every man—or boy—he signed.

You send your son off to college and you think that in a few years you might get a call, and he'll announce that he's bringing someone home, someone he wants you to meet. But then that someone turns out to be a recruiter hawking a lifetime of poverty, chastity, and obedience. What college kid in his right mind would sign up for that?

"Well," I began, turning to our guest. "I have to say that I have a few problems with the Catholic Church."

Father Saz didn't flinch. "Of course," he said. "I understand you didn't raise your son Catholic."

"That's right. We raised him Episcopalian because I couldn't tolerate the Catholic Church's stand on social issues like abortion and birth control. I couldn't condone how the church treats women. There was just so much I didn't agree with, and it didn't seem right to go on pretending that it was okay. It wasn't okay. It still isn't."

I looked around the table for a response. No one said a word. My husband, always the peacemaker in the family, looked almost as uncomfortable as the girls, who squirmed in their seats. Patrick just glanced at Father Saz and shrugged as if to say, "I told you what my mother is like."

Finally, Gary spoke up. "My wife and I were both raised Catholic and went to Catholic schools," he said almost apologetically. "We were married in the Catholic Church and baptized our children in the church. It wasn't until Patrick was about six that we decided to leave."

"He was seven," I corrected. "He had just made his First Communion, and there was this priest ..." I stopped, struck by the ludicrousness of the situation. Here I was, trying to explain to a priest why I was no longer a Catholic and trying to understand why my son not only wanted to be a Catholic, but a *priest*—a prospect I found not a little alarming.

I was thinking about this when Father Saz, no doubt trying to shift the conversation away from what's wrong with the Catholic Church (there's a lot, he had already conceded), asked another question: "Are you surprised by Patrick's interest in becoming a priest?"

My husband and I answered the question at the same moment.

"Yes," he said.

"No," was my answer.

I startled myself with that "no." I hadn't thought before saying it. But while I had not exactly anticipated the priesthood, I wasn't surprised that Patrick was drawn to the kind of life the Jesuits offer.

For years, Patrick had claimed he would be a baseball player— if Superman or Teenage Mutant Ninja Turtle didn't turn out to be viable options. As a teenager, he dreamed of one day being a doctor like his uncle, a pediatric gastroenterologist in Texas. "I could help people," he said, although he also was clearly drawn to the status that went with being a doctor. It seemed to me that he wanted to do good, but he also wanted to be part of an elite group, *recognized* for doing good.

These are aspirations I can understand. The priesthood—especially in a church I found so troubled and troubling—was something I was going to have a lot more problems with. This is my fault, I thought. I was the one who had insisted he go to Creighton; I was the one who found a way to send him there.

*   *   *   *

When it came to choosing a college, Patrick had just one preference—to be close to his girlfriend. During his senior year in high school he had fallen in love with Anne, a striking girl who looked like she could have stepped out of a Caravaggio painting, and the two of them were so cuddly and cute that the rest of the family could hardly bear to be around them.

Patrick's sisters would snort in disgust at what they considered an inordinate amount of kissing and handholding. Patrick mostly ignored them, just as he was doing his best to ignore the fact that high school would not last forever. When Anne decided to attend a small, private college in the Pacific Northwest near where we lived, Patrick declared he would go there, too. But I thought the college was too parochial, too expensive, and too close to home. Patrick needed to go somewhere where he would be challenged, where he could learn to be on his own.

Creighton, I thought, would be a good choice. It was a respected private college, not too large and not too expensive, and it offered, for a brief time, a great deal for a young man who had long talked about becoming a doctor: Undergraduates who maintained a high GPA would be granted admission to Creighton's medical school— the same medical school Gary's brother had attended. Plus, my son was only seventeen, and while I wanted him to be independent, I didn't want him to be completely on his own. In Omaha, he would be close to the sprawling Grady clan—my parents, most of my brothers and sisters, and dozens of cousins.

I knew Creighton was a Catholic university, one of two dozen or so Jesuit-run universities around the country, but that held no great significance for me. We had visited the summer before and walked around the campus, an oasis of green lawns and stately buildings on the edge of Omaha's somewhat disreputable downtown. We had stepped inside the dim cathedral-like church in the center of campus and remarked on its beauty, but there wasn't much else that distinguished the place as Catholic or even religious. There were no Jesuits in sight, and, in any event, I was far more interested in the size of classes and the state of the dorm rooms than in spotting a priest. Patrick's interest (and to some extent Gary's) seemed to be focused almost solely on the very pretty coed who was our tour guide.

A few months later, Patrick was accepted and offered a financial aid package that included a small—very small—scholarship. It wasn't enough. With three kids, a mortgage, two cars, and just one-and-a-half jobs between Gary and me, we couldn't make the numbers work. So I picked up the phone and called the financial aid office.

"Patrick is a great student," I told the disinterested man on the other end of the line. "He has high SATs and top grades in high school. He's a varsity soccer player and co-captain of the swim team. He just won a national science award. Can't you do anything?"

All of that had been taken into consideration, the man said, and there was nothing more that could be done.

"What if I told you he's interested in becoming a priest?"

I have no idea where those words came from. I had never consciously thought them before, and Patrick certainly hadn't said anything about the priesthood. He had, in fact, been insisting that he and Anne were going to get married someday, even if I did persist in sending him to godforsaken Nebraska for college. Maybe the calculating, manipulative side of my brain had taken over. It made sense: If they thought Patrick might have a vocation, maybe they would cut the price.

"That wouldn't make any difference, ma'am."

I hung up the phone, close to tears. I didn't know why, but I felt strongly that this was the right place for Patrick. I just didn't know how to get him there.

I placed another call, this time to the woman in the admissions office with whom we had met during our visit the summer before. I reminded her that when she had reviewed Patrick's file, she had said he shouldn't have any trouble getting a good scholarship. The one offered, I pointed out, was pitiful. She said it did seem a bit low, and she would see what she could do.

A couple of days later, we got a letter congratulating Patrick on his new, substantially improved, scholarship. I thanked God—and sent the woman in the admission's office flowers.

* * * *

Creighton suited Patrick. Away from his family, he seemed to be trying on new versions of himself. He gave up soccer and swimming, sports he had loved and played all his life, and signed up for fencing and choir. He joined a faith-sharing group and began helping out at homeless shelters in North Omaha and attending candlelight Masses on Sunday evenings at St. John's, the campus's beautiful stone church built in the English Gothic style of tall spires and grand arches. Bored with math and science, he enrolled in philosophy and theology classes and read Thomas Merton and Friedrich Nietzsche, the Bible and Plato.

The more he read and studied, the more interested he became in Catholicism and the more he began talking about it with other students who were amused and a little surprised to find someone in their midst who didn't know how to pray the rosary or say a proper Hail Mary. A friend taught him the rosary one day as they sat in a car in the school parking lot. Another wrote out the words for the Hail Mary on a Post-It note and slipped it into his jacket pocket.

Sometime during his junior year, Patrick called to tell us he was taking confirmation classes and needed proof that he had been baptized and had completed the sacrament of Holy Communion. At first, I was confused. Why was he taking confirmation classes when he had already been confirmed while in high school? He told us he wanted to be confirmed again, this time as a Catholic, not an Episcopalian. He was converting.

Gary and I had no strong objections to this; we had always told our children they were free to join whatever religion they liked when they got older. We located Patrick's baptismal certificate in a little metal box where we kept our marriage license and insurance policies, but the only evidence we could find of his First Communion was a single photo of him in his little blue suit. In it, his hands are folded, and his face is solemn as he looks up at the priest who is about to hand him the communion wafer. We made an eight-by-ten copy of the picture and mailed it to Omaha.

Later that year, Patrick sent home a paper he had written for a theology class in which he tried to explain what was happening to him. "I feel as though I am realizing pieces of the truth of who I am in God's eyes, who I have become thus far, who I have yet to become," he wrote. "I do not know what this means; I do not know how to react to myself or how to tell people how it is that I am changing. But I am."

I remember our conversations during this time as being mostly about money and his decision to change his major from pre-med to philosophy. I would ask what in the world he planned to do with a degree in philosophy. He would tell me there is nothing more important than figuring out the meaning of life, nothing more critical than learning how to live well. I would tell him he needed to get a part-time job. He would say, "What do I need money for?"

It was true that he didn't seem to need much. Moreover, he had a habit of giving away what little he had. We gave him a bicycle to get around campus, but when we came to visit, it was gone. He'd given it to someone who *really* needed it, he said. It was the same with the new sweater he got for Christmas and the guitar he had been so eager to learn to play.

"Damn it, I didn't give it to you to give to someone else," I would say about the latest missing item. My complaints made no impression; he kept giving things away.

One day during his junior year, he had just left the slightly shabby apartment he shared with a friend and was walking to campus to attend a meeting of his faith-sharing group. It was a cold day, and he was wearing a heavy jacket (as he describes it, "an awesome, knee-length, brown leather jacket worn with the collar flipped up like Marvin Gay"). He was praying the rosary, fingering the beads in his pocket as he walked, when he noticed two boys—barely in their teens—coming toward him. He looked up to say hello as they passed.

A few moments later, he heard the boys turn back in his direction. They drew close behind him, and suddenly he felt the press of cold metal to the back of his head. "Give us your money," one of them said. Patrick took out his wallet, which held a total of two $1 bills, and handed it over his shoulder to the boys. They grabbed it and ran. Only then did Patrick turn around.

Later that night, Patrick called home to tell us what had happened. He was calm, but I was not. I demanded that he call the police immediately—and that he never, ever, walk in that neighborhood by himself again.

Several weeks later, a detective called Patrick to say the boys had been caught. "Did he want to press charges?" Patrick asked what would happen to them: Would they get counseling; go to juvenile hall; get locked up? The officer told him they would probably go to jail, and Patrick asked if he could have some time to think it over. He waited a couple of hours before calling back to say he had decided not to file a complaint.

"Why not?" I practically screamed when he called to give me the news. "They put a gun to your head, for God's sake. You could have been killed! They should go to jail!"

His response was classic Patrick: "Mom," he said, "Nothing good would come out of it. They have enough strikes against them in their lives."

I do not mean to suggest that my son is a saint—or anything close to it. Too often, he can be domineering and judgmental, self-absorbed, and absolutely convinced he is right. He is excessively competitive and maddeningly rational. (As I write this, I can hear all three of my children saying: "And who does that remind you of, mom?" And they would have a point. If genetics didn't dictate these traits in my son, it's almost certain that seventeen years of living with me encouraged them.)

If Patrick isn't good at a game, he simply won't play it. For his sixteenth birthday, we gave him a set of golf clubs, but after a few years of humiliation, he gave up the game. To this day, he refuses to play golf. He'll walk the course with his dad, but he won't touch a club. "It's not good for me to get that angry," he says. In college, he once confessed that he felt competitive even when it came to religion: He wanted to be the "most spiritual" of all his friends.

My son has other faults. His sisters tease him about caring a little too much about his looks, and it's true he favors J. Crew shirts and fitted jeans. He runs to stay in shape, determined to keep a thirty-inch waist.

Someone meeting him for the first time might remark on his height (at five feet, seven inches, he's short compared to everyone but my brothers). They might notice the carefully groomed beard, the slim build, and stylish glasses. But what they remember is his huge smile and the way he has of looking directly at you and talking to you as if you matter. It's disarming and a little alarming the way he draws people in. At parties I have seen people who have never met him before and have no interest in Catholicism pass him around like a particularly delectable hors d'oeuvre. I don't know what they say to him or what he says to them, but I know the conversations are almost always intense. He can find out more about a person in five minutes than I can in five hours.

This is not to say that he tells people what they want to hear. He has no interest in parsing the truth, even to spare someone's feelings. "You're getting old, mom," he tells me (with love, he insists), even after I've repeatedly warned him there are some things people—especially certain people—do not want to be reminded of.

While he has far more patience with people than I could ever hope to muster, he can be severe and unbending with himself. During the summer between his junior and senior years of high school, he was picked for a soccer team that would represent the states of Oregon and Washington in tournaments in Italy, Germany, and Austria. Despite a no-drinking team rule, the boys couldn't resist taking advantage of the lower drinking age in Europe. When they went out to party at night, Patrick stayed behind in the classroom that had been made over into a dorm room, reading the same book over and over and writing in his journal—a journal I later discovered.

Reading it made me sad for my son who clearly did not fit in. "I'm not going to drink, and I feel a little out of place," he wrote. "I wish some of my friends who have values equal to mine were here ... I should go to sleep soon so that I don't see them when they come in." It wasn't until he was a junior in college that he drank a beer for the first time. (Under the Jesuits' influence, he now favors single malt Scotch.)

Surprisingly, Patrick has become less dogmatic, less rigid with others and himself under the influence of the Catholic Church. In addition to the occasional Scotch, he tries hard to listen and withhold judgment and even to let others win once in a while. He struggles to be humble, not to think about himself too much, not to ask for too much. You can see him hesitate over whether to pack the new sweater he got for Christmas, weighing how much he needs it and whether he should ask me to take it back. He'll open his mouth to disagree with something I've said and stop abruptly, willing himself into silence. He's learned to say things like, "Of course, I don't really know for sure" or "I respect what you're saying" before offering his views. He tries so hard the effort sometimes seems physical, as if he's trying to master his body along with his mind.

Of course, there are the occasional slips, the times when I can still see the youngster who could not bear to lose, the young man who competed to be the most spiritual among his friends.

One Christmas around the time Patrick entered the Jesuits, Gary's extended family gathered in Winter Park, Colorado, for a reunion. For nearly a week, twenty of us—cousins, aunts, uncles, brothers and sisters—shared a rental house. We went skiing and sledding, drank what may have been an overly large quantity of beer and wine, cooked huge dinners, and played loud, silly games.

Late one afternoon, Patrick and his cousins discovered an old board game of Risk. It's a game with a single, clear goal: world domination. It is Patrick's kind of game. For the next two nights, he and his cousins played with a vengeance. Two of the boys, still teenagers, were novices at the game, so Patrick would take them aside, drape an arm over their shoulders and offer friendly advice: "Make an alliance with me," he'd suggest. Or: "Why not leave Ukraine alone and go after Irkutsk instead? It's a much better target."

In the end, he won two straight games, and his cousins were howling in outrage. "Hey, it was all good advice!" Patrick shouted over the uproar, trying hard not to laugh. No one believed it for a minute.

CHAPTER 2

"BABY JESUITS"

"My brothers, like all of us, were sent into
a world that, when you try to love it, leaves
stretch marks on the heart. Neither they nor
we go forth alone."
PATRICK GILGER, SJ

In late August of 2002, Patrick and I flew to St. Paul, Minnesota, where he would begin his training to become a Jesuit priest. As we walked up to the low brick house on Summit Avenue, across the street from the governor's mansion where the former professional wrestler Jesse Ventura was then residing, I thought about the day four years earlier when I had dropped him off at college. He was just seventeen and not ready to let go. We puttered around his dorm room for as long as we could, then I stood up to say goodbye. He hugged me so long I thought I would have to peel him off me to get out of the room.

This time, I was the one who would have trouble saying goodbye.

On the plane ride to St. Paul, I kept asking Patrick, "Are you sure you want to do this? You can change your mind, you know. No one will think less of you." He said he was sure—at least he was sure he wanted to give it a try.

A few weeks earlier, we had received a letter telling us what Patrick would need for his two years in the novitiate:

- A normal wardrobe of school and dress clothes for winter and summer—enough to last for two years.
- A pair of black dress shoes and a dark suit if he had one.
- Whatever edition of the Bible he found most helpful.
- One credit card, with a zero balance.
- Enough spending money to get him there.
- A passport.

Novices, or "Baby Jesuits" as they are sometimes called, could bring a simple camera or a musical instrument if they played one, and they were allowed a travel alarm, small radio, or Walkman, but no personal stereos or televisions. Items such as soap, bedding, and towels would be provided. Each novice would receive an allowance of $75 a month to buy any other personal items he needed.

The list seemed pretty spartan to me, even by priestly standards, but novices were expected to begin living lives of poverty, chastity, and obedience immediately—which included "freeing themselves of material possessions" even though they would not take permanent vows for another two years.

The letter also informed us that Patrick needed "to settle his personal affairs." This didn't amount to much as he had no income to speak of and hardly more possessions than the list allowed—although he did have to part with a few favorite shirts, some books, and a lot of CDs. His student loans would be deferred and, if he stayed long enough, the Jesuits would pay them off. (If I had known that, I thought upon reading the financial boilerplate, we would have taken out more college loans!)

The Jesuits had sent along a daily schedule, referred to by the Latin word *ordo*. It started with prayer each weekday at 7:45 a.m., followed by classes with titles like "Scripture" and "Jesuit Documents." Each day, three hours or so were to be devoted to Mass, prayer, and spiritual conversations. On Sundays, the novices would go to Mass at various parishes around the city, and on Saturdays, they would clean the house. Patrick was assigned the bathrooms.

Each novice was given his own small room with a single bed, a desk, and a chair. But the men would spend most of their time in the communal areas—the chapel, classrooms, kitchen, dining room, and the two TV rooms in the basement. They would be responsible for their own laundry (machines were also in the basement), and they could check out bicycles or cars from the community if they needed to go somewhere.

Patrick's entering class of ten was one of five across the country that year with a total enrollment of about forty-five men. That's a decent size by current standards, although there were once four and five times that many men entering in a single year. Four of the novices in Patrick's class were from the US. The others were immigrants to Canada and came from Africa, South America, Ireland, and the Middle East. An additional eight men would be sharing the house; they were in their second year of training.

The Baby Jesuits were an impressive bunch: an actor from New York, an engineer from Colombia, a professional soccer player from Lebanon, a former seminarian from Ireland. The oldest was in his forties. Patrick and one other entrant, Ben, were just twenty-one.

Ben had arrived with his parents, as had the Irish seminarian and the New York actor. We were all invited to stay for dinner and orientation. Ben's mother was clearly thrilled her son was to become a priest. He was the oldest boy in the family, and as a devout Catholic mother, I imagined she had prayed for his vocation. I, on the other hand, had a lot of questions.

"When can they come home?" I asked as soon as the novice director had finished his short speech welcoming us and explaining the house rules.

"*This* is his home now," I was told. "But if you're asking when he can come to visit, novices are allowed to visit family once a year for five or six days—but there are no visits and no contact other than by letter for the first eight weeks. And they'll be spending Christmas here with us."

This was his home now? He hadn't been in the place for more than an hour. And he wouldn't be able to come home for *Christmas*? Christmas was sacred in our family. The kids could miss any other holiday without much grumbling from me—but not Christmas. Patrick had never missed Christmas. I was about to say something when I glanced at Patrick. He was sitting up very straight in his chair, bracing himself. He knew me that well. I decided that today, just this once, I would try not to embarrass him.

I managed to behave myself for the next twenty minutes or so while other parents asked questions like, "What prayers would you suggest we say for our son?" and "Is there anything we can do to help?" It was obvious to me there wasn't a single kindred soul in that room.

It wasn't until the director was reviewing the program for the next two years—we had been given a handy chart to follow along—that I risked speaking again. He was explaining something called the pilgrimage. Every novice would take a trip toward the end of the first year. He could go anywhere he chose, anywhere prayer and God directed him. It might be to the shrine of a saint thousands of miles away or it could be to a nearby Indian reservation. He would be given $35 and a one-way bus ticket and told to come back in a month. Hitchhiking was sometimes involved. The purpose, the director said, "is to trust radically in God's care for you."

This was radical trust indeed. A little too radical for me. "Couldn't you at least give them a two-way bus ticket?" I asked a little too loudly.

* * * *

Five days later, we got a letter from Patrick. "Hello! I miss you guys already," it began. "It's been hard to be here so far, but the guys are welcoming and honest and prayerful, so that helps a ton. I know that I'll change from being here; it's just the direction that I feel hasn't been decided yet. I am truly longing for clarity. Patience is what I need ... I was hoping you guys could send me my soccer boots and shorts. I'm okay other than that, I think. I love you all!!" Folded up inside the letter was a torn-off piece of paper on which he had scrawled: "Oh, yeah. Send my white Alianza soccer shirt, too! Love, P."

In another letter that fall, he wrote: "As of right now, I've been a Jesuit for one month, six days, one hour and thirty-six minutes. Not too bad so far ... (I am) trying to understand what it means to follow God fully in this world, how living this kind of life and making these choices allows me to lend/give meaning to my life ... all that stuff. (You) sent too much for my birthday. I gave most of it away." In a postscript he asks his dad to copy some Neil Young CDs for him and recommends the new Bruce Springsteen album. "I've listened to it here about fifty times and it's worth it. Okay. Love you."

His letters that first year were all like that, providing alternating portraits of an earnest young man struggling with what he is meant to do and the twenty-one-year-old kid who wants his soccer shirt, loves music, and gets excited about the fantasy football league he has started with other Jesuits.

That fall, an article appeared in the Midwest Province's *Jesuit* magazine congratulating the new recruits. There's a picture of Patrick, wearing his hair slightly spiked and smiling broadly. Underneath the photo are his name and the letters "nSJ," indicating his status as a novice in the Society of Jesus.

An accompanying write-up reads: "Gilger, 21, graduated from Creighton University this year with a B.S. in philosophy. Born in St. Cloud, Minnesota, Patrick covered a lot of ground growing up. He attended elementary school and junior high school in Louisiana and high school in Oregon. He also experienced Hispanic culture during an El Salvador immersion trip. He's traveled to Europe to play soccer and (while in college) volunteered at an Omaha parish program that feeds hungry children after school and during the summer. He has performed various leadership roles with Christian Life Community groups and on religious retreats. His interests include soccer, swimming, reading, fantasy sports, Ultimate Frisbee, and listening to music."

He volunteered with a program that feeds hungry children? He led other college students in religious retreats? How little I knew my son.

*   *   *   *

Patrick had acted so *Catholic* as a college student that for some time no one realized he wasn't actually eligible to become a priest. The church requires that men have at least a couple of years of Catholicism under their belts before they can enter an order, and Patrick had been a Catholic for only a little more than a year. Father Saz told me that when he discovered this fact, there was a bit of a scramble that involved a petition and special dispensation from Rome.

Because he hadn't been raised Catholic, my son also had some catching up to do during that first year in the novitiate. He didn't know as much as the others about the scriptures and the history of the church. Its language and rituals were still largely a mystery to him.

He took classes and read the Jesuit Constitutions, which were written by the order's founder in the mid-1500s and which set out in great detail over hundreds of pages how the organization should be run and how its members should live. (In one of those lovely turns of phrase the order still deploys, this is called "the Jesuit way of proceeding.") Patrick also spent time each week with an appointed spiritual director (a priest he was convinced found him a little annoying), and taught English to African immigrants for his weekly "apostolate," another antiquated Jesuit word referring to community service work.

About midway through their training, the novices participated for the first time in the Spiritual Exercises, a four-week silent retreat that is a hallmark of Jesuit spirituality. The longest retreat Patrick had ever made was five days; the longest he had ever been silent was possibly fifteen minutes.

He found the Exercises both exhausting and exhilarating. They included daily Masses and conversations with his spiritual director as well as visits to the gym, so there was some talking involved, but the majority of his time was spent in solitary prayer and meditation on the life of Jesus. The Exercises, which are offered to lay people as well as to members of the order, consist of four distinct segments, each of which takes about a week. The first week, as Patrick described it to me, is spent recognizing "how much you're loved by God" and acknowledging your sinfulness. That is followed by a second week of readings and vivid imaginings of Jesus' early life and ministry, during which people try to visualize themselves taking part in incidents described in the Bible. The third week is focused on Christ's passion and death, and the final week is spent contemplating Christ's resurrection and "God's loving action in the world."

A week thinking about your sinfulness? As he explained the Exercises to me, I asked Patrick what kind of sins he had to consider, given his short and relatively unsullied life. The answer had to do with pride. He came to realize, he said, that "whatever talents, whatever intelligence I have, I'm not enough. I need God."

There's a Jesuit term for this—*de arriba*—meaning "from above." The order's founder, Ignatius Loyola, wanted his Jesuits to use their talents and skills, but he also wanted them to acknowledge their reliance on things above—on God—to carry out their missions.

The Exercises traditionally come to an end with a beautiful Ignatian prayer that sums up what I think Ignatius meant and what Patrick was saying. A version of the prayer, usually referred to by its Latin name, the *Suscipe*, goes like this: "Take Lord, receive all my liberty, my memory, understanding, my entire will, all that I have and possess you gave to me. To you, Lord, I return it. All is yours now; do with it what you will. Give me only your love and your grace. That is enough for me. Your love and your grace are enough for me."

* * * *

The pilgrimage came in late January and, true to form, Patrick didn't pick an easy trek to a soup kitchen somewhere in Iowa. He chose New York City, a place where $35 arguably gets you less than anywhere else in America.

He boarded a Greyhound bus in Minneapolis and arrived at the New York Port Authority early in the evening several days later. Carrying a backpack with some clothes and a Bible, he headed to the Lower East Side where the Catholic Worker house is located. In addition to publishing *The Catholic Worker* newspaper, which has touted social justice causes since Dorothy Day founded it in 1933, the movement provides shelter and food for the homeless as well as other social services. But Patrick couldn't find the house. He walked for hours, stopping at three Catholic parishes to see if they would take him in. Three times he was turned away. "It was late," he explained. "They didn't know who I was."

Patrick didn't want to go to the Jesuits in New York. That would be too easy. But it was close to midnight and he was getting scared, so he found a pay phone and made the call. It was another fifteen-block walk to the Jesuit house, but they welcomed him in. ("Part of me wishes I had just slept on a park bench," he told me later.)

He had chosen New York because the city is home to both a lot of poor people and a lot of Jesuits. He wanted to learn what it is like to work with the poor, and he wanted to talk to other Jesuits about celibacy. How hard would it be? he wondered. How did they handle it?

He also wanted to meet Daniel Berrigan, the Jesuit priest, poet, and peace activist who was something of a Catholic rock star. It was Berrigan, along with his brother, Philip, and several others who manufactured homemade napalm and used it to destroy draft files during the Vietnam War. The Berrigans landed on the FBI's Most Wanted list, and a defiant Daniel Berrigan, who had picked up the moniker "The Holy Outlaw," was eventually arrested and spent a couple of years in prison. Patrick considers Berrigan a hero because "he really put his life on the line for what he believed." He was, in his own way, Patrick said, acting out of "love of Jesus, who preached peace."

Over the next few weeks, Patrick would attend a Bible study at Daniel Berrigan's New York City home, after which he pronounced Berrigan "the real deal." He found the Catholic Worker house (which he must have passed several times without seeing it that first night) and spent a few weeks working in the offices and cooking and sharing sleeping quarters with the homeless men who sheltered there. He talked to a lot of Jesuits, and they took him to a Broadway show and out to eat at a nice Italian restaurant. They shared their stories with him, gave him advice, and slipped money into his pocket. Money he needed. By the time Patrick arrived in New York, most of the $35 was already gone.

"What happened to it?" I asked him when he called home shortly after arriving. (It was a phone call I had insisted on.)

"Well, I gave some of it away on the bus," he said.

"You gave it away? Why in the world would you do that?" I yelped.

"Because these people I met—they need it more than me."

"Nobody," I insisted, "needs that money more than you do!"

But Patrick had resolved that while on this trip he would give money to anyone who asked for it. He would give away the clothes on his back if he was asked. No one requested his clothes, but he was walking down a street in New York one day with a $20 bill in his pocket. It was all the money he had. "I was thinking, 'Please, nobody ask me for money,'" he said. But sure enough, a man walked up and said, "Hey, man, do you have any change?"

Having none, Patrick gave him the $20 bill.

But people gave him money, too, and it wasn't just the Jesuits. "I'd meet a guy on the bus, and we'd have this great conversation, and he'd ask me what I was doing," Patrick recalled. "Then he'd say, 'Here's ten bucks; take care of yourself.'"

When he got back to St. Paul four weeks after setting out, Patrick had $35 in his pocket, exactly the amount he had started out with. "It wasn't my money," he said, so he handed it over to the house fund.

* * * *

Despite choosing New York City for his pilgrimage, Patrick actually did end up in Iowa that year. For a required "hospital experiment," he was assigned to a home for the developmentally disabled in the tiny town of Clinton, situated along the Mississippi River on the eastern edge of the state. The home is part of Clinton's L'Arche community, consisting of three houses within blocks of each other that house about twenty men and women with intellectual disabilities.

Patrick lived with the residents, referred to as "core members" because they form the heart of the community. He and other assistants cooked and cleaned and helped the members brush their teeth, wash their hands, and pray. They drove the members to their jobs, organized "walk races," and took them to the gym to train for the Special Olympics—training that largely consisted of walking slowly around a basketball court and sitting in a big circle doing stretching exercises.

Patrick, who was learning to play the guitar at the time, was a hit with the residents, especially a man with Down syndrome named Johnny. Johnny was a big Elvis fan. Patrick would pick his way through a ballad by Ryan Adams or Bob Dylan and Johnny would clap and yell, "I love it! That's Elvis! Elvis is great! You sound like Elvis!"

Another time the men and women were in the gym doing some stretches before playing a little basketball. They were all on their sides, leaning on their elbows, when Johnny's elbow slipped, and he plopped to the floor. "O-o-o-h, my ribs," he groaned. Then he immediately brightened up. "I love ribs," he announced. "Can we have ribs for dinner?" The whole place cracked up.

My son revels in these stories, and he loved his time at L'Arche. The men and women there would not be counted among the beautiful people of the world, and at best they functioned at about a fourth-grade level. But they were positive and loving in a way Patrick had not encountered before.

He was a little less enthusiastic about his next assignment—teaching World Religion to juniors and seniors at Marquette University High School, an all-boy, Jesuit-run school in Milwaukee, Wisconsin. Near the end of their novitiate training, every Jesuit must do a "long experiment"—a professional experience designed to help him figure out what career path he might choose and experience what it's like to live and work with other Jesuits in a professional setting.

This question of what *to do* is a serious one for Jesuits, who, unlike most Catholic priests, have just about every career option open to them. In the mid-1500s when Ignatius of Loyola and his roommates Francis Xavier and Pierre Favre teamed up to form the order, they had no intention of confining themselves to monasteries or parish rectories. They decided to seek God—and their life's work—anywhere and everywhere. For this reason, while some Jesuits do become parish priests, they also are artists, doctors, scientists, missionaries, carpenters, farmers, mechanics, dancers, musicians, teachers, winemakers, and economists. Coupled with the fact that Jesuits often don't wear robes or collars like most priests, this means they can be hard to spot.

Patrick wore his clerics—the black shirt, black suit, and white collar of a priest—for the first time at Marquette. It was a way to distinguish himself from his students, some of whom were only four or five years younger than he was. He remembers looking at himself in the mirror in his room before setting out for his first day of classes and thinking, *What the hell am I doing wearing this?!*

Teaching high school, he discovered, "was a little bit boring," but he enjoyed the kids, and he fell in love with Milwaukee—its old brick houses and tree-lined neighborhoods, the beer and the brats. But most especially, he fell for its baseball team.

If there's anything Patrick loves more than God (and possibly Bob Dylan), it's the Brewers. In the picture he chose for his Facebook profile page, he wore his favorite bright blue Milwaukee Brewers jacket and under "About Paddy," he wrote: "Jesuit. Lover of God, Dylan, and the Brewers." I think he had that in just about the right order.

During the summers while in the novitiate, Patrick would spend a week or so at Loyola Villa, the Jesuit summer home in central Wisconsin. The villa is nestled among white pines overlooking a lake where the vacationing priests go swimming, water skiing, and canoeing. On nice evenings, they compete to see who can hit a golf ball the farthest into the lake.

One summer Patrick was designated the "boat czar." His job was to keep the collection of old boats running and drive the older Jesuits around the lake. He also cleaned and cooked and did what he could to keep the ancient villa in repair. Jesuit brothers had built the core of the house in 1898—using only wooden pegs—and as far as Patrick could see, the entire place was a fire waiting to happen. Each summer he would pray that it wouldn't burn down on his watch.

At the villa, he said, time seemed to slow down. I think the same was true for much of the two years of the novitiate. Novices have plenty to *do,* of course, but they spend a lot of time simply being "present" in their own lives and in the lives of other people—like Johnny at L'Arche or the elderly priests spending a long summer at the villa. People like those he encountered riding a bus in the middle of the night or living at a homeless shelter in New York.

When I would ask Patrick what he was doing on one of his assignments, he would often simply say, "Being there." This notion of "being present" is one of the Jesuit concepts I find hardest to grasp. I always want to be *doing* something, and if I'm not *doing* something, I feel like I'm wasting time. This is true even when I'm with my family. "What do you want to do?" I'd ask Patrick during his visits home. "Nothing much," he'd say. "Just be with you."

It took a family game of Trivial Pursuit to make me understand. We had an unscheduled evening and clearly something had to be done. I got out the board game and ordered Gary and all three kids to the dining room table. But no one would concentrate. They were laughing and telling stories and getting up to get snacks and refill their drinks, and only occasionally actually playing the game. "It's your turn," I kept saying. "Come on, roll the dice."

Finally, Gary stopped and looked at me. "It's not about this," he said slowly, gesturing toward the game on the table. Then he spread his arms wide to take in all of us. "It's about *this*."

I think that sums up pretty well what my son learned in those first two years of Jesuit training. He came to understand the difference between this and *this*. He grew up, and he grew closer to God.

* * * *

As his time at the novitiate drew to a close in the spring of 2004, Patrick had a big decision to make: Should he petition to take First Vows, the formal vows of poverty, chastity, and obedience that would lead to another eight to ten years of training and finally ordination as a priest?

In some ways, the novitiate is a testing ground, a time to "try out" the Jesuits to see if the Society suits you—and if you suit the Society. The Jesuits don't release figures on how many men leave before their first two years are up, but if Patrick's experience is any indication, it's about one-third. About half of the remaining men make it to ordination, the time at which they become full-fledged priests. And even fewer will remain Jesuits for their lifetimes. According to a 2010 study by the Center for Applied Research in the Apostolate at Georgetown University, seventy-five percent of Jesuits in the developed world who entered in the previous three decades ended up leaving the order.

Patrick had spent a lot of time thinking and praying about which of those categories he would fall into. He was asking God to give him some guidance, some kind of sign as to what he should do. But God was not giving him an answer.

CHAPTER 3

FROM FIRST VOWS
TO LAST

"Things we lose have a way of coming back
to us in the end, if not always in the way we
expect."
J.K. ROWLING, *Harry Potter
and the Order of the Phoenix*

od hardly ever talks out loud, not even to priests. This is
why the Jesuits practice a system of making decisions they
call discernment. Basically, discernment is a way of weighing facts and feelings in an effort to figure out what God is calling
you to do.

It starts with indifference, which doesn't mean what I first
thought it did. ("What? I'm not supposed to care about what happens to me?") In a religious context, indifference is a kind of interior
freedom, a way of detaching or distancing yourself from everything
except what God desires of you, which is another way of saying your
own deepest desires. As Jesuit founder Ignatius of Loyola put it, it's
about being indifferent to "all created things as much as possible so
that we do not necessarily want health rather than sickness, riches
rather than poverty, honor rather than dishonor, a long life rather
than a short life, and so in all the rest..."

This is followed by careful attention to how possible courses of
action move you. I'm oversimplifying this, but if the idea of doing

something produces a feeling of disquiet or desolation, if it produces a loss of faith, hope, and love, that's an important message and you should pay attention. And if the thought of doing something else gives you a sense of peace or consolation—if it adds to faith, hope and love—that may be a sign it's the right thing to do.

Patrick says Jesuits have been practicing this sort of decision-making and teaching it to others since Ignatius started the order in the sixteenth century. Something about it must have stuck because the practice seems to have seeped into pop psychology.

The only time I read women's magazines is when I'm getting a haircut or pedicure, which isn't all that often. I usually skip the self-help articles (in fact, I usually skip all the articles), but one day I picked up *O, the Oprah* magazine, to pass the time while a nice Korean lady painted my toenails, and I came across an article that caught my eye. The headline read: "Martha Beck shares the four steps you need to visualize the best solution—and then make it happen."

Beck is best known for writing a book about leaving the Mormon faith in which she accuses her father, a prominent Mormon, of sexually abusing her. She then became a life coach, which is the kind of job title that always makes me a little suspicious. What exactly, I wonder, are the proper qualifications for advising others how to live their lives?

Qualified or not, Beck advises people to stop complaining about what's wrong with their lives and do something about it. The trick, she says, is to clarify your desires. You start by slowing down and really thinking about what's bothering you. Then you imagine as vividly as possible how things could change. As possibilities begin emerging, you should stop thinking and just allow ideas to enter your consciousness. Some possibilities will "leave you feeling intrigued, curious, a bit lighter. These are your preferences," she writes. The final step is to pinpoint your desires. "Thinking of a solution you'd like to see, ask yourself: *What would be even better*? After allowing an answer to come into focus, ask: *What would be even better than that*?"

Hey, I thought, this could have come straight out of the Jesuit handbook! When no one was looking, I ripped the pages from the magazine (yes, it made me feel guilty) and tucked them into my purse. When I got home a few hours later, I showed them to Patrick, who was visiting over his summer break. "Look at this," I said, waving the pages in front of him. "Jesuit discernment—right here in Oprah magazine!"

Patrick glanced through the article and grinned. "If it works, it works," he said. "But tell me, what's the big difference between this and what we've been talking about?"

While I thought about his annoying habit of asking questions designed to make me think, he held up two fingers. "In Jesuit discernment, there are *two* parties involved—you and God. The difference is that you're not alone. This," he said, pointing at the crumpled pages, "can make things worse because if you don't figure it out, you think it's your fault, that you're just not good enough. And where does that leave you?" Another annoying question, but he had a point.

Discernment is not about choosing between good and evil. Patrick says if you're considering whether to rob a store or walk on, the choice is obvious. Discernment comes into play when you have two good options, one of which may be only slightly better than the other.

The first time I heard about this discernment business was when Patrick was nearing the end of his novitiate training in St. Paul and had to decide whether to leave or petition to stay in the Society, continuing his training to become a priest. He had thought that after two years in the novitiate he would know what he wanted to do, but he was having trouble making a decision. Part of him wanted to say: "Thanks, I've had a great two years, but I'm moving on." Another part of him yearned to stay. There was, he thought, so much more to discover.

As he had been taught, he spent a lot of time trying to discern the best choice. He thought about what it would be like to live a conventional life, one that included marriage and children, and it made him feel happy. Then he imagined what it would be like to leave the Jesuits, to walk away from this order that pulled at him so strongly and had given him so much, and the thought filled him with sadness. He could be happy being a priest, too, he thought. Both were good paths, so he decided to let God choose.

"I went to prayer and said to God, more or less, 'I'm willing to be a Jesuit if that's what you want. Just tell me what to do, and I will do it,'" he said. "And then I heard a voice inside of me say: *No.* It was as clear a message as I've ever received."

God was not going to decide for him, and he was more than a little pissed.

About a week and a half later, when he had settled down a bit, Patrick decided to try talking to God again. As he prayed, he got "a very strong feeling," he said. "It was in my heart in an instant, without being formed into words first, and it said, *No, I won't tell you what to do. If you want to be a married man, I'll give you the grace to do that. If you want to be a Jesuit and a priest, I'll give you the grace to do that.*"

That answer—the freedom it represented—convinced Patrick that he could trust his life to God. "His *no,* Patrick said, "gave me the freedom to say *yes.*" Becoming a priest would be the more difficult choice, but God, he felt, had promised to take care of him.

Patrick told us of his decision one night on the phone. "Are you sure?" I kept asking him. "As sure as I can be right now," he kept saying. "I don't know how it will turn out, but I want to give it a try. I hope you understand. I hope you'll pray for me." We said we would try.

Before he hung up, he asked one more thing of us: Would we consider buying him a ring? He wanted a symbol that he wasn't available, he said. He wanted to make his commitment visible. "What kind of ring?" I asked, although I already knew the answer.

The next weekend, Gary and I visited a jewelry store to look at men's wedding bands. The salesman, looking a little puzzled, asked who the ring was for. "My son," I told him. But then realizing how odd that sounded—who, after all, buys their son a wedding band?—I quickly added, "He's becoming a priest. He needs a ring because he's becoming a priest." It was the first time I had said those words out loud, at least in public, and it struck me that this was really going to happen. "Let's go," I told Gary, and I turned and walked out of the store.

We did end up buying Patrick a ring—a simple silver band we found at a pawn shop, where the salesmen asked no questions. On the inside of the band we had inscribed his initials, followed by SJ for the Society of Jesus, and the date he was to take his First Vows. I put it in a little box along with a note: "Hope this fits. Hope you're doing the right thing. Love you."

We flew to St. Paul a few weeks later for the ceremony. It was the first time I had seen a priestly initiation of any kind, and it was the first time I had seen my son in clerics: the black suit and white collar of a priest. "What's this?" I said, reaching up and tugging the collar playfully before the service began.

I have a picture from that day of Patrick standing in a row of other young men who are also wearing black suits and white collars. Their faces are set and serious as they prepare to pledge their lives to God. Except for Patrick. My son is wearing the biggest grin imaginable. He looks ridiculously happy.

There is another picture of Gary and me taken at almost the same moment. We are sitting in a pew reserved for family, and Gary is looking straight ahead. I am resting my head on his shoulder. We are both crying.

*   *   *   *

Once a Jesuit takes First Vows, he's ready to move forward in his formation as a priest. The word "formation" is one I've always associated with football or geology, but religious orders like the Jesuits use it to describe essentially a training program for new members. It seems odd to me to talk about forming a person, as if someone has reached adulthood with only the rough outlines of a face or lacking an arm or leg. But in a sense, that's just what the Jesuits are trying to do—take the raw materials of a man and shape him into the best possible version of himself. And it takes a very long time.

To become a Jesuit priest requires, depending on a man's background and education, anywhere from eight to fourteen years, making it the longest formation process of any Catholic order (to become a parish priest typically takes four or five years) and possibly the longest of any order in any religion.

Men who want to become Jesuits begin, as my son did, in the novitiate. They spend two years working, studying, and praying, during which time they are called "novices" and sign their names with an "nSJ" instead of the fully adult "SJ" for Society of Jesus. At the end of the novitiate, Jesuits take their vows of poverty, chastity, and obedience. Some decide at this point to become brothers rather than priests. Like other Jesuits, brothers may get advanced degrees or take up a trade or profession, but they are not ordained.

Those who feel called to become priests are called "scholastics" and enter a period of graduate study in philosophy and theology. There are three of these so-called "First Studies" programs tucked away in the corners of Jesuit universities around the country: Fordham University in New York City; Loyola University in Chicago; and St. Louis University in St. Louis, Missouri. Patrick went to Loyola, where, like most Jesuits, he got a master's degree in philosophy.

I've never taken a philosophy class in my life. Philosophy, with all its esoteric contemplation and unanswered questions, just doesn't seem very *useful* to me. This is something about which Patrick and I disagree. We've been debating the question since he was a sophomore in college and decided to major in philosophy. I had hoped he would stick with his original goal of becoming a doctor—a supremely useful occupation in my mind and one with the added advantage of paying well.

Philosophy, he would tell me, is far more important. "What's more useful than learning about how to live life well? What's more important than learning how to learn?" he would say. "Philosophy teaches you to think so you don't just say things that sound pretty but are really ridiculous. What's more important than that?" (Patrick has always been hard to argue with, something which no doubt makes him a good philosopher.)

After a scholastic gets his advanced degree, he moves on to the next stage of formation, called Regency. Another of those odd Latin derivatives that are strewn around the Jesuit world, this one means to rule or direct (think of a King's Regent). In practice, however, the only thing a Jesuit Regent typically rules is a high school classroom, and only then if he's lucky.

Regents often teach in one of the many Jesuit high schools around the country, but they also do other jobs, which may include anything from driving a school bus to running a soup kitchen. During Regency, which lasts between two and three years, a Jesuit lives in a community with other working members of the order, getting a taste of what it will be like to live for the rest of his life in a community of religious men.

For his Regency, Patrick was sent to the Pine Ridge Indian Reservation on the edge of South Dakota's Black Hills. He lived with a group of Jesuit brothers and priests who run six or seven parishes as well as two elementary schools, one middle school, and one high school for children of the Lakota tribe. At various times over the next three years, he drove a school bus and taught high school classes that explored Lakota spirituality, English literature, and the history of hip-hop music—the latter a class he invented in a marginally successful attempt to engage seventeen-year-olds in conversations about culture, language, and music. He also was put in charge of the Red Cloud Volunteer Program, made up of recent college graduates doing full-time volunteer work on the reservation.

Once Regency is completed, the Jesuit begins his final stage of formation by going back to school once again, usually to earn a MDiv, a Master of Divinity degree. Patrick describes the MDiv as a practical theology degree, one meant for people who would rather be good pastors than academic theologians. Jesuits pursue this kind of practical theology at the Boston College School of Theology and Ministry in Massachusetts or at the Jesuit School of Theology in Berkeley, California, where Patrick studied for three years.

It is during this second period of theology studies that Jesuits are finally ordained. But even this is not something accomplished in one step. Jesuits are first ordained deacons, allowing them to baptize and witness marriages. They then study for an additional eight or nine months before they are fully ordained as priests, at which point they are able to perform all the sacraments, including saying Mass.

New priests are usually assigned to work in a parish or minister to the poor or sick. Some are sent overseas to teach, and some go back to school for yet another advanced degree, which can be in virtually any academic field.

Patrick's superiors encouraged him to pursue a doctorate degree, a suggestion he at first resisted. "There are so few Jesuits, why would I spend my whole thirties on a PhD?" he told me. "There's just too much to *do*." He thought he should take a job somewhere in the order's vast array of schools and churches and missions or work with young people while he was still young enough to speak their language.

He began to change his mind after more discernment, which involved long talks with his provincial, the head superior of groups of Jesuits in neighboring states that form a province. The provincial functions something like a cross between a bishop, an Army captain, a CEO, and a spiritual guide. Patrick's provincial asked him to think about what he really wanted to do, not just what he thought he should do. In the end, he agreed to go back to school, entering a PhD program in sociology at The New School in New York City.

After several years of study or work, Jesuits come to the final stage of formation called Tertianship, a term that comes, unsurprisingly, from the Latin "tertius," which means "third." This period is something like a third year of the novitiate during which a Jesuit once again studies the history and Constitutions of the Jesuits and makes, for the second time, the full thirty-day Spiritual Exercises. Only then is a Jesuit considered to be "fully formed" and ready to pursue his life's work, whether as a parish priest, a missionary, a teacher, an author, an administrator, or virtually any other career that a lay person might choose, short of managing a bar or running for public office.

Patrick's career path took him back to Loyola University, where he is an assistant professor in the Sociology Department. His students call him Father Paddy and tell him his class is worth getting up for at 8 in the morning, even if it is, as one put it, to discuss "dense sociological concepts." I have no doubt he asks them lots of irritating questions that make them think.

Teaching, research, and writing could be how he spends the rest of his career, but I somehow doubt it. When he first entered the Jesuits, I asked him what it was that he eventually wanted to do—besides contemplating the meaning of life—and he said, "Run things." This was an answer I could appreciate. Like me, Patrick thrives on being in charge. He likes to get things done—and he sees *so much* that needs doing. The Jesuits have to figure out how to best deploy their shrinking numbers, he says. Should they be teaching largely well-off kids in prestigious schools or should they concentrate on elevating those who have little or nothing? How do they reach young people, so many of whom view Catholicism—all religion, really—with profound indifference?

When he was in theology studies at Berkeley and asking himself questions like these, Patrick was struck with an idea: What if a few young Jesuits who felt as he did about the need to talk to their own generation about religion got together and started a website aimed at doing just that? They would write about movies, books, politics, sports, technology, and pop culture in all its incarnations. It would be hip and current and a tiny bit irreverent, and it would make the case that God is present in all of these things. Three other young Jesuits, Eric Sundrup, Sam Sawyer, and Jim Keane, liked the idea, and so the foursome launched *The Jesuit Post*, or TJP, and began recruiting a band of about forty other young Jesuits to contribute content.

As editor-in-chief, Patrick spent almost every spare moment he had on the site. When he wasn't editing stories or consulting with writers, he was updating, tweeting, posting, and checking audience traffic. He was using the tools of journalism to engage, persuade, inform, and sometimes just plain entertain more than 25,000 readers a week.

If Patrick and the other architects of TJP were going for eclectic, they certainly achieved it. Among my favorite articles was a tongue-in-cheek treatise on parasites that claimed even the rude and nasty parts of creation are good and beautiful, a lament about how people are more respectful in yoga classes than they are in church, and a thoughtful essay about living in an age of irony, "a time when sincerity is terrifying and pre-emptive self-defense is the first and only option."

Who could resist articles with headlines like: "I Can't Stand Tim Tebow But He Makes Me a Better Person;" "Everything I Learned About God I Learned in Spin Class;" and "Why I Feel Guilty Watching Downton Abbey, or That Creamy English Charm"?

One Christmas, TJP featured a playlist of holiday songs compiled from reader suggestions that included a standard rendition of "O Holy Night" as well as Bob Dylan's growly version of "It Must Be Santa." (I have no doubt Patrick snuck in the latter.) There was a photo contest with the title "What if Saint Ignatius had a Smartphone?" and a video clip of country western singer Thomas Rhett Akins Jr. singing about treating Jesus to a little beer and a heart-to-heart talk when He comes back—a song the editors clearly thought was pretty funny.

An obituary column dubbed "You Can't Take It With You" carried news of the famous and not-so-famous recently departed, including Egyptian democracy and the inventor of Twister, which apparently at one time was considered a pretty scandalous game.

There also was plenty of serious stuff—essays on gun violence and hurricanes, love and doubt, saints and sinners. But very little of it felt pious, and it was certainly not standard Catholic fare.

When I asked Patrick whether the Catholic hierarchy approved of all this un-orthodoxy, he pointed out the site's rather prominent disclaimer: "The opinions of *The Jesuit Post* contributors and editors found here are their own and do not constitute official statements of the Society of Jesus or the church." But he also said the site had been warmly received by almost all church and Jesuit leaders. He and other TJP editors were invited to attend a US Conference of Catholic Bishops conference in Baltimore to discuss the changing world of social media and its implications for the church. I took the catchy title for the conference, "Bishops and Bloggers," as a small sign that even the Catholic Church can be bitten by postmodernism. Perhaps this shouldn't surprise me, given that even the previous pontiff, Pope Benedict XVI, a traditionalist if there ever was one, had been known to tweet.

The point of all these efforts, Patrick said, and the point behind the whole time-consuming website enterprise, was to talk to people about God using a frame of reference familiar to them. He explained this on *The Jesuit Post*'s "About" page:

> Looking back, I think it's fair to say that I became a Jesuit so I could get closer to God. And I think it's fair to say that I was able to get closer to God because somebody somewhere could talk about God in my own language, the language of Saturday Night Live and the Milwaukee Brewers, and Springsteen. And those somebodies were Jesuits. For me, slow learner that I am, it took Jesuits talking to me in my own language about Jesus before I could even imagine getting to know Him myself.

I'm not so sure about getting closer to God, but I've been a journalist long enough to appreciate the power of language, and I understand the appeal of Saturday Night Live and Springsteen (if not the Brewers). And, Lord knows, the church could do a better job speaking to young people. Maybe, I thought, *The Jesuit Post* was on to something.

* * * *

There's yet one more step in this very long process of becoming a Jesuit. A couple of years after completing his Tertianship, a Jesuit looks for an invitation to Final Vows. Some Jesuits wait twenty years or more for this invitation, apparently without any explanation as to what took so long, but most hear much sooner. The invitation comes from Rome, from the Superior General of the Society of Jesus, often referred to as the "Black Pope" because of the power he wields and the black robes traditionally worn by members of the order.

Taking these final vows represents full incorporation into the Society. The author James Martin, who was invited to take Final Vows twenty-one years after joining the Jesuits, writes that it's something like a lawyer making partner in a law firm or a professor gaining tenure.

The vows are made at a Final Vow Mass during which the Jesuit once again pledges poverty, chastity, and obedience. This is usually followed by a private ceremony during which five more "simple" vows are tacked on. These include a promise never to change anything in the Jesuit Constitutions about poverty—unless to make it more strict—and a trio of pledges having to do with ambition. These basically say you won't strive for higher office in the church or the Society and you'll rat out anyone who does. Finally, Martin says, "We take a vow that, if we are somehow made bishop, we will still listen to the Superior General."

After all this vow-taking, some Jesuits are invited to make yet another vow—the so-called Fourth Vow of special obedience to the pope. It is this Fourth Vow that has provided endless fodder for *Da Vinci Code*-types of conspiracy theories having to do with Jesuits acting as some kind of super-secret CIA agency for the pope, sowing hatred and jealousy around the world, fighting heresy, sparking revolutions, and overthrowing governments. According to some of these theories, this final vow ceremony culminates in the initiate writing his name on a communion wafer with the point of his dagger which has been dipped in his own blood. (If you're interested in more reading of this sort, search the Internet for "Jesuit blood oath"; it makes for an entertaining forty-five minutes.)

Patrick, who has never owned a dagger, scoffs at these stories. He says the infamous Fourth Vow derives from decisions made by the first Jesuits at a time when Ignatius needed a few select men to carry out missions around the world in places like China and Japan that in the sixteenth century were remote indeed. They were to be the pope's soldiers, and, for better or worse, the military connotation has stuck. What's relevant now, Patrick says, is that Jesuits taking the Fourth Vow are promising to be uber-flexible and ultra-mobile—ready to go anywhere at any time they're needed.

Only Jesuits who have been asked to take the Fourth Vow can be promoted to the Society's highest offices, including the top job of them all—that of Superior General, the guy who is in charge of the Jesuit order around the world. This fact immediately raises my competitive hackles.

"Well, you'll surely get called, won't you?" I asked Patrick.

"I don't know, mom. I don't really aspire to it," he said, slightly exasperated with my constant striving. "I'm not aspiring to benefices or higher offices." (He really does talk this way.) "In some ways, it would be a relief to me not to take (the vow). It's hard enough for me to transition from one place to another. I'm terrible at it. I hate every new place I go until I love it."

That's true, I thought. He has never liked change. When he was thirteen and we moved from New Orleans, Louisiana, to Salem, Oregon, I gave each of the kids a journal so they could keep track of their road trip across the country to their new home. I thought it would help them with the transition; I thought I was being a good mother. On each page, I suggested a topic they could write about—what they saw on the way, something funny that happened, how they felt about the changes taking place in their lives. When I collected the journals a few weeks later, I saw that Patrick's pages were entirely blank except for one line scrawled inside the cover: "I'm sorry. I won't write in this book because I don't approve of the trip here in the first place."

If my son is called to the Fourth Vow, it will take place in secret, a fact that no doubt delights all those conspiracy theorists. As Patrick put it, "It happens in the family."

So, assuming that Patrick is invited to make this final gesture of solidarity with the Catholic Church (and the mother in me cannot fathom he would not be), I will not be there.

It will be another family—a family of brothers, of strange priests in black robes and white collars—that will bear witnesses.

CHAPTER 4

A PRIEST IN THE FAMILY

"Maybe life doesn't get any better than this, or
any worse, and what we get is just what we're
willing to find: small wonders, where they
grow."
BARBARA KINGSOLVER, *Small Wonder*

My mother was thrilled that her grandson wanted to be a priest.

She would send him little plastic statues of Jesus for Christmas and asked him to pray for her. She was an old-fashioned kind of Catholic, the kind who fears purgatory and hell and believes that unbaptized babies, the little pagan ones, go to Limbo. If she could have—if the church still allowed it—she would no doubt have spent the little money she had on indulgences, racking up extra credit to help her get into heaven.

Perhaps this is because she felt she had so much for which to repent.

When my dad was in his fifties, the Rock Island Railroad went bankrupt, and he was out of the job he had held for most of his adult life. He went to work for a trucking company for about a year; then that company went under as well. That was enough, dad said; he was tired of working for other people and wanted to start a business of his own. So, he bought a little bar in a little town in western Iowa and set up shop. It was a predictable disaster.

My dad was what you call a functioning alcoholic. He managed to get through the day (if not all the nights) relatively intact. He could go to work, drive a car, and remember to lock up the house even if he had drunk most of a fifth of Jim Beam. We were amazed he had never had an accident or been stopped for drunk driving. We called it the luck of the Irish.

At home and sober, he was often moody and uncommunicative, locking himself in his bedroom and watching TV alone for hours. But in a social situation, especially when drinks were involved (and when wasn't drinking involved?), he became a changed person. Drinking opened him up and unleashed endless off-color jokes and streams of non sequiturs that made people laugh. Drinking made him more likeable.

My mother was a different kind of drunk: secretive and careful and sly. She grew quiet and remote when drinking, as if to offset my dad's exuberance. She held herself stiffly erect and carefully enunciated every word. If you didn't know her, you might not recognize that she had been drinking at all. But we children always knew; we had become expert sleuths, attentive to a single slurred word, a slightly exaggerated gesture.

"I thought I was the type of drunk that nobody knew anything about," she once told me. "I was a very quiet drunk."

My dad would stop drinking for days at a time, but my mother, once she began, was incapable of stopping. And after they bought the bar, she didn't have to. She no longer had to wait for my dad to bring home a bottle; there were plenty of bottles to be had. And she no longer bothered to hide it.

My youngest brother, Kevin, the only child still living at home at the time, remembers stopping at the bar after school one day and finding her passed out on the floor of the small back kitchen. He propped her up and walked her home, but she couldn't make it up the four steps to the house. She fell again, this time onto the sidewalk.

When Patrick was born, I asked her if she would come help for a week or two. We were living in St. Cloud, Minnesota, far from family and friends, and I was feeling lonely and a little unsure about how to handle a newborn. She agreed right away, and a week later I drove to the airport in Minneapolis to pick her up. She arrived unsteady on her feet and reeking of alcohol. I didn't say anything—it was almost an unwritten rule in our family that we didn't talk about my mother's drinking—but I wouldn't let her hold the baby.

She behaved herself all that week, cooking dinners and cleaning the house and trying to make conversation, but I was stiff and unyielding. Arriving drunk to see her grandson for the first time seemed to me a final betrayal, and I was glad when she left. I vowed to have nothing more to do with her.

A few years later, it became clear that thirty years of drinking had taken their toll. My mother's doctor informed the family that my mother's liver was shot. If she didn't stop drinking, she would be dead within a year.

My sisters and my aunt, my mother's only sister, decided that something had to be done, so they conspired to take her to a local hospital for an "intervention," a family gathering at which she would be pressured to commit herself for treatment. My sister Stacy called and asked me to come. Everyone should be there, she said. I told her I didn't think there was a chance in hell that an intervention would work, and I didn't want any part of it. "If she wants to drink herself to death," I said, "let her." I hung up the phone.

A few months later, two of my sisters went to pick up my mother. They made up a story about a relative who had been in an accident and told her she needed to come to the hospital right away. My mother, a little suspicious, resisted until Stacy told her she had a six-pack of beer in the car and she could drink on the way. They slipped her beers all the way to the hospital.

My dad refused to participate in the intervention, perhaps out of guilt for his part in my mother's slide into alcoholism, perhaps out of fear that he would be the next in line to be pressured into treatment. But the rest of my family was waiting at the hospital when she arrived. They formed a circle around her and, one by one, they told her what her drinking had done to their lives.

My sister Patty talked about the time when she was a teenager and mom and dad had decided to sell the family home in Omaha, Nebraska, and move to Iowa to run the bar. One day the real estate agent called and said he was bringing some interested buyers to see the place. Patty knew mom was in no shape to be seen, so she thought fast: She got mom out of bed and took her to the garage, where she hid her behind a stack of tires and made her promise to stay there until the showing was over.

My brothers and sisters spoke of shame and embarrassment and the missed milestones of their lives—the birthdays and graduations and plays and games that were ignored or overlooked. They talked about being forced to grow up too soon, of never knowing what to expect.

When it was her turn to speak, Stacy told her, "I want a real mom. I want a mom who cares about herself, a mom I can talk to. I want a mom who's here. You're not even here. You don't care."

They gave her the papers that would commit her to treatment for three months, but my mother wouldn't sign. She said she didn't have a problem and didn't need help and would never forgive them for what they were doing to her. But my brothers and sisters wouldn't budge. If she didn't commit herself, they told her, they would have nothing more to do with her; she would never see her grandchildren again. "You're choosing booze over your family," they said. My sisters believe that the threat of losing her grandchildren is what finally got through to her. But it also could have been the tears. By the end, everyone was crying.

"Oh, okay. I'll stay for a little bit," she told them finally. "Overnight maybe."

* * * *

My mother loved treatment.

"I was the only woman there with all of these wonderful men," she said, the old flirtatiousness lifting her face into a grin.

She stopped drinking and taking pills, and within a few weeks the shakes stopped, too. She spent a lot of time thinking about the reasons she drank, but she wouldn't concede that it was a disease out of her control, and she wouldn't blame her parents or my dad or anyone else for her drinking. "You've got your own free will," she said firmly.

After she got out of the hospital, she went to an Alcoholics Anonymous meeting, something the hospital staff had strongly recommended. But she never went back. "These people telling all their sob stories," she sniffed. "I thought, 'Geez, go get a life.'"

It is to my mother's credit that she never drank seriously again. She had a few drinks over the years—to test herself, she said, to prove she was not really an alcoholic. But she never really seemed to need it. She went back to work, selling photo packages over the phone to make a little extra money and found that she was good at it. She could make friends with anyone, she claimed, and it seemed to be true. One of her phone friends, an elderly woman who lived alone, became a regular at her Thanksgiving table.

She completed *The New York Times'* crossword every week, tore through John Grisham novels, and never, ever, missed an episode of "Lost" or "The Bachelor." And she surprised me by being, if not exactly an attentive grandmother, a fun and loving one.

When we brought the kids to visit, which was not often, she would smother them with kisses, teach them to play pool, and give them free reign of her house. They would spend entire afternoons concocting outrageous dishes using every ingredient in her kitchen, then move to the bathroom where they plundered her makeup, painting their faces and sometimes hers as well. She wrote them long letters on their birthdays and sent them waggling Hula dolls and other unlikely Christmas gifts that made them laugh.

But after my dad died, she grew quiet and withdrawn. She had complained incessantly about him when he was alive ("I have to do everything for him;" "He's such a baby!"), but she missed him when he was gone. She didn't seem able to focus on anything; she could barely get out of bed in the morning. Her doctor gave her a prescription for antidepressants, which we tried to argue her out of taking. We reminded her that she was an addict and that she had gotten by for more than a dozen years without them, but it did no good. She said she couldn't live without them.

When I called her, which was every week or two after my husband pestered me, I would hold my breath and wait for her first words, the ones that would tell me in an instant what kind of call it would be. On some days she was bright and chatty. She talked about her cat, which had hidden in the cupboard and wouldn't come out. The bushes needed trimming and the air conditioning was threatening to go out. My brother wasn't talking to her and she didn't understand why. She never once asked about me or my family, but I was used to that.

Those were the good calls. On other days, her words were slurred and sloppy, her sentences hopelessly incomplete. I would ask how many pills she had taken, if she had been drinking, whether she had bothered to eat that day. These were questions I had been asking since I was a teenager, but I no longer really listened to the answers.

I would see my mother about once a year, at a baptism or wedding or funeral, and I was always struck by how small she had become. This was not just a metaphorical smallness; she was literally shrinking. At eighty-two, she was several inches shy of five feet and weighed barely 100 pounds, the consequences of osteoporosis and a diet that largely consisted of cigarettes and TV dinners.

It seemed to me that she was shedding parts of herself. She stopped buying things, stopped wanting things. She no longer did the crosswords or consumed books like she used to, and she hardly ever left the house, not even on Sundays when a deacon from her church would come to the tiny trailer where she lived and place the host on her tongue while the cat watched. Her world circled in on itself like a drain, and her life shrank to a single room, a television set, a carton of cigarettes. I tried to be understanding. She was old; she didn't feel well; she wanted to be left alone. And I reminded myself that the distance between us wasn't new. She had long ago lost interest in who I am.

She didn't cry once in the days following my dad's death, not even at his funeral. "I know I should feel something," she told me at the funeral home where my dad lay in his open coffin, looking nothing like himself. "But I don't feel anything." Patrick seemed to be the only one who could reach her. She would lean against him and pat his arm and say, "I'm so glad you're here."

It was at my dad's funeral that I saw for the first time what Patrick would be like as a priest. The pastor of my parent's home parish happened to be a Jesuit, and when he found out Patrick also was in the Society, he was happy to have some help.

Patrick was the one who led the rosary at the funeral home and encouraged people to share memories of my dad. And that night, as my sisters and brothers and their children and their children's spouses crowded into Stacy's house to eat pasta and drink beer and talk, Patrick went down to the basement and, surrounded by a decade's worth of discarded toys, wrote a farewell for all of us.

The sermon he read at the next day's funeral Mass was a warm and funny reminder that my dad was the kind of person, who, no matter how irreverent, no matter how many bad priest jokes he told, always kept God (and the Chicago Cubs) close to his heart. At his best, Patrick said, John Grady was childlike but not childish; he was someone who loved fully and lived large.

After the Mass, after they wheeled my dad's casket out of the church into a bitter cold January morning, we drove to the graveyard where Patrick sprinkled holy water on the casket and spoke the final, solemn prayers for the dead.

"Patrick was wonderful," my sisters whispered to me as we left the cemetery. He *was* wonderful, I thought. He's really good at this.

Patrick was close to my parents, especially my dad. He hadn't known them well until he started college in Omaha. But every Friday night during his freshman year, they would pick him up, hungry and a little homesick, from his dorm and treat him to dinner at the Village Inn. Always the Village Inn.

Patrick thought my dad was hilarious. He would tell Patrick stories about how he would sneak into Cubs games in Chicago when he was a kid and how he was once ordered to drive a train during a railroad strike even though he hadn't the foggiest idea how to drive a train. He delighted in a story about going shopping for a bra for my mother. When the sales lady asked what size she was, he held out his hands, palms up, and said, "About the size of two fried eggs." He liked to tell Patrick—and anyone else for that matter—about the time he ate an entire block of cheese and was backed up for weeks.

After their Village Inn dinners, Patrick and my folks would play cards for hours, my dad bidding wildly. At least a half dozen times during a game of 500, my dad would survey his hand and pronounce: "These cards look like a mad woman had diarrhea!" This was guaranteed to make Patrick laugh.

When Patrick was a senior in college and had just declared his intention to enter the Jesuits, my dad, then in his mid-seventies, had surgery to repair a vein in his leg. His circulation wasn't good, and he'd been having trouble walking for a long time. The operation went well, and he seemed fine, other than being a little fuzzy from the anesthesia, when I talked to him that night on the phone. But the next day he started having trouble breathing and everything began to go very wrong very quickly: His organs began to fail—first the bladder, then the kidneys. He was placed on a respirator and slipped into a coma. One of his nurses took my sisters aside. "If it was my father," she said. "I'd gather the family to say goodbye."

A priest gave my dad Last Rites while I was on the plane to Omaha. During that long flight, I kept thinking about something my dad had said a year or two earlier when I had asked him if death frightened him. "I'm not afraid to die," he had told me without hesitation. "I just don't want to be there when it happens." Well, if he couldn't avoid being there, I thought, the least I could do was be there with him.

For the next five days, the members of my family took turns sitting at his bedside. There were so many of us—children and grandchildren and great-grandchildren—that we filled the waiting room where we had set up camp with board games, books, and snacks. Nurses and aides and janitors kept poking their heads in and saying: "You're *all* Gradys?"

Several days into this vigil, a new priest came by and asked if we wanted my dad to have Last Rites, a final blessing before he died. My mother, perhaps thinking it wouldn't hurt to double dip, agreed.

All that week we tried to get answers: Would he wake up? What were the chances that he would recover? Was there any chance at all? But no matter how we posed the question, the doctors all said the same thing: "We can't be sure. Wait and see."

One morning, a young doctor we hadn't seen before took us aside. There had been no change, he said. It was time to talk about removing the respirator. My dad had always said he didn't want to be kept alive by artificial means, but taking him off the respirator meant that in all likelihood he would die.

We were still debating the question of the respirator that night when I flew home. I had to get back to work, and Patrick, who had been spending his Christmas break with us in Arizona, was coming that night to take my place at the hospital and then return to classes at Creighton for the spring semester. We would miss each other by a couple of hours. I hugged my family goodbye and told them to call me the minute anything happened. On the way home, I thought about what kind of funeral my father would want and where he would like to be buried.

Late that evening, standing at my father's bedside, Patrick took off the Celtic cross he was wearing on a chain around his neck and wrapped it in his grandfather's fingers.

Over the next couple of days, my dad, against all odds, began to get better. His kidneys—the organ the doctors were most worried about—seemed to be functioning again, and they thought it was safe to take him off the respirator. If he couldn't breathe on his own, they would re-intubate him. That night, my dad was talking to me on the phone.

"Damn it, dad!" I said, "I was there for five days, and you have to wait until I leave to come out of a coma?"

"It was Patrick," he croaked.

"It *was* Patrick," my mother insisted.

My dad lived for another ten years, and despite Patrick's protests ("Well, grandpa," he would say with a grin. "Maybe I helped a little, but I think you're just too tough to die."), my parents never budged from their story: Patrick and his cross had saved my father's life.

Like many Catholics of their generation, my parents saw most of their children and grandchildren drift away from the church. With one or two exceptions, we are no longer the kind of people who believe in the healing power of a Celtic cross. We don't see the point of dragging ourselves to Mass on Sunday mornings. And while some of my siblings were married in the Catholic Church and had their children baptized, their children—my nieces and nephews— generally don't bother even with that. The premarital classes required by the church take too much time; the churches are too hard to book.

But when we're together, whether it's for a wedding or a funeral or just a family gathering, they look to Patrick. Will he say grace before the meal? Can he talk to a troubled nephew or niece or daughter or son and see if he can't straighten them out? Will he say a prayer for them?

When my eldest daughter, Dana, was married a few years after my dad's close call, we imported one of Patrick's friends, a priest from the reservation in South Dakota, to perform the ceremony, with Patrick in an assistant's role since he was not yet ordained.

Father Phil fit right in. He stayed with us in a rented house and drank beer and played cards with my sisters late into the night. They soon forgot he was a priest. The night of the reception, he mingled and danced for a while, then, worn out from several late nights in a row, excused himself and went back to the house we had rented to get some sleep. My sisters weren't going to let him get away with that. They showed up around midnight and banged on his bedroom door, my sister Patty yelling, "Phil, get your butt out here and play some cards!" He did.

Patrick used to tell his youngest sister, Lauren, that she couldn't get married until he was ordained and could perform the ceremony himself. Lauren promised to wait. Meanwhile, other family members began lining up. The first wedding Patrick performed was for his cousin Katie and her fiancée. They asked him to do the honors one Christmas at a Gilger family ski vacation in the mountains of Colorado. We were all gathered in the big family room of our rental house when Katie and Sam made the announcement. "Patrick has agreed to marry us," they said.

As everyone applauded and cheered and wiped their eyes, I thought: I'm just beginning to learn what it means to have a priest in the family.

CHAPTER 5

SHANTY IRISH

"Home is where they let you live."
JASMIN DARZNIK, *The New York Times*

Lots of people have difficult childhoods, parents who were either too absent or too much *there,* if you know what I mean. My parents fit into neither of these categories: They managed to be there and to be absent pretty much at the same time.

I am the second oldest of eight children in a big Irish Catholic family. "Shanty Irish," my grandmother on my mother's side called us. Grandma, of sturdy German Catholic stock, was a formidable woman with firm opinions. She didn't smoke, drink alcohol, or wear pants. She had a closet full of house dresses and a drawer full of rosaries. She fasted during Lent, collected holy cards, lit vigil candles for a dead daughter, and went to church every Sunday. She kept her teeth in a jar of water next to her bed at night. She hardly ever smiled.

In her mind, my father's sole redeeming quality was his religion—and even that was a lukewarm approbation. The way the Irish practiced Catholicism was a little too raw, a little too *pagan,* for her. Men, in general, I think, were a little too pagan for her.

Every summer, my mom and dad would take the family for a visit to my grandparents, leaving one or two of us children to spend our summer vacation with them. It was about a two-hour drive from our home in what we thought of as the big city of Cedar Rapids to the tiny town of Ossian in northeastern Iowa. There would be four or five or six of us children, depending on the year and the latest birth, vying for my mother's lap or jockeying for space in the backseat, all of us reeling from my dad's cigar smoke. He would roll his window halfway down when we complained, but it didn't help much. We would arrive woozy and disoriented.

I remember my grandmother stepping onto the front porch, the screen door swinging shut behind her, when the car pulled up outside her house. She would wipe her hands on her apron and stand there, waiting for us to come to her. My father never would. He would stand next to the car while we children swarmed around our grandmother and then into the house, banging the door, shouting for our uncles, racing each other to the bathroom.

After a few awkward minutes, my dad would say, "Well, I guess Frank must be up at the bar. I think I'll go join him for a cold one." This was calculated to produce maximum irritation. Frank, my grandfather, undoubtedly *was* at the bar, something my grandmother had waged a forty-year battle over and did not care to be reminded of.

My father never went willingly into that house, and neither would he go to church while we were in town—not because he didn't go to church but because he wouldn't go to *her* church. The only times I remember him stepping foot into Ossian's St. Francis De Sales Catholic Church were for my grandfather's funeral—at which he genuinely mourned—and then years later for my grandmother's funeral. He would remark afterward that the single greatest satisfaction of his life was the fact that he had outlived her.

My father was stiffly polite in my grandmother's company, a sure sign of the depth of his antipathy since the more he liked someone the less polite he tended to be. My very proper grandmother, on the other hand, came dangerously close to swearing when he turned his back.

The lifelong animosity between the two of them was almost

certainly my mother's fault. As a young wife, she would call her mother every time she and my dad had an argument. She would complain about his drinking and his "appetites," his unkind words, his thoughtless tendencies. My dad was certainly capable of all those things, but it was never a fair fight when it came to my grandmother: She was interested in only one side of the story.

On those few occasions when she came to our house—usually after the birth of another baby—my dad would do his best to confirm her worst opinion of him. He would disappear for hours and then show up, more than a little tipsy, with an expensive present for my mother or us kids.

One year it was a swing set—our first—and we screamed with joy as he began, none too steadily, to assemble the contraption. While he struggled with the perplexing jumble of screws and poles and planks, my grandmother watched from the kitchen window, furiously scrubbing dishes in the sink and muttering what was to become one of her favorite pejoratives: "Oh, there he is: Big Pockets Johnny."

The name stuck. The only problem was, Johnny had far more children than he had pockets—or cash to put in them. He worked as a clerk for the Rock Island Railroad, a job that never produced quite enough money to cover the needs of a family whose size was unrestrained by birth control. I remember my mother sitting at her little wooden writing desk at the end of each month, a stack of bills in front of her. "Should I pay the doctor or the dentist this month?" she would ask my dad before writing out a check for $10.

Johnny bought groceries on credit at a mom-and-pop grocery store a few blocks from our house until the store went under and he was forced to switch to the supermarket, which did not extend credit, even to a charming Irishman with a brood of little kids to feed. Our home was perpetually short on food and overfull with children. I'm not saying that we starved, just that we subsisted largely on cold cereal, bananas, and peanut butter and jelly sandwiches—the only reliable items of food to be found in the house.

Each weekday night, my dad would call home before he left work and ask my mother what he should pick up at the grocery for dinner. She would dictate the list—hamburger, canned tomatoes, canned tuna, canned peas—between long drags of her cigarette. One of her favorite dishes was something she called "Matilda's Surprise," a concoction of elbow noodles, tuna, and canned tomatoes. She came up with the name one day when, exasperated with children constantly tugging at her and yelling, "Mom! Mom!" she announced she was tired of being called mom: We should call her Matilda instead.

I have no idea where she came up with Matilda. My mother's real name is Irene Christine, a dreamy, lyrical name to which she always had profound objections. As a child, she managed to convince everyone, including her parents, to call her Pat instead. It was a chirpy, modern name that she felt suited her much better.

It seems to me that Pat yearned to be modern—and as different from her own mother as she could manage. My grandmother was, admittedly, a hard act to follow. She tended a huge garden, canned food, sewed her own clothes, baked her own bread, and raised seven children with almost no help and very little money. She held herself to a strict schedule—laundry on Monday, ironing on Tuesday, baking on Wednesday, mending on Thursday, cleaning on Friday, confession on Saturday, and Mass on Sunday. She fed the chickens every morning, collected their eggs every afternoon, and slaughtered them herself when the time came.

Every chore was executed according to her own precise rules. Clothes were sorted and soaked and pressed twice through an old wringer washer before being hung to dry on the big clothesline stretched across her backyard—the jeans upside down with the legs spread so they would dry evenly, shirts pinned by the collars and elbows, socks toe-up next to their mates. The effect, especially in a stiff breeze, was eerily human, as if a chorus line was about to start up. The clothes, like everything else in my grandmother's life, danced to her tune.

My mother did none of these things. She never possessed a

clothesline or raised chickens or baked anything from scratch. She cleaned the house only when the mood struck her and held to no particular schedule, except possibly to get dinner on the table each night.

She was the kind of person who was perfectly comfortable in the midst of chaos. The house could be overrun with kids from the neighborhood, the kitchen floor so sticky it was like treading on tree sap, dishes piled up in the sink, laundry everywhere, and my mother would be nestled in the corner of the couch, reading a book and smoking a cigarette, leaving a telltale smear of red lipstick on each butt.

We lived in a tract house—one of those cheap, efficient, box-like affairs thrown up in suburbs all over the country after World War II. It had three tiny bedrooms, a kitchen, a living room, a hallway, and a bath. No basement, no garage, no porch, no trees. My dad painted the house pink, and my mother planted a bed of petunias in the front yard, a raucous display of purple and pink and red and white. That paint and those blossoms were the main things that distinguished our house from every other one on the block.

*   *   *   *

In 1963, there were eight of us living in the little house on Linwood Street—my parents and six children—one boy and five girls—with a seventh on the way. We children split two bedrooms between us, me sharing the upper berth of a bunk bed with my younger brother.

Even in that neighborhood of working-class families overrun with children and perpetually short of cash, the Grady family stood out.

My dad coached the eighth-grade basketball and baseball teams in exchange for tuition at the local parochial school so we children could get what he referred to as a good Catholic education. He soon grew friendly with the two priests who ran the school and church, and it was our house the priests came to on Friday nights, bearing a bottle of Jim Beam and playing cards late into the night.

Our house was always full of people. Neighbor ladies would sit at the kitchen table drinking coffee and gossiping for hours with my mother on warm summer afternoons. They would scurry off before their husbands returned home from work, but afterward, when everyone had been fed and the dishes had been cleared, they would come back, husbands and children in tow, to talk some more while the men drank beer and we children played hide and seek and chased fireflies in the dark.

My parents seemed young and glamorous compared to the other adults who crowded into our home. Mom, slim even after all her pregnancies, wore high heels and tight skirts and smelled of perfume and lipstick. My dad, with his closely cropped curls and crooked smile and Irish charm, clearly adored her. When he drank too much, which was often, he would attempt to twirl her around the tiny living room, repeating over and over for his children's benefit: "Your mother: She's a *beautiful* woman."

Mom was different from the other mothers in the neighborhood in one other important respect: She had a job. She was a nurse at the local Catholic hospital, in charge of the overnight shift in the emergency room. She would put on her crisp white uniform and peaked nurse's cap and head to work shortly after we kids had gone to bed each night. She would return just before we awoke, as my dad was leaving for the railroad yard.

This was her bedtime. While she slept, my brother, sisters, and I fed and dressed ourselves and tried to keep quiet. My older sister, Sandy, and I were expected to watch the little ones, but at seven and eight years old, the most we could do was to try to keep them from wandering into the street. We weren't always successful even at that. One day, my sister Pam, a chubby and cheerful five-year-old, escaped. Stark naked, she ran down the street, joyful and free, until I tackled her and dragged her back to the house. When I told my mother about it later, she laughed.

We were constantly inflicted with pinworms, a shameful malady that kept us awake at night scratching our butts. With our hand-me-down clothes and home haircuts, our once-a-week baths and bare feet, we looked civilized only when compared to the only other Catholic family on the street—the Lesmeisters.

The Lesmeisters had even more children than we did, but in reverse genders: six boys and one girl. They lived in a long, low house down the street that appeared to have been built in pieces, bedrooms alternating with rooms jammed with carpentry tools and workbenches, alternating with other rooms so filled with *stuff* it was impossible to distinguish their purpose.

Mr. Lesmeister spent most of his time in one of the workrooms, smoking a pipe and carving walking sticks, toys, and oddly shaped chairs. He hardly ever spoke, and he was practically deaf—a blessing, perhaps, considering the circumstances. His wife could usually be found in the kitchen, located somewhere in the center of the maze. It seemed to me she was always standing at the stove over a pot of water peeling potatoes—and cutting away half of the potato along with the skin. She would be barefoot, the soles of her feet black with grime, a cigarette dangling from her mouth, the ashes threatening to tip into the potatoes.

The Lesmeisters' oldest child, Mike, and I were in the same grade at St. Ludmila Elementary School. The school and the parish were named after a Czech saint, a noblewoman and the grandmother of Saint Wenceslas, he of "Good King Wenceslas" song fame. Ludmila was reputedly strangled with her own veil by two men hired by her daughter-in-law to get rid of her. It was not a story we learned from the nuns.

The Sisters of St. Francis ran the school. It seemed to me that they ran *everything,* including the two young priests who frequented our house and were ostensibly in charge of the parish. Father Zachar and Father Paisley acted a little in awe of the nuns in their black veils, black lace-up shoes, and black robes with long black rosaries dangling from their waists. All that black made the tight white wimples framing their faces all the more stark and amplified their expressions—all you could see was their mouths, their eyes, and their arched eyebrows.

Once a year, the nuns would cancel classes and herd us all into the cafeteria to watch "The Song of Bernadette," a black-and-white movie that seemed dated even in the 1960s. The other kids, especially the boys, would groan and throw kernels of popcorn at each other when the nuns weren't looking, but every time the room went dim and the scratchy image of Jennifer Jones as Saint Bernadette flickered onto the screen, I was *there*, in 1858 France. I *was* Bernadette, stoically suffering from tuberculosis and kneeling in a grotto, waiting for the Virgin Mary to appear. It's possible, I thought, that I could be a saint.

The last scene of the movie always made me cry. Bernadette is on her deathbed. The tuberculosis, a mysterious disease that has only made her more beautiful, has just been discovered, and the nun who has persecuted her for years has finally repented. The "beautiful lady," whom Bernadette has not seen since childhood, appears once more. Bernadette reaches out her arms and cries, "I love you! I love you! Holy Mary, Mother of God, pray for me," then falls back on her bed, dead.

For several months after these showings, I would concentrate very hard during our morning children's Mass on the life-sized statue of Mary that stared out at us from beside the altar. I willed her to move—to give me just a little wave, some sign I was special, that I had, as the nuns would say, a "calling." But no matter how hard I stared and squinted and purposefully blurred my vision, Mary wouldn't budge.

Besides becoming a saint, my other ambition was to read every book in the bookmobile that visited our corner of southwest Cedar Rapids during the summers, and at this I came closer to success. My mother, a voracious reader, would take us there once a week. We each had our own library card—a prized possession and the first form of ID I owned—and we would check out five books at a time, the maximum number allowed for a child.

I read books about saints, of course. Saint Therese, the Little Flower of Jesus, was my favorite, possibly because she was, unlike me,

sweet and compliant—and also because she died young and beautiful. But I also read *Uncle Tom's Cabin, Gone with the Wind, Little
Women,* and endless Nancy Drew books.

Reading was a way to escape my noisy, messy family, which
just seemed to get noisier and messier with each passing year. There
always seemed to be another baby, another party, another bottle of
whiskey being cheerfully drained around the kitchen table. With a
book, I could lie mostly undisturbed on my top bunk and shut out
everything but the words on the page, sounding out the ones I didn't
know. For a long time, I mispronounced words because I had never
heard them spoken; I knew them only from the pages of a book.

Years later when I read *Angela's Ashes,* Frank McCourt's book
about growing up Irish Catholic in New York, I was startled by
the descriptions of poverty, the children starving while their father
spent his welfare checks on drink. But I recognized immediately the
Irish excess, the deep-seated compulsion toward drink and melan-
choly and self-destruction that I saw in my own father, who grew
sweeter and sadder with every drink he took. And I recognized a
child's longing for order in a household that could, at any moment,
swell into chaos.

But at the time, I could not name what was wrong with my family. All I knew was that except for the Lesmeisters, who seemed to
belong in a category all their own, other people did not live the way
we did. My friends had beds—and sometimes even bedrooms—to
themselves; their mothers made them after-school snacks; their
houses were clean; their clothes fit; and their parents could keep
their names straight. Their lives were predictable and orderly in a
way I could never count on.

I was ten or eleven when I realized something else: While my
parents still had friends over, still threw parties and played cards
with the priests, they no longer seemed to need company to drink.
They didn't need a reason at all.

CHAPTER 6

STARTING OVER

"I wear dark glasses to hide my eyes; there are
secrets in them I can't disguise."
BOB DYLAN, "Long and Wasted Years"

About the time I turned ten, the Grady clan packed up and moved to Omaha, Nebraska, to a slightly bigger house in a somewhat nicer neighborhood. My dad had his first white-collar job as a sales representative for the Rock Island Railroad. He wore shirts and ties to work and took clients to lunch, writing off the expense to a company account—along with bottles of bourbon he slipped his best customers at Christmas.

It was a pretty spectacular rise for someone who started out as a manual laborer loading cargo onto dusty boxcars, and to my dad, the new job meant a toehold in the middle class—the first time anyone in his family had gotten close to making such a claim. His father, my grandfather, had also made a living loading and unloading trains for the Rock Island. It was brutal work that ended one day when something he was pulling off a cargo car slipped and hit him on the head. The concussion killed him.

My dad was born two weeks after the funeral service. With a new baby and a one-year-old son at home, Rita Gaffey had little choice but to marry again. The man she settled on ran a small grocery store and supplemented his income by sneaking out at night and stealing whatever the railroad hadn't locked up. He would often take my dad's older brother, Francis, with him on these forays, teaching him that the only way to get ahead in the world is to take what you want and avoid getting caught. At least this is the way my dad always told the story. In his version of events, his stepfather wasn't just a thief, he was a drunk and a bully who hit his wife and beat his kids. My dad couldn't get away fast enough. In 1943, he joined the Navy, and a few days after turning eighteen, he left Iowa behind and headed to San Francisco for training. A few months after that, he was on a ship in the South Pacific.

He never willingly came into contact with his stepfather again, and he only rarely saw his older brother, who had turned reckless and untethered, wandering the country in a drunken haze and occasionally turning up at the houses of relatives to ask for money. One day, Francis, or Junior, as most people called him, knocked on the door of our house in Cedar Rapids. My mother, seeing who it was, stopped my dad before he could answer. "You can't let him in," she said.

Junior died a few years later. He had just turned thirty-eight years old. A book of family history that traces the Grady family's emigration to the US during the Irish potato famine lists Junior's cause of death as kidney failure, although it might just as accurately have stated that he drank himself to death. Junior's five children, born of either two or three different women—no one seems to be sure of the number, although there's general agreement that none of them were fit mothers—were turned over to a Catholic orphanage and eventually adopted into new families.

My dad had wanted to take in his nieces and nephews himself, but money was scarce, and he and my mother already had a slew of children of their own, with more arriving pretty much on schedule every other year. I remember playing with my cousins in the backyard of our house in Cedar Rapids while my parents discussed the matter. We never saw them again.

Moving to Omaha felt like a new start for all of us. Our split-level house had a willow tree in the front yard with big branches where I could hide and read books, and it had a basement complete with a built-in bar. We put the pull-out couch in the basement, and that room with the bar became my bedroom, which I shared with my older sister.

There was money for an extension phone in the basement and a color TV—our first—in the living room. My mother, who was expecting her seventh child, didn't have to work any longer, although she still juggled paying the doctor and dentist bills.

We joined the local Catholic parish, St. Joan of Arc, where four of us, ranging from kindergarten through the sixth grades, were enrolled in school. This new school required no uniforms, which was both liberating and deeply disturbing, given that my wardrobe was limited to a total of about five items. The nuns who were assigned to us wore modern habits with skirts that ended mid-calf, revealing a shocking glimpse of black stockings, a sign, I hoped, that other liberalisms might be forthcoming. Perhaps there would be fewer punishments (the popular ones being sharp applications of a ruler, even sharper tugs on the earlobes, and the occasional expulsion to the closet). Perhaps they would smile more.

As it turned out, however, these nuns were just as serious and sour as the ones at my old school—with one remarkable exception: Sister John Marie.

Sister John Marie was young and pretty—at least as much of her as I could see, which was a slim waist and ankles, round cheeks, blue eyes, bright smile. She was the first teacher I ever had who seemed genuinely interested in making learning fun. We had class elections, art contests, science fairs, and a student newspaper. Best of all, Sister John Marie would read to us for thirty minutes every day after recess. *Charlotte's Web* was my hands-down favorite. Not only did the animals talk, they made me feel like I was hearing language for the first time. Every day when the half-hour was up, we begged for more.

Because there weren't enough nuns to go around, one of my younger sisters, Becky, had a lay teacher who we thought looked exactly like Julie Andrews. If Sister John Marie was pretty, Becky's second-grade teacher was indisputably beautiful. St. Joan of Arc's young assistant priest must have thought so, too: He spent a lot of time in her classroom, and students began tittering about how the two were in love. One day neither showed up for work, and that Sunday, the senior pastor, Father Meister, a stoic German who reminded me of my grandmother, announced to the congregation that the two of them—assistant pastor and second-grade teacher— had run off together. We thought this all very exciting and romantic, but Father Meister just looked worn-down and sad. We should pray, he said, for both of them.

Prayer was something I had been thinking about for some time when the scandal of priest and teacher hit our parish. Despite the promise of our family's improved circumstances, the chaos at home was growing, and it didn't seem to me there was anything God or anyone else could do about it.

* * * *

Away from her friends and stuck at home without a job or car, my mother, never the housewifely type, began to get panic attacks. Years later, she described these attacks to me as terrifying: "You think you're dying. Your blood pressure shoots up, your adrenaline shoots through your body, and you just kind of gray out and you wonder: What can I hang onto to keep my mind?"

She wanted to go to confession, remembering the calm it brought her to kneel before a priest and list her sins and receive forgiveness. She thought it would erase everything; she would feel whole and pure and good again. And she did try. She would go to church on Saturday mornings and get in line with the old ladies and the little kids waiting their turns to enter the tiny cubicle where the priest sat behind a curtained grill. She practiced the words: "Bless me father, for I have sinned. It has been a year since my last confession. These are my sins ...." But then the panic would rise in her throat, and she would flee, sins intact and feeling worse than ever.

One day she decided a little drink might help. And it worked. The alcohol blunted her senses and gave her enough confidence that she could wait in that long, slow line and bend to her knees in the dark and tell the priest everything—everything except the fact that she was slightly drunk and the only courage she possessed came from a bottle.

My dad's new job involved a certain amount of socializing, and socializing in the 1960s, as the television series "Mad Men" convincingly portrayed, invariably involved drinking. He would take a client out for lunch, and they would have a couple of highballs, as he called them, and then, feeling good and wanting to feel even better, he would stop to buy a bottle on the way home.

"Come on, Pat. Have a drink," he would say, dangling the bottle in front of her. Even if she had tried to say no, it probably wouldn't have worked. My dad did not like to drink alone.

My father was not the kind of man who hugged his kids or told them he loved them. He was mostly silent around the house, except when he lost his temper, and we were rarely able to predict when that might happen. We often tiptoed around him, ducking when we got too close, fearful of a slap or a push. When he got angry and hit us, my mother, the nurse, would look up from the stove or the sink and say, "Don't hit them on the head, Johnny. You could hurt them," then calmly return to whatever it was she had been doing.

But when he drank, my dad never hit us. He would alternate between joyous nonsense, telling us the world was as simple as "ABC" and then proceeding to slur the entire alphabet, and a sentimental moroseness that usually ended with him singing "Danny Boy"—at least the parts he remembered—over and over until we begged him to stop.

My mother, on the other hand, was a quiet drunk. She seemed to become more bland and less sure of herself even as my dad's personality expanded, engulfing the entire family. It was if there wasn't room for anyone else. And so they would finish off the bottle, and the next morning my dad would get up, get dressed, put cereal on the table, grab a cup of coffee, and head off to work, seemingly hangover free.

Not so my mother. She would still be in bed when we left for school. My older sister or I would change the baby's diaper and give him a bottle of milk, then crack open the door of the bedroom far enough to tell her that we were leaving, that the baby was in his crib. On really bad days, she barely got out of bed at all.

For a long time, we didn't speak about what was wrong with our mother, not even to each other. At least for me, there was an element of denial in the silence. If I didn't think about it too much, if I didn't put into words what was right in front of me, I could almost convince myself it wasn't real.

I recall quite clearly the day I stopped pretending. I was fifteen. I was in the kitchen cleaning up after lunch when mom stumbled out of her bedroom. She went to the refrigerator, took out some leftover stew and dumped it into a pan on the stove. She was standing there, spoon in hand, not saying a word, when I heard a sound like air escaping from a balloon and then the sickening thud of her head striking the floor.

I remember dropping to my knees, lifting her head, screaming for help. I remember trying to wipe the streaks of brown gravy off her pink nightgown.

It must have been only a few seconds before she came around. I helped her up and back to her bedroom, but I was shaken and worried that something was terribly wrong. The doctor's number, written in my mothers' neat cursive, was taped to the wall next to the phone. I made the call. The panic must have been clear in my voice because the receptionist put me through to the doctor right away. "Has she been drinking?" he asked almost immediately. "Did she take any pills this morning?"

I didn't know about the pills, but I was pretty sure she had been drinking. Still, I couldn't bring myself to say the words, not when I had never spoken them before, even to myself. All I could manage was a weak "I don't know." I must have been given some directions, some reassurance or advice before hanging up the phone, but I don't remember what it was. I do, however, remember my dad calling a few minutes later.

"Did you phone the doctor?" he demanded. "Did you tell him your mother's been drinking? Why didn't you call me first?"

I wasn't sure if my dad was more angry at me or my mother, but it was clear to me why I was at fault: I was guilty of betrayal. I had named something that all of us had agreed, through years of silence, would not be named.

I had been wary of my mother for some time before this happened. I was careful not to get too close or ask for too much, but after what my dad called her "fainting spell" in the kitchen, I no longer tried to pretend that everything was okay. I still didn't talk about what was happening in our house, but I grew distant, sarcastic, and angry with her. I would stay that way for a long time.

* * * *

Years later, when I was a mother with three children of my own and working on a project about alcoholism for the newspaper I was managing, I interviewed my mother and several of my siblings. I was writing about the devastating impact alcoholism has on families— the devastating impact it had on my own family. I wanted to know how it had happened. "When did the drinking get out of control?" I asked my mother, who had been sober for several years by then. "When did you know you couldn't live without it?"

She said drinking had been part of her life since high school when she and her friends would sneak a flask of bourbon into school dances. She told me about her first date with my dad —how the two of them got up to dance and my dad was so drunk and so funny people threw pennies at them. She explained that she never tried to stop him from drinking—that instead, she joined him because she didn't want to be like her own mother who nagged her husband endlessly about the evils of alcohol and was never any fun. And she talked about how she felt after all those evenings when she and my dad would share a bottle.

"I would get so sick I didn't think I could live the next day," she said. "That was when I discovered a beer would help the next morning."

The morning beer may have been good for hangovers, but she was still feeling depressed and anxious, so she went to see her doctor, who prescribed Valium. This was even better than a beer. She could take a pill and within a few minutes she would feel calmer. And she could still function. She could face the mounds of dirty clothes, the squalling baby, and the thousand other thankless tasks required of a woman with too many kids, all without a hangover. Valium became the most important thing in her life.

On bad days, she would take four or more pills, but then, panicked that she would run out before the prescription could be refilled, she would force herself to ration them. That's when she began to drink between doses, downing a beer or a glass of vodka with a veneer of orange juice. The combination of drinking and pills seemed to erase her more completely than ever. The part of her I had always loved the most—the vivacious, smart, flirty part—became increasingly absent. She was, as my youngest sister, Patty, put it, "partly dead."

It was the youngest members of the family—Patty, Kevin, Stacy, and Creighton—who were hurt the most. When things grew really bad, when the drinking and the pills eclipsed everything else in the household, I was in high school and could usually escape to a friend's house for a night or the weekend. They were too young to escape, and I was too young to give them much thought.

Patty, a blonde, sunny child, says her earliest memory of mom is coming home from kindergarten one day with some paper mâché maracas she had made in school. She was very proud of them and wanted to show them off, so she went into the bedroom where mom was sleeping and woke her up. "She took one of them and she threw it against the wall and broke it," Patty said. "That was probably the first time I realized she wasn't like other moms."

Kevin, the last of the brood, was a skinny kid with bad eyesight and bad teeth who collected beer cans and struggled in school. He says it was years before he realized mom had a problem. "I never saw her drink," he said. "She just slept a lot. Everybody just thought mom was tired."

The rest of us knew better. On weekends, dad would organize the older kids into search expeditions for her hidden bottles. I found nearly a dozen once—bottles of vodka and Jim Beam stashed in empty Tide boxes on the laundry room shelves. There wasn't a single drop left in any of them.

Stacy remembers finding a half-filled bottle during one of these hunts, but before she could turn it in, my mother intercepted her. "Mom gives me this sob story about how this is her only way to relax and she has this horrible life," Stacy said. "She made me feel so sorry for her that I didn't tell dad I'd found it."

About half an hour later, Creighton found the same bottle. With all the authority of a brother two years older, he handed it over to dad. Stacy still remembers how furious that made our mother. "I can remember her yelling at Creighton and telling him, 'I'm never doing your laundry again or cooking your meals, and you're a horrible son.' We were sent on those hunts nearly every weekend, Creighton and I," she added. "He was nine or ten at the time. I was only seven or eight."

But not long after the bottles had been emptied into the sink, my dad, defying all logic, would come home with another one. Soon he would be urging my mother to join him for a drink.

After one such evening, dad passed out in the front yard. I don't remember how he got there, but I remember there was snow on the ground and we children were worried. "Shouldn't we go get him and bring him into the house?" we asked our mother. She told us to leave him out there; he could freeze to death for all she cared. When he woke in the morning, he was still lying in the snow, but he was covered with a blanket and there was a pillow tucked under his head. Stacy had snuck out of the house in the middle of the night to care for him.

It was typical of Stacy to try to fix what could not be fixed. At number six on the list of Grady children, she had grown up fast. From the time she was twelve, about the time I moved out, it was she who did the Christmas shopping, coaxing money out of dad and walking to a nearby strip shopping center to buy dime store presents to put under the tree. She was the one who made up the Easter baskets and did the back-to-school shopping so Patty and Kevin would be supplied with pencils and notebooks. Many nights it was Stacy who made dinner.

My parents didn't show up to see her graduate from high school. They didn't make it to Patty's graduation either. They stayed home and drank.

Over the years, our house, which I had always thought of as too full of people, had become a place to be avoided. My older sister and I watched for our dates from the living room window and ran outside the moment the boys pulled into the driveway. We posed for prom pictures at friends' houses. We became mascots of other people's families.

Children of alcoholics, or COAs, as they're called by the people who research such things, respond in different ways to their damaged childhoods. They may become social extroverts, always trying to please people as a way to win approval and attention. Some become highly competitive perfectionists, intent on being in control. Others become super responsible; they are the ones who, like Stacy, parent younger brothers and sisters or who marry alcoholics, believing they can rescue them. Still others become self-destructive, acting out in socially irresponsible ways.

It's an easy matter to place every one of my brothers and sisters into these categories. It's easy to place myself. I became both a pleaser and a perfectionist. I tried hard to impress my teachers and was rewarded with A's. I sought out friends from well-off families, families that seemed absurdly normal to me, and copied the way they dressed and the way they talked. I took a series of part-time jobs and spent my Saturday nights babysitting, using the money to buy clothes that helped me fit in with my new friends and saving the rest for college. I joined the youth group at church and went to Mass every Sunday.

I think that for a long time, I tried to save my family by being good. When it finally became clear to me that nothing I could do would make things right—that there was, in fact, nothing to be done—I decided to save myself instead.

I had just graduated from high school and had enrolled in classes at the University of Nebraska's Omaha campus, a commuter school a few miles from our house. To get there, though, I would need a car. I bought one with a $400 cash scholarship awarded by my high school and asked my dad if he would cover the tuition.

"You're a girl; you don't need to go to college," he told me before writing the check. I had expected both an argument and a capitulation; my dad had always been the kind of person who would say the wrong thing and then do the right thing, but, still, the words stung. My brothers had little interest in academics, and I doubted either of them would even want to go to college. But I did. College for me was an escape, a chance to live a different sort of life altogether among people who knew nothing about me or my family, and with that check I now had everything I needed to make it happen.

One day I packed everything I owned into the back of my car and told my parents I was moving into my own apartment. A friend of mine had offered to share her tiny place situated over a drug store near the campus. I could have the pull-out couch. My parents didn't ask where the apartment was, and I didn't tell them. I hugged my little brothers and sisters goodbye and drove away, feeling guilty about leaving them but also feeling magnificently, unimaginably, free.

I cut ties with my old high school friends, who had all gone off to real colleges, the kind with dormitories and frat parties and weekend keggers. I quit the Catholic youth group I belonged to and stopped going to church. It wasn't that I had lost my faith, exactly. I still called myself a Catholic if anyone bothered to ask, and I didn't seriously question the main tenets of the faith. Catholicism was too deeply drilled into me for that. But the church, like my family, was wound up in a past I was intent on discarding. Choosing to stay with one and not the other felt to me like hanging from a jungle gym by one arm. I had to let go.

My new church was the school newspaper office, and my new friends were long-haired guys who thought of themselves as radicals. They liked to smoke dope and read e. e. cummings and write angry diatribes against the world in general and the college administration in particular. They scared me a little, but their anger also felt clean and justified. The adults in my life—at least the ones I was supposed to be able to count on most—had been largely a disappointment. It seemed to me that they fell into two categories: There were my grandmother's type—pious, unbending, and often unkind—and my parents' sort—selfish, undisciplined, and careless of who got hurt.

I didn't want anything to do with any of them. I didn't want to be German or Irish, Catholic or non-Catholic, sister or daughter. I didn't want to be the good girl any longer. If I could have changed my name I would have.

I was starting over.

CHAPTER 7

FITS AND STARTS

"There is no fear in love. But perfect love drives
out fear ..."
SAINT JOHN THE APOSTLE, 1 John 4:18

urely there must be people who wake up one day and decide they are finished with religion and that's it, they're done. But I think that more often leaving the faith you grew up in—like leaving the family you were born into—is something that happens in fits and starts and never feels quite done. Pieces just keep surfacing like the knees of a Cypress tree, jutting out in unexpected places.

I didn't go back home for a year after packing up and moving into that no-bedroom apartment over the drugstore. I didn't go back to church until the day I got married.

Gary and I met in a class on feminist literature during my junior year in college. There were only three guys in a class filled with women, and I remember thinking what cool guys they must be, how enlightened, for being willing to spend an entire semester reading Doris Lessing and Virginia Woolf. Only later did the lopsided odds occur to me: Where else were they likely to meet so many young, single women?

Gary was the slouchy, silent guy with a brown mustache and long, frizzy Jesus hair who sat in the back of the room. He invariably dressed in jeans, T-shirts, and a frayed jean jacket with a pack of Old

Golds sticking out of the pocket. I was a little surprised when he asked if I wanted to work with him on a project that we had been assigned exploring stereotypes about women, but he said he knew how to shoot video, so I agreed.

He lugged the heavy camera equipment and figured out how to make it work, and I interviewed sorority girls, the underpaid secretaries at the Mutual of Omaha insurance company —and my mother. This was during my ardent feminist years when I favored a T-shirt with the words "Women are Not Chicks" printed across the front and refused to wear a bra or makeup. I pressed my mother hard. "Wasn't the Catholic Church really just a patriarchal institution designed to oppress women?" I asked. "Had she really wanted eight—*eight!*—children?"

She was unperturbed. "Which one of them do you think I should have given up?" she asked.

Gary was not the guy I planned on marrying. I did not, in fact, plan on getting married at all—at least that's what I told myself and others. I would graduate from college and move to Washington, DC, and if *The Washington Post* wouldn't hire me, I would go to work for a high-powered Congressman. I would wear heels and carry a briefcase to work and drink wine and sail the Chesapeake on weekends. I had had a taste of those things during a summer internship in college, and I had vowed to get back to Washington and out of Omaha and its endless split-level houses bowing to the prairie winds as soon as I had my diploma in hand.

For these reasons, I was skittish when it came to men and relationships, apt to bail at the first sign that things were getting serious. But unlike the other boys I dated, Gary didn't demand anything of me. He just shrugged when I told him I was dating around, and when I went further, telling him I didn't want to see him anymore, he shrugged again and walked away. A week later, he called to see if I wanted to catch a movie, and it all seemed so low-key, so safe and uncomplicated, that my "yes" was almost a reflex.

Less than a year later, I found myself walking down the aisle without ever having repeated that "yes," at least formally. This is because Gary never proposed. My children don't believe me when I tell them this story, but it's true. He and I had moved in together— in part because we both needed roommates to share the rent. We found an apartment in a little brick building next to a railroad track not far from campus. When the trains passed, as they did several times a day and almost every night, the entire building would shake. The trains came so close we could practically reach out the bedroom window and touch them.

Gary was as easy to live with as he was to date, and he was an incomparably better roommate than any of the girlfriends I had shared apartments with. He never sulked or picked a fight, he cleaned up after himself, and he let me watch "The Waltons" without comment.

A few months after we moved in together, one of us—neither of us remembers which one —said something like, "Well, what do you think? Is it time?" The conversation ended with an agreement that August would, indeed, be a good time. I canceled a date with a very good-looking young man I had just met and began planning the wedding.

I realize now how careless this must sound, but I was not a careless person, not even in 1975, not even at age twenty-one. Marrying Gary felt like the sensible thing to do, and looking back, I think it may have been the sanest act of my life. What we felt wasn't a head-over-heels infatuation; it was direct and simple and lasting. I knew that I would be safe with him, that I would be home.

My parents had met Gary once or twice and while I didn't bother to ask them what they thought, they did manage to convey a certain distaste for the length of his hair and the peace symbol he had plastered on the side of his 1967 Volkswagen Beetle. I didn't tell them that he also volunteered for George McGovern, played the guitar, and listened to The Mothers of Invention and other music that was nearly as incomprehensible to me as it would have been to them. I figured they had enough to digest.

When we told them we planned to get married, my dad pulled Gary aside for a little chat. "Do you have any idea what she's really like?" he asked between pulls of his cigar. "Do you know what you're getting into?"

"Yes, sir," he said. "I think I do."

Although neither of us had strong feelings about marrying in the Catholic Church, we had both been raised Catholic and having a church wedding would make our families happy. A few years earlier, my older sister, Sandy, had gotten married in a friend's living room. The service was performed by a long-haired minister who may or may not have been credentialed but was certainly efficient. The entire ceremony took about five minutes, after which my sister and her new husband exited the room to a recording of the Beatles' "A Long and Winding Road." My mother, who showed up only under threat of being denied contact with any future grandchildren, did not take it well.

Getting married in a church seemed to Gary and me more permanent and somehow more serious than the alternatives. We would feel less like two kids just a few years out of high school who had decided to get dressed up and throw a party. Besides, I was beginning to realize this was very likely the only wedding I would ever have. One night shortly after we had agreed on the big day, I remarked that if the marriage didn't work out, we could always get divorced. I was joking —sort of —but Gary didn't think it was the least bit funny. "I don't believe in divorce," he told me.

I gulped and made arrangements for us to attend the pre-marital sessions required by the Catholic Church. Our counselor was the stoic German priest I had known since the fifth grade, which sounds a lot more convivial than it was, given that the sessions consisted largely of lectures on handling finances (the man's job, of course) and how men and women have very different needs. "Was he talking about sex?" I asked as we left the last session. "I think so," Gary said. "But I'm not really sure."

I was more concerned about whether Father Meister would

remember our names at the critical moment. Throughout the preparations, including the rehearsal the night before the wedding, he called us Agnes and Henry, and I wasn't entirely certain we wouldn't be married as Agnes and Henry. It was a relief to me when he got it right during the ceremony.

* * * *

We spent the first few years of our marriage in Lincoln, Nebraska, a place that in the late 1970s was just beginning to discover the 1960s. The first Black state legislator had been elected and was wreaking havoc at the statehouse, women were organizing support groups and talking about equal pay, and twenty-somethings like us were embracing Buddhist economics and feeling pretty smug about living more simply than our oh-so-materialistic parents. Gary and I planted a garden, turned down the thermostat, set up a compost pile, and bought a small Japanese car.

I got a job with the University of Nebraska's Cooperative Extension Service writing press releases and columns about ways to save energy and the merits of the metric system, among other pressing issues of the day. It wasn't the kind of writing I wanted to do, but it meant I could study for a master's degree in journalism—free of charge by virtue of being a university employee.

Gary worked in the university's student affairs division, organizing concerts, lectures, and coffee houses for students only slightly younger than he was. He loved music, and I think he would have left with one of the many bands that passed through Nebraska in those years except that he was now a married man, albeit a married man who wasn't sure what he wanted to do with his life. Over the next few years, he would sell real estate (a spectacularly unsuccessful venture) and start a small remodeling and repair business (something he was very good at), but he never really seemed focused on a career. He would define his success in other ways.

I, on the other hand, was very much set on having a career, and

I wanted it to be in journalism. In high school and then in college, I had fallen in love with the daily urgency and the implicit power of newspapering. Like many other young people in the post-Watergate era, I was drawn to a profession that had demonstrably changed the world. Newsrooms were an added bonus—clubby and raw and filled with smart, interesting, and often downright eccentric people. It would be fun, and my days would be filled with words.

I also wanted a family. This was not obvious to most people. When Gary told his mother we were going to get married, she asked him if he was sure. "You know she's not the kind of woman who is going to want kids," she said. This was not something we had talked about. That night Gary said he had something to ask me: Did I want children someday?

"Sure," I said.

"How many?"

"Not many; maybe four or five," I told him. It didn't seem like that many to me. He almost passed out.

I was perfectly confident that I could have both a career and a family, and not just any family, but a perfect one—the kind I had longed for when I was five and ten and fifteen years old. Maybe I wanted to make up for the past; maybe I just had something to prove.

One day about three years after that conversation about children, and with about as much thought as I had given to getting married, I threw away my birth control pills. It was time, I told Gary, for us to have a baby. He said that sounded fine to him; he had just been waiting for me to be ready. We thought it would be a matter of months before I got pregnant, and I was already redecorating our extra bedroom in my head and picking out names. I'd like a boy, I thought, someone I would raise without sexual stereotypes. I'd give him a doll. I'd teach him to be nurturing. But I didn't get pregnant. What was supposed to be easy—what my mother had done eight times without trying—would take us almost three years.

The specialist we consulted advised taking my temperature every morning and having sex when the thermometer indicated rather than when the mood struck us. We tried cold showers, boxer shorts, infrequent sex, and frequent sex. We spent our days circling around one another, careful not to say anything hurtful, cautious about the marriage.

Eventually, I was scheduled for exploratory surgery. The doctor made a small incision below my gut, just large enough to see whether things were as they should be. He sewed me back up and pronounced me fine. Only then did it occur to anyone to check Gary's sperm count. One day he went into a small room with two *Playboy* magazines and emerged with a small vial of sperm—too few sperm, as it turned out.

I got the news in a phone call one night after work. The urologist had a lot to say, but I remember only one sentence: "I suggest you look into adoption."

For the next two years, I became a person deranged. The sight of a baby in a stroller moved me to tears, and it seemed as if babies in strollers had suddenly sprouted everywhere. Pregnant women were worse. Their pregnancies were so *excessive* somehow, as if they were making a point of their fecundity, my lack of it.

When one of my younger sisters announced to the family that she was pregnant with her first child, I blurted, "Well, don't expect *me* to be excited about it!" Incapable of graciousness, I vented my anger on myself. Locking myself in the bathroom one day, I pounded my abdomen furiously with my fists. The bruises lasted for days.

After a while, we stopped trying, almost stopped hoping. I looked for reporting jobs and took the only one I could find—as the farm reporter in St. Cloud, Minnesota. Gary quit his job, and we put our house up for sale and drove to central Minnesota just after Christmas in 1980. He left me there, ensconced in a single room in an old boarding house filled with college students while he returned to Nebraska to wrap up our lives there. He promised to return in a month, no more than two.

Alone in that boarding house, in a bedroom so cold and drafty I taped up newspapers over the windows, I realized I had missed my period. It's probably just the stress of moving and a new job, I thought, but, just in case, I bought a cheap kit at the drug store and took a pregnancy test. When it came out positive, I bought another kit and took the test again.

I sat in the bathroom for a long time holding that test stick in my hand, checking over and over to see if the results had changed. I felt as if someone had just granted me a reprieve from a life sentence breaking up rocks—a feeling of relief that was quickly followed by one of pure terror. How in the world was I going to do it? How was this even possible? Here I was with a new job, no house, no friends, an absent husband, and almost no money, and I was *pregnant*?

I called Gary. "I'm pregnant," I told him.

"That's impossible," he said. "How do you know?"

"I took a home pregnancy test. I took *two* home pregnancy tests. The little sticks keep showing positive."

"Have you been to the doctor yet? Have you had a blood test?"

"No. I took two pregnancy tests, damn it!"

"Go to the doctor; then call me back." He hung up the phone.

Approximately nine months later, after a labor of thirty-six hours, Patrick was born, his head tapering almost to a point from being stuck in the birth canal for so long. Afterward, when I felt sane again, I marveled that there wasn't something wrong with him, that he hadn't suffered from a lack of oxygen, that in every way except that cunning little cone head he seemed perfectly normal.

It wasn't long before I began to question what normal meant.

CHAPTER 8

AN ACCIDENTAL LIFE

"Alice laughed. 'There's no use trying,' she said.
'One can't believe impossible things.'

'I dare say you haven't had as much practice,'
said the Queen. 'When I was your age I did
it for half an hour a day. Why sometimes I've
believed as much as six impossible things
before breakfast.'"

LEWIS CARROLL, *Through the Looking-Glass*

My sister Stacy sees auras and talks to dead people, but I have never believed in the supernatural. I have a difficult enough time believing in God. But even I have trouble explaining what happened the day Patrick was baptized.

We had arranged to have the service in Manson, Iowa, where one of my younger sisters lived at the time. It was about halfway between our house in central Minnesota and eastern Nebraska, where most of my family lived. We planned to celebrate Thanksgiving dinner and the Baptism on the same weekend, and my sister Becky had convinced her parish priest to preside.

The day was bitterly cold—gray and overcast with not even a hint of sun. We bundled up Patrick, who had just turned two months old, and made the short drive to the church, a low-slung brick building unobjectionable enough on the outside but with one of those unfortunate stripped-down interiors—all blonde benches and bleached walls—that came into vogue after the Second Vatican Council in the 1960s. The effect was antiseptic, I thought, with none of the color and warmth and grandeur of older, more traditional churches.

But it had a baptistery installed as part of a remodel in 1952, along with a bathroom, kitchen, and new furnace, none of which were in evidence. The baptistery was just an alcove, a small, square room open to the church on one side and with big panes of gold and green stained glass reaching to the roofline. A slender baptismal font was positioned in the center.

There was no one else in the church as the family gathered in a circle, Patrick in the arms of his godparents, a pair of college friends who had driven up from Omaha for the day. They softly repeated "I do" as Father Thom asked them to state their belief in God and the Catholic Church. Then, just as the priest dipped a hand into the water and sprinkled the first drops onto Patrick's head, pronouncing the words, "I baptize thee in the name of the Father and of the Son and of the Holy Spirit," the sun broke through the stained glass and a beam of light shone directly onto the baby at the font.

We looked at each other and laughed a little nervously. My mother made the sign of the cross. Father Thom grinned and said, "God must have something special in mind for this baby."

As we left the church—no sun in evidence—I put the incident out of my mind. To me, it was just that—an incident; somewhat unusual perhaps but easily enough explained. It was a cloudy day; the sun came out for a moment. Nice touch.

At the time, the only marvel that interested me was my son. I had grown up taking care of younger brothers and sisters, but I was pretty certain at least some of what I had learned was wrong and possibly harmful, so I read every baby book I could find. By the time Patrick was born, I could discuss with some conviction the merits of cloth diapers, homemade baby food, and treatments for diaper rash. I knew what he was supposed to do (smile, sit up, stand up, talk, crawl, and walk) and when he was supposed to do it. I took to heart admonishments not to over discipline, overindulge, overfeed, or overstimulate.

I was not, however, in any way prepared for what I felt. I expected to love my baby, of course, but I did not expect to *be* in love in the overwhelming, all-consuming way that new mothers and fathers often are. You simply could not have convinced Gary or me that there had ever been a more perfect little being than our sunny, whip-smart son.

This is not a condition that is appealing to most people, and not just because enthralled parents generally make poor conversationalists. We had become ordinary in a way that surprised friends and family who thought of Gary as the long-haired hippie and me as the Barbra Streisand character in "The Way We Were"—the idealistic one who is set on changing the world. In truth, we had often thought of ourselves that way. Now I was getting up at 6 a.m. to work the early shift at the newspaper so I could pick up Patrick mid-afternoon. Gary had cut his hair and was selling real estate. We were all in bed before 10.

Our friends, meanwhile, were pursuing lives of determined unorthodoxy. They got married in corn fields and went off to live in communes; they took up residence in remote Rocky Mountain cabins and learned to ski; they fled to Wyoming and took up saddle-making or escaped to New York to try acting.

We were to become an unconventional family by accident.

* * * *

When Patrick was three, I took a job in New Orleans. I would be bureau chief for *The Times-Picayune* newspaper in the River Parishes a few miles upriver, which means generally west and a little north of the Crescent City. It was like moving to another country, one populated with sugar cane fields, oil refineries, and chemical plants, a country where people engaged in strange behaviors like hunting alligators, throwing beads at people, sucking the heads of crawfish, and baking small plastic babies into cakes.

I was pregnant with our second child (a pregnancy that was almost as much of a surprise as the first one), and as we drove toward New Orleans, I asked Gary if he would consider postponing a job search and staying home until we had settled in. It would be a year at the most, I said, and I'd be making enough money that we could get by. He agreed it was the sensible thing to do.

We settled in LaPlace, Louisiana, a gritty little town that was once the site of one of the largest slave uprisings in the country, in a two-story house on a cul-de-sac bordering a manmade lake swarming with what the natives brightly referred to as nutria, but which looked to me an awful lot like large rats. I went to work directing local news coverage, which in Louisiana meant lots of stories about dubious politicians and their even more dubious antics, while Gary stayed home and cleaned and cooked and played Legos and Lincoln Logs with Patrick and took care of Dana, our newborn daughter.

To say that people regarded us as strange would be an understatement. This was the mid-1980s and we were, after all, in the Deep South—in a state that even in that part of the country was widely regarded as ... a little slow to change. When Gary started hanging diapers on the clothesline he had strung up in our backyard, it was as if we had posted a sign: "Husbands Beware: You Could Be Next!"

Indeed, the other husbands in the neighborhood didn't have much to say to Gary. But their wives had plenty to say to *them*: Why didn't they ever do the laundry/watch the kids/change a diaper/vacuum the house/wash the dishes/take out the trash/mow the yard/paint the house?

I remember going to fetch Patrick one day from his best friend's house two doors over. The best friend's mother, Marilyn, a tiny woman who couldn't have weighed more than 100 pounds, was up on a ladder trying to paint the ceiling. I took one look at her and demanded, "Where is Danny?"

Danny, her husband, was out fishing in the bayou. Danny was always out fishing in the bayou—when he wasn't out hunting in the bayou or pulling a shift at the oil refinery. Marilyn, on the other hand, held down a full-time job as a receptionist, raised two girls virtually by herself, and did all the housework *and* the yard work. We had a talk, Marilyn and I. I gave her a lecture on equitable distribution of labor and washed out her paint brushes for her.

In return, Marilyn taught me how to make gumbo, the official cuisine of Louisiana, a kind of soup-stew made with leftovers and served over rice. The trick to a great gumbo, she told me, is the roux. You heat up oil in a pan, add flour, and cook until the mixture is two seconds from burning. She also provided valuable translation services, explaining why people haul their ladders with them to Mardi Gras parades (they sit their children on top so they are in a better position to catch beads) and why King Cakes, those colorful, oval confections served throughout the Carnival season, have little plastic babies baked into them (they represent the baby Jesus in anticipation of Easter).

A year-and-a-half later, Gary was still at home taking care of our own babies when I got pregnant for the third time. Our first child was a miracle; the second a surprise. This one was a sign it was time to take matters into our own hands. Gary volunteered to get a vasectomy. It was a simpler and cheaper procedure than me having my tubes tied, he said, and I wasn't about to argue with him. As soon as Lauren was born and the two of us were home safely from the hospital, he made the appointment.

The children and I went with him to the doctor's office one day while I was still on maternity leave. We had been told the surgery would take no time at all and we could wait while it was being performed and then, assuming all went well, drive him home. Gary, who seemed entirely unfazed by the whole thing, filled out some forms and was ushered into a back room to await the doctor. That's when the receptionist at the counter beckoned me over.

"You need to give your consent before the doctor will perform the surgery," she told me. I had not expected this, but I had gotten used to things being a little different in Louisiana. Maybe, I thought, this was another of the state's unusual laws, like the one that allows people to drink and drive—provided they're not *drunk* and driving. I asked the woman what exactly it was I was being asked to sign.

As she began to patiently explain the fine print, I stood there, juggling Lauren in one arm, pushing Dana back into her stroller with the other, and telling Patrick he couldn't possibly have to go to the bathroom again. The woman regarded us all for a moment, slid the paper toward me and said, "Just sign here, honey." I did.

I was still on leave a few weeks later when the newspaper transferred me to a larger bureau in St. Tammany Parish on the other side of Lake Pontchartrain, just east of New Orleans. Patrick was enrolled in a first-grade class for gifted students—a program I had insisted he be tested for even though children his age weren't typically accepted into accelerated programs. I liked the idea that he would get one-on-one attention and be exposed to material far more advanced than that usually given to first graders, but my real motivation was to get him out of nap time, during which he never napped and often got into trouble. In the gifted program, he would be spared naps and could spend the time in another classroom with a teacher who let him chat away as much as he liked. Patrick loved it.

Dana, who was even more sociable than her brother and yearned to go to school, started preschool at a program called Mothers' Day Out. For a small fee and an agreement to work at the school one day a month, moms could drop off their children several mornings a week. Only in our case, it was dad who dropped off—and dad who showed up to work on the appointed volunteer day. The night after Gary worked his first shift, the woman who ran the program got a half dozen phone calls from mothers, all with the same question: "Why was there a man in my child's classroom today?"

Gary took all of this with equanimity. He is not the kind of guy who gets worked up about things. In fact, he's one of only a handful of people I have ever known who truly do not care what people think of them, which explains a lot about the way he dresses, which is to say cheap and on-hand. I once came home from work to find him wearing a new sweater. "Guess where I got this?" he asked me. I looked at him, looked at the sweater and said, "On the street." He was incredulous: "How did you *know*?" he sputtered.

I sometimes complain that my husband is the cheapest man in America, but the truth is he's not miserly at all. It's just that waste offends him. He doesn't see any sense in using more than absolutely necessary. This mindset applies to everything from clothes (thus his preference for Goodwill over any other store) to plastic bags (we wash, dry and reuse them, even the free ones that come from the grocery store).

Gary has held part-time jobs over the years, but mostly his career has consisted of taking care of me (some would say nearly a full-time job in itself) and our children. Our kids didn't question why their dad stayed home and mom worked. It seemed natural to them that it was dad who bought the groceries ("made groceries" in New Orleans' parlance), cooked dinner, took them to the doctor, scheduled their play dates, and checked their homework. He drew the line at playing Barbie dolls with the girls, but otherwise almost anything was a go. I would come home from work some nights and find Gary stirring something on the stove, his fingernails painted bright red or pink. The girls had insisted, he said; he had such nice big fingernails for them to practice on.

I loved my job, but I did sometimes feel a little jealous of the time Gary had with our children, the times I missed. Still, deep down, I knew that he was better with them than I would have been. He was more patient and more attentive, more playful and better at saying no.

I freely admit that I am not one of those mothers who live for her children. My children, in fact, claim it is often hard to get my attention. I have a tendency to ask a question and fail to listen to the answer. I'm apt to wander in and out of conversations. I'm often late and easily distracted. I spend too much time working and not enough time with my family.

The last point was brought home to me one afternoon when I left the office early, arriving home well before the usual expected time of half-past dinner. Dana and her best friend were sitting in the middle of the living room playing with dolls. "Hi, mom," Dana said casually. Her friend looked up at me in surprise, then leaned over to Dana. "I didn't know you had a mom," she whispered.

"Of course, she has a mother," I said a little too sharply. After that, I was careful to make it home a little earlier at least a few nights a week.

I like to think that while I spent a lot of time focusing as a journalist on other people's lives, I was there for my children at the critical times—when they were hurt or floundering or heading for trouble. I like to think I knew them to their cores and there was nothing they could do or say that would surprise me. But, of course, I was wrong, especially when it came to Patrick. In ways I found it hard to put my finger on, my son seemed different from other children. While he could be playful and silly, he more often did things with a seriousness and purpose that seemed out of proportion to his age and that I found difficult to understand.

When he was six, he decided we should read the dictionary from beginning to end. We started with an illustrated *Sesame Street* dictionary, but he said that was too easy, so we took up "the big people's dictionary," as he called it, reading a page or two each night. He would fall asleep as I explained the meaning of words.

It wasn't long before he discovered *The Hobbit* and then *The Lord of the Rings*. I wasn't sure how much of these books he understood (I wasn't sure how much I understood), but I suspect now that it was the idea of an impossible quest that appealed to him, the notion that clear evil and imperfect good will inevitably clash and it is this collision that shapes the world and gives it meaning.

Patrick's other childhood passion also involved hard-pitched battles with clear winners and losers, only these battles took place in real life—on a playing field. For several years, baseball occupied his every waking moment. He bought and traded baseball cards like a miniature stockbroker and counted the days until Little League started, speculating endlessly about what position he would try out for and who would make the team. When he was seven and playing his first season, he got hit hard in the eye with a baseball. "I have to go back!" he kept wailing as we drove to the hospital. "My team needs me!" A few years later, he began playing soccer, a sport he would stick with until discovering Ultimate Frisbee in college.

Most of all, he hated to lose—at anything. When he was little, I would try to beat him at board games just to teach him that he couldn't always win, an effort I had to largely give up by the time he was ten because there wasn't a game, including chess, he couldn't beat me at.

Like many eldest children, Patrick was mature beyond his years, comfortable with adults and responsible to a fault. In fact, I sometimes felt like *he* was the adult and *we* were the children. On the rare occasions when we hired a babysitter, he would ask what time we planned to be home, and he would be standing at the front door, arms folded, at the appointed time. "You're late," he would say. "You were supposed to be back ten minutes ago."

He seemed so intent on the truth that I resolved never to lie to him. One year a few weeks before Christmas, shortly after he had turned eight, he said he had something important to ask me. It was about Santa Claus, he said, and he wanted me to tell him the truth. Was Santa real? I remember bending down to look into his face, weighing whether he was ready for such a large dose of reality, wondering whether an eight-year-old didn't deserve a few more years of make-believe. "Do you really want to know?" I asked him.

Patrick remembers this moment as vividly as I do. "I was only eight!" he has said to me more than once. "Why did you tell me there was no Santa Claus!"

"Because you asked me," I tell him a little defensively. But in truth, he so infrequently acted like a child that I sometimes forgot he was one. And when I did remember, I would start worrying. Wasn't he a little too intense, a little too prone to extravagant passions and fervent friendships? Would he ever be able to negotiate a middle ground?

I should have realized my son would be no different when it came to religion. We had joined a Catholic church in Louisiana, not because we were particularly religious but because it seemed to us that serious parenting required a least semi-serious churchgoing. If our children decided to drop out of the Catholic Church when they were older, that was fine, but, in the meantime, we felt a little religion wouldn't hurt and could very possibly help them develop a moral compass—or at least a sense of purpose beyond satisfying their own impulses.

This was fine in theory until Patrick was nearing the age of seven, the traditional age at which Catholics make their first confession (now called Reconciliation) and their First Communion. What I remember most about my own First Communion is wearing a white dress several sizes too big (a hand-me-down from my older sister), a white veil (also passed down), and white shoes (breathtakingly new). My parents invited all our relatives and threw a party in the backyard during which I refused to remove one inch of white. I think I would have slept in that dress if they had let me.

By the time my son was in training for the traditional Catholic sacraments, girls were discouraged from wearing miniature bridal costumes and nobody was required to wear white. I bought Patrick a suit—his first—in pale blue and quizzed him on his catechism, which hadn't changed at all as far as I could tell. There were still mortal sins (the kind you go to hell for) and venial sins (the slightly less serious kind for which you might end up in purgatory), and only good Catholics were sure to get to heaven.

Patrick was a wreck, nervous about the sins he would confess to the priest (what sins could he possibly have? I kept thinking) and worried about walking to the front of the church to receive the communion host for the first time. (This is in contrast to my youngest, Lauren, who made her First Communion, so to speak, several years later by sticking out her hand and grabbing the host the first time she had the chance.)

Serious and pale, Patrick managed to make it through the ceremony without throwing up, and we hosted a little party for him afterward. The following Sunday, he got up, put on his little blue suit and asked when we were leaving for Mass. It was, he reminded us, a mortal sin to miss Mass on Sunday.

After that, Gary and I took turns accompanying our son to church while the other stayed home with Dana and Lauren. Taking the girls inevitably meant spending most of the service in what was impolitely but accurately called the cry room, where we would stuff them with Teddy Grahams and pace back and forth in front of the window separating us from the rest of the grown-ups—the ones without children or whose children miraculously obeyed—watching as they mouthed words to a service we couldn't hear.

It was my turn to take Patrick one Sunday when the pastor, an innocuous man who tended toward sleepy sermons and warm handshakes, cut short the usual reflection on that day's Gospel to talk about money. The church needed it, he said, and it was our obligation to give it. Pledge cards were handed around, and the priest made a little speech about how women who happened to be there unaccompanied by their husbands should take the card home and have their husbands fill it out because men are responsible for a family's finances.

I was incredulous. Expecting gasps of outrage (this was, after all, the late 1980s), I looked around the church. No one seemed to be paying particular attention: A handful of other solo moms were trying to contain their toddlers. One stuffed the card into her purse.

I took my card and started writing. In very small print, filling every bit of available space, I told the priest exactly what I thought. I wrote that I, not my husband, was the breadwinner in our household and my husband stayed home and took care of our children while I worked to support us. And I didn't need my husband to decide how much money we should give to the church or to anyone else, and if I consulted him, it would be because we should make financial decisions together, not because he should make decisions for me.

I think I might have squeaked a little because at one point Patrick pulled at my blouse. "Mom, what's the matter?"

"Nothing," I hissed and kept writing.

When the service was over, I grabbed Patrick's hand and pulled him down the aisle. We marched up to the priest (at least I marched up to the priest; Patrick was just trying to keep up). Handing him the card, I said, "Here's what I think about what you said, and I'm not coming back." I didn't wait for an answer, and I didn't go back.

I had walked away from the Catholic Church before, but that had been more of a cessation than a conclusion. I had still thought of myself as Catholic; I was just taking a pause. I could change my mind whenever I wanted. This time, leaving felt permanent and irreversible, as if I was renouncing citizenship in my native country. It carried with it feelings of nostalgia and small pangs of homesickness, but it also felt right. For years I had doubted whether the Catholic Church was a place where I could ever feel comfortable again.

It seemed to me that when it came to women, the church's approach was nothing more than a series of no's. No, you can't use birth control; no, you can't have an abortion regardless of how dire the circumstances; no, you can't be a priest; no, you can't even step on the altar—it's reserved for men. All of those no's added up to one thing in my mind: I wasn't equal. I wasn't even very welcome.

I thought briefly about giving up formal religion altogether, but Gary, an idealist with a strong practical streak, worried that without a strong religious foundation, our children would grow up deficient somehow; they might even join a cult. He wasn't kidding, so we began to look around.

We visited several churches, including another Catholic congregation, before eventually settling on an Episcopal church, small and with, I thought, a much more enlightened view of the world. These

Episcopalians embraced birth control, married clergy, and female priests. They welcomed gay members, valued a decent choir, and said as little as possible about abortion. In other ways, though, they seemed more Catholic than the Catholics. There always seemed to be copious amounts of incense floating around, and people still knelt at a railing before the altar to receive communion. It reminded me of the church I grew up in.

Instead of a cry room there was a children's Mass, and when it was over, about halfway through the blessedly quiet adult Mass, the children would march up the aisle, faces bright and fingers clutching that day's art project. They would scan the pews, looking for their parents and, when spotting them, rush into their arms, waving their noodle Noah's arks and glittery pictures of apostles.

The only thing I missed was the comfortable anonymity of the big Catholic churches in which I was raised. Here, people noticed if you showed up or not, what you wore, whether you brought a casserole to the church picnic or volunteered to teach Sunday school. I felt conspicuous. I felt obligated. Still, we stayed, making friends and contributing our share of casseroles.

One week, Patrick's Sunday school teacher took me aside. She wanted to talk about Patrick. She said she had never had another child in her class who took the church's teachings so seriously, who seemed so open to God in his life. I nodded vaguely as she talked, thinking about my eleven-year-old son who spent too much time playing Nintendo and who loved tormenting his little sisters. He would wrestle Dana and Lauren to the floor and pin their arms to their sides, then lean down and suspend long drops of drool over their faces while they watched and screamed helplessly.

"You don't understand," the woman insisted, coming closer and enunciating every word. "He's *really ... deeply ... * spiritual."

She was right. I had no idea what she was talking about, so I thanked her politely and wandered off. I didn't bring up the conversation at home because there didn't seem to be much to say—she was probably an overzealous Sunday school teacher thankful for a single preadolescent boy willing to sit still long enough to listen to her.

"He's a good boy," I thought, and put it out of my mind.

*   *   *   *

Later that year, Gary began lobbying to leave Louisiana. As he ticked off the reasons—a crumbling public school system, rampant political corruption, high crime rates, and pollution—all I could think of was that those were precisely the reasons I liked it so much. Louisiana was a great place to be a journalist. Where else could you cover a governor's race that pitted a former Ku Klux Klan leader against an incumbent who publicly questioned the resurrection of Jesus and declared the only way he could lose the race was if he was found in bed with either a dead girl or a live boy? (To be fair, the incumbent, one Edwin Edwards, made it clear that he did not expect to go to heaven. He did, however, eventually go to jail.) Besides being a journalistic promised land, I reminded Gary, the cost of living was low, the food was great, and no other people on earth threw such good parties.

But I knew I was defeated when the next Mardi Gras rolled around. We were standing on a corner taking in the spectacle of floats and marching bands and trying to keep the kids from running into the street in pursuit of stray beads, doubloons, lace panties, and plastic dog turds when the Chalmette Strutters came by. The krewe was made up mostly of eight- and nine-year-olds wearing sequined tops and tiny shorts, bright red lipstick, and piles of makeup, their hair teased to impossible heights, and they were dancing to the song "Let's Get Physical" in the most suggestive way imaginable for eight- and nine-year-old girls.

Gary looked at our two young daughters and then at me. "Is this what you want them to be?" he asked.

Dana, who always had an eye for spangles and sparkles, was

pulling at my sleeve. "Can I have one of those, mommy?" she asked, pointing out a particularly skimpy outfit.

"Ok," I said to Gary. "You've got a point."

The next year we moved to Salem, Oregon, where I took a job as managing editor of the newspaper, and we settled into a little house in an historic neighborhood that wound up and down a lush hillside where blackberries grew wild in the summers and children wandered freely from house to house. All three of our kids could walk to their schools on weekdays, and we could walk together to the Episcopal church on Sundays. We would make our way down the hill, the girls twirling their skirts and swinging their plastic purses while Patrick hurried us along so as not to be late for his altar boy duties. I don't remember now whether it was his idea or ours that he become an altar boy, but he didn't seem to mind assisting the priest during Mass—or the fact that the long white robe he got to wear made him look like a character in a Star Wars movie.

The girls joined the children's choir and the bell choir and competed to be angels in the annual Christmas pageant. Patrick signed up for a class to prepare for confirmation, a ritual that would initiate him, at age twelve, into the Episcopal Church as an adult member. I noted that he approached the ceremony as soberly as he had his First Communion, with the same sense of something momentous happening, but I doubted the parallel occurred to him. In fact, I doubted he remembered the Catholic Church at all.

CHAPTER 9

THESE MEN CALLED JESUITS

"Some people say a lie is just a lie;
But I say the cross is in the ballpark.
Why deny the obvious, child?"
PAUL SIMON, The Obvious Child

My favorite Jesuit, other than my son, of course, isn't a real Jesuit at all. He's not even a real person. Emilio Sandoz is the tortured main character in Mary Doria Russell's science fiction classic, *The Sparrow*. Sandoz and three other Jesuit priests are chosen by the Society of Jesus to travel to the planet Rakhat using an interstellar vessel made from a small asteroid. Only Sandoz returns, with strangely elongated fingers and despairing of God.

While I know of no Jesuits who have ever actually traveled to other planets, the story rings true in an important way: Jesuits have been confronting alien cultures almost since the Society was formed.

Ignatius of Loyola, a Catholic nobleman from the Basque region of Spain, founded the Society of Jesus in 1539 along with six other young men, all of whom were eager to convert souls to Christianity and rekindle the faith among those already Catholic. By the time Ignatius died in 1556, the company had grown to more than a thousand members and was running churches, hospitals, schools, and missions throughout much of Western Europe as well as Brazil, India, and Japan.

Wherever they were, they adapted to the native culture. While other missionaries condemned the customs of countries like China and Japan as pagan, the Jesuits adopted local language, clothes, food, and drink. They went out of their way to incorporate each country's customs and beliefs into Catholic ceremonies, sometimes to the consternation of the Vatican.

In seventeenth-century China, for example, Jesuit missionary Matteo Ricci essentially became a Mandarin in order to understand Chinese culture and win acceptance at the imperial court. He adopted Mandarin dress, spoke Mandarin, wrote a book about the similarities between Catholicism and Confucianism, and allowed that there was a place for the veneration of ancestors. Centuries later, another Jesuit, Pedro Arrupe, became something of a Japanophile. He was posted to Nagasaki in the years before World War II and was there when the atomic bomb was dropped. After the war, while Superior of the Jesuits in Japan, Arrupe tried Zen meditation, Haiku, Japanese calligraphy, and tea ceremonies. He learned to speak Japanese and published eight books in the language.

Jesuits have always been highly pragmatic when it comes to winning friends and influencing people—especially people in power. One story widely told about Francis Xavier, a contemporary of Ignatius, describes how he was dispatched to Japan as a missionary but was having no luck with the local elite, who were decidedly unimpressed by this foreigner with his humble clothes and soft-spoken ways. Xavier decided to change his approach. He dressed up in fine clothes, gathered a large entourage, and presented himself to the local authorities along with gifts that included a pair of velvet slippers and a watch. It worked. He was given permission to preach.

Xavier and the Jesuit missionaries who followed him pursued a kind of ecclesiastical expansion, converting hundreds of thousands of people around the world, ranging from Iroquois Indians in Canada to the Guaraní tribes of Paraguay. Some of these conversions lasted no longer than a generation, but many others have endured to the present day. The Philippines and much of Central America, South America, and Africa are Catholic due in no small part to their efforts.

Along the way, Jesuits accumulated an impressive list of firsts that seemingly have little to do with converting souls. They made the first modern maps of China, pioneered the study of Sanskrit in the West, and created the first grammars and compiled the first dictionaries in Japanese, Vietnamese, and the languages of the Philippines and many Native American tribes. They introduced the printing press to India and Western science and astronomy to China. They also communicated Chinese knowledge and philosophy to Europe, which included translating Confucius' works into European languages.

They were among the first Christian scholars to embrace secular sciences such as mathematics, physics, astronomy, archeology, linguistics, biology, and chemistry. They developed telescopes, discovered comets and binary stars, and mapped the equators of the moon. (Fun fact: thirty-five craters on the moon and thirty-two asteroids are named for Jesuits.) They laid the groundwork for the development of calculus and germ theory, pioneered the use of computers for linguistic and literary analysis, and were among a group of researchers to first detect excess atmospheric radiation.

Jesuits also built performing arts theaters across Europe and, in 1640 in Quebec, they founded the first theater on the North American continent, eventually adding accoutrements such as a trapdoor and the sheer curtains known as the scrim. They are credited with everything from laying the foundation for the modern ballet and teaching the French how to make porcelain to inventing the first megaphone, introducing umbrellas to Europeans, and reforming the Gregorian calendar. Because of Jesuits, a native Peruvian cure for Malaria, cinchona bark or "Jesuit bark," more commonly known as quinine, spread around the world and saved untold lives, including that of the emperor of Japan.

Jesuits have been counselors to kings and emperors and chiefs, and they have educated the children of kings and emperors and chiefs. They have brokered political alliances, arranged royal marriages, and negotiated peace treaties. All of this has not been enough, however, to keep them out of trouble. Almost since their founding, they have managed to offend large numbers of people, including a fair number of Catholics and, perhaps more significantly, no small number of popes. To gain support for their missions across Europe and around the globe, the early Jesuits struck a number of alliances with kings, queens, dukes, and duchesses, but currying favor with secular power meant occasionally getting on the wrong side of the pope, not to mention *rival* kings, queens, dukes, and duchesses.

Even more problematic, the church of Ignatius' day was an institution caught up in fierce religious arguments and rivalries over matters that few people would think worth bothering about today, including how often the faithful should receive communion and how many hours a day a priest should spend praying. The Jesuits tended to take unorthodox views of such matters, especially when it came to how priests should behave. This is apparent in the Jesuit Constitutions, the document that still guides the way members live and work, in which Ignatius set out a remarkably moderate course.

Jesuits would not live in cells like members of monastic orders. Each member was to have his own room, large enough to fit a bed, desk, books, and other personal items. The main meal of the day was to be served family style, accompanied by wine, and each house was to have a room set aside for recreation. Jesuits were to exercise, eat healthily, get plenty of sleep, and wear decent clothes. A healthy man, Ignatius observed, could be of more help to his neighbor than an unhealthy one.

Members of other religious orders might go on brutally long fasts, doing without food or even water until their bodies broke down, but Ignatius had done some fasting of that sort early in his religious career and decided it was counterproductive. He advised Jesuits to be reasonable about their fasts and instructed them to see a doctor before embarking on one at all. And while other religious communities had jail cells where disobedient members could be whipped or scourged, Ignatius wrote no penal code into his Constitutions.

When it came to prayer, Ignatius was concerned not that members wouldn't pray enough but that they would spend too much time praying. A young man entering the Jesuits was allowed no more than one hour a day in prayer or meditation. There was just too much else to do.

While Jesuits took vows of poverty, chastity, and obedience like other Catholic religious orders, Ignatius' view of poverty, at least, was a practical one. He didn't want members to have to spend all their time begging, nor did he want them living richly. This "middle way" is one the Jesuits have attempted to observe ever since.

Ignatius was big on one other thing: He really didn't want Jesuits climbing the church ladder. Perhaps he thought it would be corrupting, or he just wanted his men to be available in a way that bishops, tied to dioceses and geography, could not be, but he was adamant on the point. He wrote into the Constitutions a special vow required of all Jesuits that they will not aspire to higher church office. The wording could not be clearer: "I will not ambition, not even indirectly, to be chosen or promoted to any prelacy or dignity in or outside the Society; and I will do my best never to consent to my election unless I am forced to do so by obedience to him who can order me under penalty of sin." Every Jesuit still takes that vow, which goes a long way toward explaining why there had never been a Jesuit pope before Pope Francis.

But Ignatius was also a pragmatic man, open to bending the rules when the occasion required, and even during his lifetime there was at least one Jesuit bishop. Typically, such a promotion happens when the reigning pope steps in. He taps a Jesuit on the shoulder, the Jesuit reminds him that he has taken a vow not to be elevated in the church, and then the pope has his way. Once this occurs, all doors are open. A Jesuit who becomes bishop can then be named a cardinal, the highest church office next to pope and the body from which new popes are selected. (At the time of Pope Francis' appointment, there were four Jesuits cardinals, not counting Francis himself, but all but one of them was too old to take part in the papal election, and the one besides Francis who could have participated was too sick to make the trip, making Francis's election all the more remarkable.)

Once a Jesuit is made a bishop or cardinal, he is only nominally a Jesuit. He is no longer active in the order and no longer answers to the Superior General, the head of the Jesuit order, although Ignatius did suggest that a Jesuit who finds himself in an elevated position "keep an open ear" to the Jesuit General's counsel.

In any event, it seems clear that Ignatius' strategy was to steer his members away from traditional posts of authority within the church and focus instead on what he considered the order's real work—to "help souls" on the streets and in schools and hospitals and brothels—wherever people spent their lives.

It didn't always turn out the way he intended, however. Ignatius spent a good deal of time navigating papal politics and the shifting secular alliances of his day. He and his order would be in favor with the powers-that-be one day and then a new regime would take office, and all bets were off—a pattern that would repeat itself over the next several centuries and would culminate in the suppression of the Jesuits by Pope Clement XIV, a former Franciscan, in 1773.

It wasn't so much that Clement hated the Jesuits as that he was under considerable pressure from France, Portugal, and Spain, where the Jesuits had powerful friends and even more powerful enemies, to rein in the rich and influential order. Consequently, on July 21, 1773, Clement signed an official order called a papal bull that officially disbanded the Society. Jesuit property was confiscated, the Superior General was thrown into prison, and Jesuit priests were told to join other orders. Only in Russia, where Catherine the Great decided to ignore the pope's demand, did the Society continue. The ban in the rest of the world lasted forty years before another pope acted to restore the order.

The following 150 years or so were a conservative time for the Society, at least in Europe. Jesuits managed to stay pretty much on the side of the ruling monarchies while putting much of their energies into the US, Africa, India, Central and South America, and the islands of the South Pacific. During this time, the Jesuits were closely associated with Ultramontanism, a movement within the church that emphasized papal authority and centralization.

In the twentieth century, especially after the Second Vatican Council in 1965, the order began to shift to advocacy for political reform on behalf of the poor. And, as they became increasingly aligned with disenfranchised elements of society, members began to come into conflict with the governments and institutions that caused, or at least contributed to, the terrible circumstances endured by the people they were supposed to serve.

Encouraged by their own experience and set free by the Vatican, the Jesuits became, in the view of many, increasingly radical. During the 1970s and 1980s, a number of Jesuits were instrumental in the development of liberation theology in Central and South America. Their premise was that freeing people from injustice and oppression was a necessary part of doing God's work, and it led them to identify with revolutionary movements in places like Nicaragua and El Salvador.

This was dangerous business. In 1989, soldiers dragged six Jesuits who had been critical of the El Salvadoran government out of their beds and shot them, then went back into the house and killed a housekeeper and her fifteen-year-old daughter. The summer after he graduated from college, Patrick visited the graves of these martyred priests as part of a trip sponsored by the Jesuits at Creighton University. He needed to go, he said, in order to understand what it really means to believe in a God of the poor.

The Marxist overtones of liberation theology did not go over well with the church hierarchy and neither did a growing social activism on the part of Jesuits in more developed countries. In the US, peace activist and Jesuit priest Daniel Berrigan—the one who prompted Patrick's pilgrimage to New York—encouraged resistance to the Vietnam War, and he and other Jesuits loudly advocated for economic justice for the poor.

The Polish-born Pope John Paul II, a staunch anti-Communist, was especially critical of such efforts. In 1981, apparently believing the Jesuits had become too independent, leftist, and political, he suspended the normal workings of the Jesuit Constitutions in what some call the second suppression of the order. He also removed reform-minded Pedro Arrupe as Superior General, replacing him with an Italian Jesuit he trusted more. It was two years before the Jesuits were once again allowed to elect their own leader.

The next pope, Benedict XVI, was not as openly hostile toward the Jesuits as his predecessor, but he appeared to harbor some doubts as well. One of his first actions upon taking office was to remove the editor of the New York-based Jesuit *America* magazine, known for its sometimes less-than-orthodox coverage of controversial issues such as birth control, priestly celibacy, and the ban on women priests. Benedict also pressured the Jesuits to pledge "total adhesion" to Catholic doctrines such as divorce and homosexuality. The fact that Benedict was replaced with a Jesuit must have been as big of a surprise to him as to everyone else.

*   *   *   *

From the start, the Jesuits intended to be different from other Catholic religious orders. They did not want to be confined to parish churches or to be monks tied down to one place chanting the liturgy for hours a day. They were not trained for ceremony but for ministry.

One of the earliest directives issued to members was to "see God in all things." They were to imitate Jesus and the disciples by going out into the world, preaching and doing good works. The early Jesuits promptly set out to establish orphanages, hospitals, and schools. They worked with the sick, the poor, prisoners, and prostitutes. And when it was the best way to reach people, they sang and produced plays.

Because they would be part of the world rather than separate from it, Jesuits did not have an official habit like other religious groups. The Constitutions give only these instructions as to what constitutes proper attire: "First, it should be proper; second, conformed to the usage of the country of residence; and third, not contradictory to the poverty we profess."

The common priestly dress of the day was a black cassock, a long gown wrapped around the body and tied at the waist. During the missionary periods in North America, native people began calling Jesuits "Black Robes" because of this dress. Today, most US Jesuits—when they wear clerics at all—favor black pants with a black shirt to which is attached a Roman collar, a white strip of cloth or plastic that buttons or snaps onto a regular shirt collar.

Ignatius' Jesuits differed from traditional religious orders of the day in two other significant ways: their focus on education and the meditative, almost mystical approach to prayer that is known as the Spiritual Exercises.

The clergy in the sixteenth century were not particularly well educated, and Ignatius himself didn't become a university student until he was in his thirties, but he wanted his recruits to have a first-rate education. And he wanted them to teach—not just theology but philosophy, Latin, Greek, classical literature, sciences, and the arts—to anyone who wanted to learn. The first religious order of the Catholic Church to take on formal education as a major part of its ministry, the Jesuits were running seventy-four colleges on three continents by the time Ignatius died in 1556.

Over the next two centuries, Jesuits would go on to establish what a member of the order, John W. O'Malley, in his detailed account of the Jesuits' early years, calls "a remarkable network of more than 800 educational institutions, primarily in Latin Europe and Latin America, but also in other parts of the world, a truly unique phenomenon in the history of education."

Today there are more than 3,700 Jesuit colleges or universities in more than seventy countries around the world, including twenty-eight in the US. These include Georgetown University in Washington, DC; Fordham University in New York City; Boston College; Gonzaga University in Spokane, Washington; and the various Loyolas in Chicago, New Orleans, and Los Angeles. In addition, Jesuits operate about sixty secondary schools in the states that prepare mostly high school boys for college. These schools have educated scientists, writers and lawyers, CEOs and generals, US presidents and cabinet members, ensuring the Society's continued influence and, some would stipulate, power.

The other important Jesuit innovation is contained in one of the world's most famous books, *The Spiritual Exercises*, a kind of teacher's manual containing meditations on the life of Jesus, prayers, and mental exercises. These Exercises, developed by Ignatius based on his own spiritual awakening well before the founding of the Society, were to be conducted under the guidance of a trained director, typically over a four-week period—in effect, creating the modern notions of a retreat and spiritual direction.

The Exercises initially brought Ignatius into conflict with church authorities, who thought them a little scandalous and possibly heretical. This was at a time when Protestantism was on the rise, and Catholic leaders were intent on warding off any signs of unorthodoxy. For them, religion was about correct thinking on dogma and acting according to strict rules. The Exercises were about feelings, desires, and getting close to God in a deeply personal way. The person guiding the Exercises was not to try to influence the outcome in any way, leaving it to God to do the teaching. Moreover, this experience was to be open to anyone, not just clergy.

Ignatius used the Exercises to recruit members, but his ambition was to reteach all Christians how to pray. That is still the goal of the Jesuits, who conduct versions of the Exercises for thousands of people around the world every year.

However, Ignatius never thought that prayer alone was enough.

His directions for the Exercises include the words Jesuits have been repeating for more than five centuries: "Love ought to manifest itself in deeds rather than words." People are to complete the Exercises and then go out and *do* something—preferably something Jesus or the disciples would have done.

These two calls—to contemplate and to act—became the central tenants of the Jesuit order, and they are in large part what distinguish the Jesuits from other religious orders. They are, I believe, what attracted my son to the Jesuits and what keep him there.

* * * *

When Patrick went to Creighton University, he had never heard of the Jesuits, and at first, he didn't know what to think. Who were these men who seemed so worldly and so other-worldly at the same time? They could probe philosophy one minute and dissect basketball scores the next. They were deeply religious but not in an in-your-face kind of way. And perhaps best of all for an idealistic young man, they were rebels and reformers: They wanted to change the world.

The risk, the radicalism of it all, appealed to him. These were not men who settled for comfortable lives in suburbia. They lived zealously, with conviction and purpose. It made Patrick think of the Paul Simon song "Obvious Child" about a man who has chosen a conventional life filled with fun and money and even love but finds no meaning in it. "Who wants to live like everyone else?" he thought.

Many young people feel this call to act—to live differently than their parents, to do good in the world. But what struck Patrick most about the Jesuits was that they made this kind of life possible. They painted a picture of what the world should be like and then created a system, an order that, he says, allows people to "live in a certain way, in a way that makes it easier to be good."

Moreover, the Jesuit conception of what could be accomplished in the world struck him as rational, defensible, and real. This wasn't just Jedi fantasies (although George Lucas apparently has hinted that the Jedi with their black robes, strict rules of discipline and purity, years of training, and dedication to the Force, were modeled on the Jesuits).

Patrick thought that what the Jesuits offered was more than fairytale stuff or feel-good introspection. It was grounded in history's great philosophers like Saint Augustine and Saint Thomas Aquinas and continues to be shaped by modern Catholic thinkers like Charles Taylor and Alasdair MacIntyre—people who believed the world can be understood and changed and did their part to change it.

Patrick remembers walking out of his first philosophy class, the one all Creighton students are required to take, and thinking "How come no one ever taught me *this* before?" He was equally impressed with the way people around him talked about God. His best friends in high school included evangelical Christians and Mormons who were good people and talked about God but "not in a way that was compelling or intellectually rigorous," he said.

These Jesuits were different. And Ignatius blew him away. As Patrick relates the story, Ignatius was a guy who basically set out to be a saint. "He does what he thinks you have to do to be a saint—he gives away all of his belongings, wears rags, fasts, prays, goes off on a pilgrimage, and cuts himself off from the world. And the result is that he feels terrible. He literally almost commits suicide. He thinks, 'God was telling me to be a saint, and this is what it means to be a saint, and I do it, and it feels awful, and I want to die.'

"The only part he was wrong about was what it means to be a saint. And he was so stubborn! As soon as he let go a little bit and let God speak to him and say, 'That's not what it means,' he found his way. And later in his life, after the Jesuits had been founded, he would stand on the roof of the curia (the Jesuit house) at night and look at the stars and cry at how beautiful the world is and how he could possibly be loved by the God who created this. He had to learn that you have to be loyal to your own experience of God. He doesn't want you to be a saint somebody else's way, but your way."

Listening to him, I remembered a line from a book by Anne Lamott in which she asks a friend what can be done in the face of powerlessness and despair. The friend tells her that the key is to "show up, wear clean underwear, say hello to strangers, and pray that we might cooperate with any flicker of light we can find in the world."

For Patrick, Ignatius of Loyola and the long, strange history of the Jesuits was that flicker of light.

CHAPTER 10

CHASTITY, POVERTY, AND OBEDIENCE

"He who is unmarried cares for the things of
the Lord—how he may please the Lord. But he
who is married cares about the things of the
world—how he may please his wife."
I CORINTHIANS 7:25

hen I tell people that my son is a priest, I can count on one of two reactions. First, there are those who say, "You? You have a son who's a priest?" These tend to be people who know me, and the better they know me, the more emphasis there is on that word *"you."*

I am, admittedly, an unlikely candidate to be the mother of a priest. A journalist for more than twenty years, then an educator of journalists, I am a skeptic, a cynic, a scoffer. I'm comfortable in newsrooms and courtrooms and bars. I'd rather hike a mountain than go to church.

"Yes," I tell these people. "Some things just can't be explained."

The second reaction I get when people learn my son is a Catholic priest is a little more nuanced but no less curious. "Really?" they say. "You mean he can't get married?" What they're really wondering, I suspect, is whether he can have sex.

A lot of people never marry and still manage active sexual lives (some might say to excess). What's unusual about Catholic priests is that they're not allowed either marriage or sex. Let me repeat: No sex. Ever.

I don't know about anyone else, but I find that proposition almost unimaginable, especially in twenty-first century America when it's nearly impossible to turn on the TV, go to a movie, open a magazine, walk on a college campus, or enter a mall (think Victoria's Secret and Abercrombie & Fitch) without encountering sex—people dressing for sex, people talking about sex, and sometimes people actually having sex—right there in front of you. What must that be like for a celibate man?

This is not a comfortable topic for a mother and son, but when I've broached it (as a journalist I've grown used to asking untoward questions), Patrick has tended to shrug it off. It's not that he doesn't think celibacy is a big deal. It is, he says. And it doesn't mean he's suddenly become asexual. He points out that he's as likely—perhaps more likely—to pick out a pretty woman in a crowd as any other heterosexual man. But celibacy is both a practical consideration for men like the Jesuits who live together in communities (just imagine the chaos that would erupt if partners, wives, and children began moving in) and a means to develop the kinds of relationships with others that are nearly impossible if sex is involved.

I think it's true that men and women who practice celibacy well—who have, in other words, found a way to be both abstinent and psychologically healthy—tend to be open to others in ways that people rarely are. Poet and writer Kathleen Norris says this is one of the things that surprised her most during the many months she spent living in a Benedictine monastery. The monks, she writes, have a talent for friendships. They learn to listen "without possessiveness, without imposing themselves." They just seem more available, more open, and more willing to see others as they really are.

I think this is what Patrick means when he talks about "the beauty of celibacy," but he also means that being a single man, without the attachments of a wife or family, gives him more time and space for other things.

Celibate is a word that historically applied to all unmarried men, but in the twentieth century it came to mean someone who abstains from sexual activity. In the Catholic Church, the principle is the same: Priests are expected to be both celibate (unmarried) and abstinent (refraining from sex). It was with some relief that I read the church doesn't expect men to be asexual—i.e. not interested in sex. They are just supposed to control their impulses.

Jeff Sullivan, one of Patrick's close college friends who joined the Jesuits a few years after he did, said that in some ways he feels he's "more of a sexual being" now as a celibate man than he ever was before. Jeff had several serious relationships with women before joining the Society, and he notes that "I know what I'm missing." But being celibate has made him more aware "of what the body does and what it says. I notice boundaries with women, my own desires and what they're rooted in. A guy who is having sex whenever he wants doesn't have to reflect on that." Celibacy isn't just about being a better priest, he said, it's about growing as a human being, about better "understanding my spirit and soul."

There's another aspect to this that isn't widely recognized, Jeff said. Giving up sex also is about giving up "this whole American sense of what it means to be a man"—to win women, to get ahead in the world. "You have to learn to think outside of yourself, outside of your culture and the way you were raised," he said. In other words, celibate men must learn how to be un-macho in an extremely macho world.

If you think of celibacy as being profoundly countercultural, it's not surprising that so many people have a difficult time understanding it. Neither is it surprising that so many people assume that anyone who chooses celibacy is just plain foolish, or worse—perverse. It's almost a given that celibacy contributed at least in part to the sex abuse scandals that have shattered the Catholic Church in recent years. As Bill Keller, the former *New York Times* executive editor and columnist, has written: "Celibacy—by breeding a culture of sexual exceptionalism and denial—surely played some role in the church's shameful record of pedophilia and cover-up."

Keller also points out that at least some of the apostles were married, as were most clergy, until the eleventh century when the rules were changed. And if the rules were changed once, they can be changed again. Some hoped this would happen during the 12 years of Pope Francis' papacy, and while Francis did once call celibacy requirements for priests a "temporary prescription" in the western Catholic Church, the prospect went no further than a study group.

Meanwhile, celibates like my son have to deal with no small amount of incredulity, if not outright suspicion, which may be understandable but sometimes has the effect of making a celibate's life—already a lonely one—even more isolated.

I don't think Patrick cares a lot about being seen as a man's man. He has lived with his father too long for that. I believe the harder part of celibacy for him is learning to live without the kind of intense emotional relationship with another human being possible only through physical intimacy. Even harder, I think, is giving up the chance to have a family, of holding his own babies in his arms.

No matter where he is, Patrick notices babies. We can be in line to order coffee, walking through a museum, or pushing a cart through a grocery store and he'll spot one in his mother's arms or peeking out of a pack strapped to her dad's back. It's like the stuffed toy glow worm he had when he was small—something bright and warm lights up inside of him.

He doesn't often approach these babies. That's too creepy for a single man, especially for a priest in these tendentious days, but you can tell he wants to. And when he's around his sisters' or his friends' babies, when he doesn't have to worry about what people think, he'll get down on the floor with them and play like a kid. He holds them so close it seems as if he's inhaling them.

When my daughter, Dana, and her husband were expecting their first child, they joked that Patrick seemed to think of the baby as his own and if she ever disappeared, they would know exactly where to look. When they told him that, he laughed out loud and said, "You bet it's my baby. I can't wait!"

A priest's love for God is supposed to take the place of the human craving for sex, a spouse, a family, and to some extent it does. Patrick tells me that while he may never have the kind of relationship Gary and I or Dana and her husband have, he feels very loved. He's a part of many families who treasure his place in their lives. It occurs to me that this is one of the reasons priests are called "Father."

There's another reason Patrick says he doesn't feel alone: He has God for company. He genuinely feels that God is always within reach, that He listens to him and loves him deeply. He doesn't say things like this often because he knows it makes me wince a little. I do not have a close personal relationship with God. I have a difficult time believing He's interested in me at all.

I try hard to accept that God fills a critical space in my son's life. I'm even thankful for it. Plenty of people don't have anyone—spiritual or corporal—to fill the holes. I hope that it's enough, but I can't help thinking that as much as my son finds company with God, he can't take God out for a movie on a Saturday night or read the papers with Him over coffee the next morning. In these ways, I think most people would agree, God makes a pretty lousy companion.

Gary has more trouble with this than I do, not just because he's uncomfortable in general talking about God but because he just doesn't understand why anyone would give up sex—at least without trying it first.

Before Patrick entered the Jesuits, just before he turned twenty-two, he and his dad were spending a weekend afternoon watching a baseball game on TV. In the middle of the game, without preamble, and without making eye contact, Gary suggested that perhaps Patrick should experience sex before deciding to give it up. "You don't know what you're missing," he said. "It's great." This was followed by a few seconds of silence, then Gary's voice came floating up from the couch: "Really great!" Patrick laughed and told him he appreciated the concern, but he was just fine, thank you very much.

None other than Friedrich Nietzsche endorsed the benefits of sexual restraint, writing, "The re-absorption of semen by the blood

... perhaps prompts the stimulus of power, the unrest of all forces towards the overcoming of resistances." In other words, he was saying it makes you strong, which is presumably why some athletes refrain from sex for days or weeks before a competition. Despite the lack of any scientific evidence, they believe abstention will make them more aggressive, more formidable, on the field or in the ring. This isn't all that different from what Roman Catholics have been saying since about the fourth century.

The belief is that a celibate, chaste priest will be a better priest. He will be better able to concentrate on what's important—God and the church—without the distractions of wives or girlfriends or partners of any kind. Additionally, the argument goes, a priest is the person of Christ, and since Christ was single, so should be the priest. (This is essentially the same as one of the main arguments against women becoming priests. Christ was a man; ergo, priests should be men.)

But celibacy is more than that, too. Catholic priests talk of celibacy as a kind of love, an "agape" love that is unconditional and self-sacrificing—and ultimately freeing. It is, in the words of the Notre Dame priest Monsignor Michael Heintz, a love "willing to give itself wholly and without reserve, a love so free that forgetting itself, it gives itself away." Celibacy is not better than the love of spouses for each other or parents for their children, Heintz says. It's just different.

A priest who fully subscribes to the church's teaching on celibacy and abstinence will give up another sexual practice that is not discussed as widely but on which the church has expressed strong views. The Vatican tells us in no uncertain terms that masturbation is a "grave disorder," in large part because sex is supposed to be for the sole purpose of procreation.

In 2012, the Vatican denounced a book written by Sister Maragaret A. Farley, a respected feminist Catholic theologian, for failing to adhere to Catholic teaching. In *Just Love: A Framework for Christian Sexual Ethics*, Farley addresses same-sex relationships, marriage, family, divorce, second marriage—and masturbation, writing that the latter "usually does not raise any moral questions." (She was talking about female masturbation, but I'm assuming the principle applies to men.) The church's response was lengthy but can be summed up in five words: "Her opinion is not acceptable."

When I asked Patrick about the Jesuits' view of masturbation, he just laughed. Apparently, there are some things I can figure out for myself.

* * * *

Chastity, of course, is not the only vow a Catholic priest takes. There also are the not-insignificant matters of poverty and obedience. Together they make up a trio of pledges that are so at odds with American culture that we may as well be talking about polytheism or the divine right of kings. But while being chaste is pretty much an either-you-are-or-you-aren't proposition, the same is not necessarily true of being poor and obedient. At least for the Jesuits, poverty and obedience are relative matters.

When my son joined the Jesuits, it was a pretty big step up the standard-of-living ladder from being a college student (admittedly a college student on a very tight budget). The novitiate in St. Paul was not luxurious—much of the furniture had been donated and some of it was on the shabby side—but the house was comfortable and located in one of the toniest neighborhoods in St. Paul. There was a cook who prepared most weekday meals, a fully stocked kitchen, and several cars that, while far from new, were available for novices to check out. The residents had their own library and chapel, cable TV, a makeshift ping pong table, two pianos, and several guitars.

But the novitiate was poor indeed compared to the Jesuit residence at Loyola University in Chicago where Patrick began studying for a master's degree after completing his two years of novitiate training. The residence was an imposing five-story brick building that housed about forty Jesuits and was located approximately fifty yards from Lake Michigan. The dining room was stunning—gleaming wood tables with white tablecloths and tall windows that looked out on an expanse of green lawn that paused dramatically at the lakefront. The house had leather couches, a fully stocked bar, a massive kitchen, and a lounge with rows of recliners facing a big-screen TV. The Jesuits were served by a staff of cooks and janitors and two young handymen who did everything from painting to tidying up. Clothes were picked up for dry cleaning, and a tailor visited regularly.

The room Patrick was assigned on the third floor of the house had high ceilings and tall windows that provided a magnificent view of the lake. He remembers walking into that room for the first time carrying two small suitcases containing everything he owned. He set them down, looked out the window, and started laughing. When I first saw the house on the lake, I laughed, too. I felt like the novice in a story that is popular with the Jesuits. The joke goes like this: A first-year novice is visiting a large Jesuit community on a feast day when a grand dinner is being served. The novice sees the immense dining room, the silverware, flowers, glasses of wine, and plates of filet mignon and announces: "If this is poverty, bring on chastity!"

(I should note that the Jesuit residence at Loyola has since been torn down to make room for a new student library and the priests were moved to a new building a few blocks away. It, too, is beautiful, but without a view of the lake.)

At first, Patrick chafed at his surroundings. He was a little embarrassed and a little frustrated that there was "so much nice stuff." He and a few other young, idealistic Jesuits newly emerged from the novitiate brought up the issue in group meetings. They didn't want for anything, they pointed out, and shouldn't poverty be about wanting for things? And weren't they further alienating people who already believe that religion is filled with hypocrisy? At the least, Patrick said, "We ought not to say we're living in poverty if we're living like a middle-class family" or better.

Powerless to change the big things, the young Jesuits satisfied themselves with small gestures. They made sure the house was buying fair trade coffee, and they gave things away whenever they could. But eventually, Patrick's indignation cooled. He said he came to the realization that some *things* are necessary. Without computers and books and a comfortable place to study or gather with others to talk, eat, and pray, the community couldn't do the work of teaching and ministering to others. As Saint Thomas Aquinas once put it, "Possession of a few goods is important for a well-ordered life."

The other thing Patrick realized is that living in a community with dozens of other men means you don't always get your way. "I'm not my own free agent," he told me when I asked him about this. "I don't get to live with nothing or invite homeless people in off the streets."

He got his chance to live more simply in 2007 when he left Chicago for South Dakota to begin his Regency on the Pine Ridge Indian Reservation. Other than a cook who prepared dinner several nights a week, the priests were pretty much on their own. They did their own grocery shopping and cleaning and ate most of their lunches in the school cafeteria.

The two-story house in which the reservation priests live was built in the late 1800s of red bricks made from local clay and lime. The bricks are so soft that generations of students have etched their names into the walls. Inside, mismatched furniture is set off by macramé plant holders and macramé wall hangings. The kitchen has one wall built of brick, one covered with brick-patterned wallpaper, and a third constructed of plywood. Just about everything, from paint to linoleum, is peeling.

When I saw the kitchen for the first time, I turned to Gary and said, "This would be a great project for you. You should come back and tear out the entire thing and start over." Patrick was nonplussed. "Hey, what's wrong with the kitchen?" he demanded.

The truth is: He loved that house. He loved its history and quirkiness and the funny, warm, and committed men who lived there. "That's what makes a house a community," he has told me more than once. "Not what it looks like."

The Jesuit residence at the Jesuit School of Theology in Berkeley, California, where Patrick moved next to study and prepare for ordination, ranks somewhere between Loyola and Pine Ridge on the comfort scale. It's a nice house that sits on "Holy Hill," a collection of religious schools for various Catholic orders as well as Eastern Orthodox, Muslim, the Church of Jesus Christ of Latter-day Saints, and several Protestant denominations such as Episcopalian, Baptist, and Unitarian.

The converted duplex where Patrick lived may once have been beautiful but over the years has come to look exactly like what it is—a house filled with a bunch of single guys with peculiar decorating ideas. When we first visited, the living room consisted mainly of couches and TVs, and one of the sets was a 1985 model with wood paneling, which was subsequently replaced with a flat-screen TV. "Thank God," Patrick said when announcing the purchase to us. "It was impossible to watch the NBA on that thing."

The linoleum in the kitchen was cracked, and one cabinet door, which had come unhinged, was propped against a wall. The over-sized refrigerator overflowed with leftovers and the remnants of takeout meals.

Still, it would have been impossible to mistake it as anything other than a religious house. There were holy cards taped next to the bathroom mirror and religious prints hanging on almost every wall. Caravaggio's Doubting Thomas and one of Henry Tanner's brooding images of Mary reigned over the couch and the dining room table. A jet-black bobble head of Saint Ignatius wobbled crazily from its perch on an end table.

James Martin, SJ, acknowledges that Jesuit poverty doesn't always look like—well, poverty—at least in the way we usually think of poverty. In his book *The Jesuit Guide to Almost Everything*, he writes that the goal is for all Jesuits to live simply on a limited budget, but what that looks like varies from house to house and from Jesuit to Jesuit. But even Jesuits who live in nice residences with cooks and handymen share almost everything with their brothers and own almost nothing individually. They get a monthly stipend to cover essentials like shampoo, shaving cream, and other personal items, and if they need something bigger, like a pair of winter boots or a plane ticket, they usually have to ask their superior for permission—and the cash.

Simply put, a Jesuit can never own his own car or house or boat. He can't buy stock or collect a paycheck. Anything he earns, whether it's from teaching a class, winning an award, or publishing a book, goes back to the Society.

Sometimes this distance from materialistic things can be useful. When Patrick was doing his regency at Red Cloud Indian School, the economy was in a tailspin and donations to the school were dropping at an alarming rate. Bob Brave Heart, one of Patrick's good friends and the superintendent of schools, was having trouble balancing his budget. He had made some painful decisions and was within $5,000 of his goal when he hit a wall. He just didn't know what else to cut.

"Hey, aren't I under your budget?" Patrick asked him one day. "Why don't you cut my salary?"

"By $5,000?" Brave Heart asked. "You'd really do that?

"Sure, go ahead," said Patrick, who didn't actually know how much the Jesuits had included in the school's budget for his position since he never saw the money. But he was pretty sure it was more than $5,000. Brave Heart balanced his budget.

I don't think I began to understand what poverty would mean for my son until the day he took his First Vows after completing the novitiate. We had just left the church in St. Paul where he and a dozen other men wearing black clerical suits had pledged chastity, poverty, and obedience. Afterward, we made our way to the basement for sandwiches and iced tea and congratulations. But just as we sat down, an older priest took Gary aside and told him there was a piece of paper he needed to sign certifying that Patrick could never be our beneficiary. He could not own anything in common with us, serve as executor of our estate, or receive an inheritance from us when we died. He would have nothing except what the Jesuits gave him.

This does not concern Patrick in the least, nor does it worry his sisters, who joke that it just means more for them. My initial reaction was outrage that the Jesuits were interested only in getting Gary's signature. Apparently, mine didn't count, even though I was the family's primary source of income and Gary and I owned all of our property in common. Their mistake, I thought. I had made no promise; I could give my son anything I wanted. But then I realized it wouldn't make any difference. My son wouldn't accept anything from me. In fact, he doesn't want anything. Poverty is not a vow he is ever going to have a problem with. Obedience, however, is another matter.

When Patrick was in the novitiate, he worried aloud about this third vow, and his concern struck me as odd since he was always compliant as a child. I think the most rebellious he ever got was during high school when he came home one day with his head shaved. It turned out he had done it in support of a classmate who had cancer and lost his hair during chemotherapy.

Patrick didn't always listen or pay attention ("You wanted me to clean my room?!" "I was supposed to call home?!"), but my husband and I can't think of a single time that he flat out defied us, and we can't remember ever seriously disciplining him for misbehaving. But he has always been stubborn. When he has made up his mind about something, he's usually sure he's right, and it can be very difficult to persuade him otherwise. This is where the Jesuit pledge of obedience gets sticky for him. He doesn't like the idea that someone else—even a Jesuit superior—might be right and he might be wrong.

Like poverty, the Jesuits have their own interpretation of obedience, and it's one that has changed considerably over the years. It used to be that Jesuits didn't get much of a say in what they did or where they went. (Purportedly, one of the oldest Jesuit stories is about a mortally ill novice on his deathbed who asks the novice master for permission to die.)

In his book, Martin writes that until the mid-1960s, many American Jesuits learned of their assignments each year by reading the "Status," a piece of paper that was pinned to their house bulletin boards on July 31, the feast of the order's founder. (The bulletin board is still a staple in every single Jesuit house in the country, despite the advent of text messages and emails). Sometimes, the Status contained assignments that came as quite as a surprise, as when one Jesuit who had never in his life studied chemistry was assigned to teach just that in a Jesuit high school. But generally, there was no arguing—each man just did what he was told.

Since the Second Vatican Council more than a half a century ago, much more emphasis has been placed on what the individual Jesuit wants to do. Now, each person meets with his superior to discern the matter. The two discuss options, followed by prayer, followed by more discussions, followed by more prayer in an attempt to figure out God's will in the matter.

Usually, a priest and his superior end up pretty much agreeing on a course of action, but like the military, it's the superior officer who has the final say. Perhaps the most famous example in modern history is the case of Father Robert Drinan, a Jesuit who was the first Catholic priest to serve as a voting member of Congress. Drinan had represented Massachusetts for a decade when Pope John Paul II decided priests should not be involved in politics. Drinan was ordered not to run for reelection in 1981, so he left a career he loved. He lived out the rest of his life as a law professor, author, human rights activist, and Jesuit—but not a public official.

My son's experience wasn't nearly as dramatic, but it, too, changed the course of his life. After finishing his master's in philosophy at Loyola University Chicago in 2007, Patrick had hoped for an assignment teaching philosophy. He imagined a life of the mind— classrooms filled with erudite students debating Kant's *Critique of Pure Reason* and intense coffeehouse conversations about the relevance of God in an increasingly secularized world. His superiors said that might be good, but was he aware that the Jesuit-run schools on the Pine Ridge reservation in South Dakota were sorely in need of help?

The reservation was not a proposition that appealed to Patrick, who much prefers a big city to the country, especially a part of the country with hardly anyone in it. He didn't want to teach high school again. He imagined an intellectual desert cut off from civilization, and a visit to Pine Ridge did not persuade him he was wrong.

In the end, he pleaded with his superiors, "Please do not send me to the reservation." But like a good Jesuit, he added, "And if you do, I will try my damnedest to love it there." His superiors listened and said they would pray on it. Then they sent him to the reservation. They pointed out to him that he had often talked about social injustice and how the church's work with the poor was an important part of what had drawn him to Catholicism in the first place. This was his chance to see what it was like to minister on the margins, to help where he was most needed. It would be good for him.

Patrick had encountered a handful of other no's during his formation. Once he was denied permission to attend a friend's wedding out of state, and he was told he couldn't come home to sit with his grandmother for a week when Gary and I were going to be out of town. But these were mere annoyances. He was now facing a real test of obedience: Why should he go somewhere he didn't want to go to do something he didn't want to do when he had worked so hard and sacrificed so much?

He was, he said, "in a very dark place. It's hard because there are times when you think what you want is the right thing, and if you think what you want is the right thing and you're still not getting it, and the voice of your superior is supposed to be the voice of Christ—something's wrong. Either my feeling is wrong, or my superior is wrong."

In the end, he said he accepted the assignment because he felt the directive came out of love and concern for him and because he knew he was needed there. And before long, he learned that it was his initial feeling that was wrong. Of all the places he has been sent to live and work, he has loved the reservation the most.

This experience of obedience taught him that free will isn't necessarily freeing. What is more freeing, he said, "is to realize that everything you want isn't the right thing and sometimes you have to trust that others know what is best for you and what God wants for you."

I don't think I could ever put myself so completely in the hands of others, but I can imagine what a relief it might be. And it helps me to remember that the word obedience comes from a Latin word that means "to hear."

This, I think, is what Jesuit discernment really means—to listen to someone or something other than your own inner roaring, to open yourself up to the possibility that maybe getting what you think you want doesn't always get you what you really want.

CHAPTER 11

LOVE, SEX, AND MARRIAGE

"Can a man take fire in his bosom, and his
clothes not be burned? Or can one walk upon
hot coals, and his feet not be scorched?"

PROVERBS 6:27-29

To enter the Jesuits, you first have to pass a psychological exam. This is presumably to keep out pedophiles and other kinds of sexual predators as well as men who, if accepted, could spell trouble—men with anger management issues, for example, or someone who's convinced he's God.

The evaluations are designed to assess mental stability and personality traits. Patrick was given the Rorschach inkblot test as well as the Myers-Briggs Type Indicator and the Minnesota Multiphasic Personality Inventory and asked to fill out a psychosexual life history questionnaire and submit to a diagnostic interview.

One of the questionnaires, Patrick said, was made up of a long series of mundane questions and then, just when you were feeling a little bored, up would pop one like: "Do you ever feel there is a tight band around your head?" and "Do you ever hear voices telling you to do something violent?" This may be hyperbole, but it provided an endless source of amusement to Patrick and the other young men entering the novitiate.

Other questions were aimed at ferreting out a Jesuit hopeful's sexual predilections: "Were you ever sexually abused as a child? At what age were you when you first became interested in sex? Have you ever had sexual interest in men, boys, or children? Have you ever engaged in unusual sexual behavior?"

Despite the official position of the Catholic Church that it will not admit to seminary or ordain "those who practice homosexuality, present deep-seated homosexual tendencies or support the so-called 'gay culture,'" the Jesuits appear to have a more relaxed attitude. Every Jesuit I've ever questioned about this has said the same thing: As long as a man is celibate, his sexual orientation doesn't really matter.

Patrick, as always when taking a test, aced it. Heterosexual in orientation and emotionally stable (although inclined to see things in a positive light, indicating a reluctance to deal with negative emotions), he was, the evaluator concluded, an all-around suitable candidate.

With the church so desperately in need of priests (the number has dropped by around forty percent in the US since 1965, and more than 3,500 parishes no longer have priests in residence), it's hard to imagine that any except the most extreme cases get turned down. But it does happen. It happened to a young professor who I assumed was a Jesuit when I met him during a visit to a Jesuit university on the East Coast. Jesuit-educated since high school, he taught theology to college students. He didn't wear black or sport the white collar of a priest, but Jesuits often don't. He was sophisticated, engaging, and urbane like most of the other Jesuits I have met.

When I asked him if he was a member of the order, he laughed and said "No, but not for lack of trying." He had applied to become a Jesuit, taken the tests, filled out the questionnaires, and completed the interview. In the end, he was told he had not resolved his sexual orientation, something he needed to do before he could be accepted. And the church, he said, turned out to be right. He had grown up denying he was gay, trying to fit into a culture that "valorizes a kind of red-blooded hyper-masculinity." Celibacy was a way of avoiding the issue and, when that was no longer possible, he had to confront who he was. A few years later, he came out, moved in with his partner, and began writing about the place of homosexuals in the Catholic Church.

When I tell people my son is a Catholic priest, I often can see the question in their eyes. "No, he's not gay," I sometimes say before they can ask. I do this not because I would object if he was gay but because I resent the assumption. I have so far refrained— barely—from adding, "No, he's not a child molester, either." I can see that question in their eyes as well. And who can blame them? It is estimated that there were more than 100,000 victims of sexual abuse at the hands of Catholic priests in the US from 1950 to 2020. Thousands upon thousands of broken promises, of lives irrevocably damaged.

The Jesuits have not avoided the sexual abuse firestorm that has engulfed the Catholic Church. One former Jesuit priest, Donald J. McGuire, was sentenced to serve a twenty-five-year sentence for molesting teenage boys—abuse that court records show his superiors knew about for four decades. A popular leader of spiritual retreats around the world, McGuire was a spiritual adviser to Mother Teresa, among others. He died in prison. Another, James Talbot, was one of five Catholic priests in the Boston area who were convicted and sentenced to prison. Talbot admitted to abusing nearly ninety students over a period of several decades.

Like other religious orders, the Jesuits allegedly protected their problem priests. In some cases, they moved such priests to Native reservations and small villages, in effect, hiding them and making a vulnerable population even more vulnerable. In 2011, the Oregon Province of the Jesuits agreed to pay $166 million to settle claims made by nearly 500 Native Americans and Alaskan natives who were sexually or psychologically abused as children while attending the order's schools in the Pacific Northwest. It was one of the largest settlements in Catholic Church history.

There is no evidence that this kind of abuse took place on the

Pine Ridge Indian Reservation in South Dakota, where Patrick reluctantly headed in 2007, but the shadow of the sexual abuse scandal hovered even there, where Jesuits have been successfully running schools since 1888. It made the priests, some of whom have lived and worked on the reservation most of their lives, alert to boundaries, wary even of hugging the children in their care. This is especially sad, Patrick pointed out to me, because these are often the children who most need to be hugged.

Red Cloud is burdened with another shameful legacy, one shared by hundreds of Indian boarding schools run by the Catholic Church in the US and Canada from the late-nineteenth to mid-twentieth centuries. The children of the Oglala, Lakota, and Sioux tribes were forcibly separated from their parents and sent to live at the Holy Rosary Mission, where they were compelled to give up their traditional language, dress, and culture. Some never left. They are buried in the Holy Rosary Cemetery perched on a grassy knoll above the school with a view of the prairie beyond.

* * * *

The Pine Ridge reservation is a beautiful and terrible place. Situated at the southern end of the Badlands along the South Dakota-Nebraska border, it is immense—roughly the size of Connecticut—and abjectly poor. More than eighty percent of adults are unemployed, and more than fifty percent live below the federal poverty level, making it one of the poorest places in America. Infants are five times more likely to die here than elsewhere in the country, and the adolescent suicide rate is four times the US average. Fewer than thirty percent of children finish high school, and adults live shorter lives than anywhere else in the US. With those kinds of statistics, it could be Bangladesh. Add in alcoholism, which affects an estimated eight out of ten families, and it's worse than Bangladesh.

The reservation has been dry, meaning no alcohol has been sold there, for all but two months of the past century. No matter.

For almost all that time, Pine Ridge residents had a steady source of alcohol along its southern border in the tiny town of Whiteclay, Nebraska. The town's four liquor stores sold somewhere between 11,000 and 13,000 cans of beer and malt liquor *every day* until the Nebraska Liquor Control Commission revoked their licenses in 2017. The ban hasn't stopped people from drinking, however. Residents simply drive to towns further from the reservation, and local police report that bootlegging is on the rise. The most popular variation is clear booze disguised in plastic water bottles. The going rate? Ten bucks a bottle.

The Jesuits keep no alcohol in the house they share on the reservation—highly unusual for Jesuits, who are known to appreciate a fine bottle of Scotch. Patrick wouldn't even have a beer when he left the reservation to meet friends in nearby Chadron, Nebraska, or grab a pizza in Rapid City, South Dakota. He didn't want anyone to see him drink; he didn't want to set a bad example.

He struggled that first year on the reservation. He was twenty-six years old when he arrived fresh from a college campus teeming with other young people. In Chicago, he had access to concerts and jazz clubs, coffee shops, and museums. He was within driving distance of Milwaukee and his beloved Brewers. He was accustomed to living within a large community of Jesuits, many of whom were close to his own age. Suddenly he found himself in a distant outpost on a remote reservation where it was almost a two-hour drive to Rapid City just to see a movie or shop for a pair of shoes. Pine Ridge, a town of just over 600 households, was ten minutes away, but the business district consisted mostly of a supermarket and a gas station. When a Subway sandwich shop opened, Patrick was as thrilled as if the Lakers had come to town.

He lived with ten or twelve fellow Jesuits, some of whom were decades older than him. At eighty-two, Brother Bill Foster had been there the longest. Bill was Red Cloud's carpenter. He made bookshelves, tables, and picture frames for the house and white crosses for the cemetery, even though his hands were so arthritic he could barely bend his fingers. He wore overalls and plaid shirts and favored steak and ice cream for dinner.

Not far behind Brother Bill in age was Brother Mike Zimmerman, who has spent most of his adult life at Red Cloud, taking care of the grounds, patching boilers and buildings, and keeping the place running—pretty much, as the saying goes, on a wing and a prayer. He's the kind of man who puts on a cap and blue overalls every day and takes care of whatever it is that needs to be done. He's the kind of a man who doesn't bother to distinguish between work and prayer because for him, they are much the same.

Patrick admired Brothers Bill and Mike and the other Jesuits at Red Cloud, and he figured he could grow accustomed to the living arrangements. Much harder was getting used to the funerals. There was Casey, who had just finished his first semester at college, and Anita, who was six weeks out of high school and trying to figure out what she wanted to do with her life. Both died in one-car accidents on remote reservation roads. Then there were the suicides, kids hanging themselves, leaving their family members to discover their bodies suspended in closets. When an old person died, it was almost a cause for celebration—a life had been fully lived.

During his phone calls home, Patrick talked about the heartbreaking funerals, how lonely he was, and how hard it was to teach English to high school students, many of whom had little interest in school and even less in writing. He didn't think he was very good at it. He said he was praying a lot and taking long runs; he could run a long way without seeing anything more than tall grass and prairie dogs. But as the months passed, his spirits lifted. He was assigned to drive the school bus, traveling long distances each morning to fetch children from all over the sprawling reservation. When he described these mornings, it was easy for me to picture the children straggling from their homes toward the bus, small, solemn figures drifting unhurriedly down long driveways framed by giant tractor tires. Still half-asleep, they would climb the steps, mumbling a response to Patrick's whispered greeting and then huddle in their seats, waiting for the bus to warm up and for the gentle jounces of the ride to lull them back to sleep.

He loved the kids, and he loved the raucous Lakota high school basketball games, especially when he was tapped to be the play-by-play announcer, revving up the willing crowd and shouting "Yamni!" the Lakota word for "three," each time a Red Cloud player made another long shot.

As often as he could, he participated in a sweat lodge, or Inipi, ceremony, a Lakota tradition going back centuries. Huddled in the dark around steaming and glowing rocks, he would sweat and chant and sing and pray with men who had become his friends, men with names like Roger White Eyes and Alvin Slow Bear, men who were teaching him that pain is not without purpose, that suffering can have meaning.

The reservation, he was learning, can be harsh and unforgiving, but it is also a place inscribed with simple and unexpected joys.

*　*　*　*

One day after he had been at Red Cloud for a couple of years, Patrick called and said he had something important to tell us. "I've fallen in love," he announced.

"In love?" I imagined some kind of vision or rapture, a religious epiphany of the kind I could never hope to understand. Christ, I thought, now he's really gone off the deep end.

"Mom," he said more insistently. "I've fallen in love with a woman."

Unable to utter more than two-word responses, I repeated, "A woman?"

She was part of the Jesuit Volunteer Corp, an organization of lay people who work for one or two years in community service in cities and towns and missions around the country. The volunteers commit to living simply ("free from material distraction") while focusing on spirituality, social justice, and service.

There were about twenty volunteers on the reservation, most just out of college and looking for something meaningful to do with their lives for a few years before heading off to graduate school or gainful employment. The volunteers taught classes, ran after-school programs, coached athletic teams, and drove school buses, among other chores. Most lived in a former convent—a small house next to the elementary school playground. Although a group of haphazard trailers that once surrounded the convent had been hauled away long ago, the area was still known as trailer row.

Patrick had been spending time with one particular volunteer, and they had discovered they had a lot in common. She liked to debate philosophy and theology, she believed the world's wrongs could be corrected, and she wasn't interested in a comfortable life. In other words, she was a lot like my son. I could easily imagine her being a Jesuit if such a thing was allowed. Because it decidedly is not, she had majored in theology, volunteered at Red Cloud—and fallen in love with a Jesuit.

Patrick was torn between wanting her and wanting to be a Jesuit, and these polar choices were tearing him apart. "I want both," he said.

"You should be able to have both," I told him. "It's cruel to force anyone to make this kind of decision." I couldn't resist adding that Episcopal priests are allowed to marry, and the world needs Episcopal priests, too. Subtlety has never been my strong suit.

The Catholic Church has been moving imperceptibly—and I'm talking millennia here—toward accepting married clergy. The Eastern Catholic Church, which has its own leadership separate from the pope, have long allowed the ordination of married men as priests. And since Vatican II in the mid-1960s, the Roman Catholic Church has allowed married men to become deacons, serving as assistants of sorts to priests. In the early church, deacons were often assigned the practical aspects of running a church—managing property, distributing alms, collecting offerings, and paying the bills, so to speak. In modern times, Catholic deacons have taken on many traditional priestly duties, including preaching, baptizing, marrying, and distributing the Eucharist, but they cannot say Mass, hear confession, or anoint the sick. They are perpetually confined to a sort of second tier of priesthood.

Although many Roman Catholics aren't aware of it, the church also has accepted married Protestant clergymen into the priesthood since the 1980s. These are men who have converted to Catholicism and who have convinced church authorities they are called to become priests. And in 2009, the church announced a move to absorb Anglicans into the church, which includes allowing former Anglican clergy who are married to serve as priests.

In the US and other developed countries, opinion polls of Catholics show widespread support for a married clergy. But despite these clamors for change, the most one can hope for is that it could happen ... one day. It almost certainly is not going to happen in my son's lifetime. And even if it did, Patrick and many others think marriage should be allowed only for parish priests, not Jesuits or other orders built around communal living. Sharing a house, praying, and working together, Patrick notes, are all a big part of what it means to be a Jesuit.

About six months after Patrick's proclamation of love, Gary and I flew to Rapid City to visit the reservation and meet the young woman for whom Patrick had such strong feelings. He was nervous, and Gary thought the whole thing more than a little awkward, but I was curious and just a little bit hopeful. Deep down, I think I was rooting for her.

Patrick brought her to the room we had been assigned, down a dark hallway in the section of the rambling residential quarters set aside for guests. Gary said hello and shook the hand of the pretty, delicate young woman and then escaped as quickly as he could. Patrick left with him, and the young woman and I sat on the bed while I peppered her with questions: How long had she been on the reservation? Why did she come? Did she like it? What did she plan to do next?

Her answers were as simple and straightforward as her appearance: clear expression, little makeup, long brown hair tied in a loose knot at the base of her neck. She seemed comfortable in her own skin. I liked her. Later, after Patrick had come to fetch her, he returned to the room and asked me what I thought. "I think she's perfectly delightful," I said, and I meant it.

For months the relationship ricocheted back and forth. The two of them would cut off contact, deciding it was too painful to talk with or see each other, then they would decide it was too painful not to.

Patrick told his superiors that he was in love and was having a hard time. He suggested it might be best if the two of them were separated, something that could be accomplished by transferring him to an assignment far from the reservation. His superiors were sympathetic but unalarmed, reminding him of what he had learned in the novitiate back in St. Paul: If you're living the Jesuit life well—if you're interacting with other people in meaningful ways, if you're living in the real world—you're going to fall in love. The question was: What did he want to do about it? Running away was not making a decision, they told him. He had to take time to figure out what God had in mind for him. Patrick decided to give it a year.

Over the next several months, he spent a lot of time agonizing about whether to remain in the order or leave. He would sit down every morning to pray "and open up my heart and just feel hurt and pain," he said. "I just felt crushed." He kept wondering whether he was being punished and why God was testing him—until it occurred to him that he had it all wrong.

"At some point, it became clear to me that God was doing something important in the midst of this darkness and this wasn't some punishment He was inflicting on me," Patrick told me. "The hurt I was feeling wasn't about being a Jesuit at all. It seemed to me that either suffering has meaning or it doesn't, and either God is active in that or He's not." In other words, he thought that what he was experiencing was necessary in order to be the kind of priest he wanted to be—the kind who can understand pain and loss.

As the year drew to a close, Patrick made up his mind to continue with his formation as a Jesuit. It was easily one of the most difficult decisions of his life—in no small part because he knew how much it would hurt the woman he loved.

I think it was how his superiors dealt with the situation that tipped the scales. Patrick had always said that of the three vows—chastity, poverty, and obedience—obedience was the hardest for him. Strong-willed and opinionated by nature, it was difficult for him to put himself in the hands of others. But when his superiors supported him without alarm, when they spoke of God and left all options open, Patrick couldn't resist doing what he felt deep down he was being called to do.

There was also the matter of why. Patrick felt the experience—the "darkness" of these months, as he put it—was much more than a simple test of his vocation. He kept thinking about what his time with the Lakota had taught him—that pain has a purpose. When faced with pain, he had come to learn, a person has two choices: try to escape or pray. And when the pain gets worse, when the heat of the glowing rocks makes you want to tear off your skin, pray harder.

The Lakota believe that those who willingly endure such suffering are able to ease the suffering of others, especially the young and the old who can't endure the pain on their own. Thus, the sacred Lakota phrase *mitakuye oyasin*, meaning "all my relatives" or "all my relations."

When he looked around the reservation, Patrick saw that "too many kids knew what it was like to suffer—to wake up and have to take care of a little sister or brother because their parents had not come home or were passed out from drinking." He had no idea what it was like to grow up like that. "I had everything," he said. But after a while, after his exhaustive struggle with love, he no longer felt he had everything. He felt changed, and the Lakota, he thought, understood that something fundamental had shifted inside of him.

"It was like they could look at me and say, 'It's hard, Paddy,' and they would know I also knew what it was like to suffer and that I wasn't holding myself apart from them," he said. "I still didn't know what it was like to go through what they were going through, but I knew what it was like to hurt."

And that, he is convinced, will make him a better priest.

CHAPTER 12

COMMUNITY LIFE AND OTHER ADVENTURES

"Happiness is having a warm, caring family—in
a city nearby."
GEORGE BURNS

Imagine living the rest of your life in a series of houses, each with a different set of roommates, none of whom you choose for yourself. Some of these roommates are people you like very much, and some are people you can't stand. A few of them are people you would like a lot more if you didn't have to share a bathroom with them or encounter their leftovers in the refrigerator.

This pretty much sums up community life for most Jesuits.

Patrick is the alumnus of a half dozen Jesuit communities in as many states, and he undoubtedly will live in many more, as most Jesuits tend to live fairly transient lives. Most of the communities he has been a part of have been small—a dozen or so guys who take turns cooking and cleaning, running errands, doing the dishes, and shopping for groceries. Some days they may see each other only on the way in or out of the house as they head to jobs and classes. But there also are frequent communal meals and shared prayers and plenty of time spent watching basketball and football. There are female visitors (although they don't wander into the bedrooms) and the occasional barbecue, complete with beer and brats (or, in the case of the California Jesuits, wine and cheese).

While this isn't what you would call *Animal House*, neither is it the kind of life led by monks, who also live communally but tend to be more isolated from the world, or by parish priests, who often live by themselves. Almost all Jesuits, even university presidents, live in communities, except in the rare case when a man is missioned on his own somewhere—usually to a foreign country—in which case other members of the order joke that he is "residing elsewhere."

This has been the case since 1534 when seven college friends vowed to stay together after finishing their studies in Paris. They called themselves "*amigos en el Senor*," friends in the Lord. Patrick says these first Jesuits didn't so much set out to start a religious order as their friendship built one.

Jesuit communities in the US range in size from a half dozen to several dozen, which gives members a lot of experience living with others. And when it comes right down to it, sharing space with a bunch of other people, even nice, intelligent, spiritual people, presents all the problems you would expect with a single exception often noted by visiting mothers and sisters: In Jesuit communities, it's okay if no one remembers to lower the toilet seat.

Priests, it turns out, can be just as eccentric, sloppy, petty, boring, and annoying as anyone else. There are the guys who finish off the crackers and put the empty box back in the cupboard or who rip open sacks of potato chips with their teeth, leaving gaping holes in the middle of the bags. These things drive Patrick crazy. He can describe with great feeling the time he discovered a big blob of rice stuck to the dining room wall and the occasion when he dug into the fruit bowl only to find four blackened banana stems still held together with a ribbon of green tape. He still can't figure out how someone managed to extract the bananas and leave the tape and stems behind.

Then there are the guys who never empty the dishwasher, who shrink your best sweater by throwing it in the clothes dryer when you meant to lay it out to dry, and who buy so much junk at the grocery store that there's no money left in the food budget at the end of the month. And we haven't even gotten to the cars yet.

Most Jesuit communities have a fleet of cars, with the size of the fleet varying according to the size of the community. When Patrick was there, about 100 Jesuits lived on Holy Hill in Berkeley spread out over six buildings, and they had at their disposal some twenty-five cars, all in various stages of repair—or to put it more accurately, disrepair. Patrick is not the kind of guy who cares much about cars, but even he was taken aback by what he ended up driving.

"Sometimes I feel like a schlep showing up at a ritzy dinner in a beat-up Toyota Corolla without hubcaps," he said. "It ought to make me feel proud, but the truth is I feel both ways."

A large part of the reason the cars are so crappy is that the drivers come from all over the world and have what might generously be called eclectic driving habits. Some have never driven before at all, having recently arrived from Rwanda or Vietnam or another country where driving is not something everyone is expected to do. A few years before Patrick arrived, the Jesuit community at Berkeley was excited to get two new cars. One of them was totaled almost immediately.

Even more annoying are the guys who always check out the nicest car and the ones who forget to put the keys where others can find them or leave a car with an empty gas tank. (Knowing Patrick, I have no doubt he is occasionally one of these guys.)

Living with people from all over the world presents other challenges, ranging from hygiene to food. Some men who come from other, less compulsively scrubbed, cultures have to be introduced to the American concepts of deodorant and daily showers, and some seem to have never before entered a kitchen. If a neophyte cook puts something particularly awful on the table, the housemates might adjourn to a nearby restaurant, followed by a friendly chat with the newcomer about something called a recipe.

The diversity of many Jesuit houses, largely the result of men from around the world coming to the US to study and work, does have the advantage of expanding the palate. During his three years at Berkeley, Patrick lived with British, Korean, Vietnamese, Rwandan,

Nigerian, Spanish, Mexican, and Colombian Jesuits, plus one guy who grew up speaking Lithuanian in Cleveland. He learned to love slow-cooked pork carnitas, fried plantains, squid ink pasta, and—his favorite—Phở, the spicy Vietnamese noodle soup. These are not dishes he had ever encountered growing up when his dad was the primary cook and the repertoire was pretty much limited to meat loaf, spaghetti, tacos, and tuna noodle casserole.

Patrick had told us the house at Berkeley felt like home to him, and when Gary and I visited I understood right away what he meant. We stayed in the basement guest room for a few days, wandering up the stairs for coffee in the mornings and joining the residents around the long dining room table for dinner at night.

I had imagined if not a somber place at least a quiet one with a long list of rules posted on the refrigerator door and young priests holed up in their rooms doing their theology homework. What I found instead was surprisingly social and informal. All day long and well into the evening, there was a steady thrum of visitors, male and female, wandering in for a chat or a cup of coffee. One group would be splayed across the living room couches watching a game on television while another would be having a lively conversation around the dining room table. Almost always someone would be foraging for food in the kitchen, whether they actually lived there or not.

The Jesuit residence at Pine Ridge was a much different community, if only because of the ages of the men who live there. Most of the men at the house in Berkeley were thirty or so; his housemates at Red Cloud were almost all over fifty—and some, like Brothers Bill and Mike, were much older. Living with so many generations is unusual enough, but living with generations of people who aren't even related to you is almost unheard of. Young Jesuits can find this hard to get used to, especially when the older Jesuits are set in their ways, or worse, have never seen an Adam Sandler movie. As Patrick once wryly observed, sometimes you just have to go elsewhere for your entertainment.

But new members of the order also find that living with men

old enough to be their grandfathers can provide a reassuring sense of history and community. They are evidence of lives well spent, and, moreover, they model what it looks like to age gracefully. "I have lived with so many guys who were immensely talented and charismatic and important in 'their day' but now live with chronic pain or simply don't have a big audience anymore," Patrick said. "And the humility that most of them show by the way they live their lives is just awesome to me."

When a Jesuit dies, a holy card is mailed out to members of the Society. On the front of the three-by-five card is the deceased man's name and a photograph, and on the back is a prayer that held meaning for him. In a 2012 article for *America* magazine, Patrick wrote that he had three of these cards taped to the wall of his room. All commemorated men—grandfathers really—who he had come to know and love.

One card was of a laughing, red-faced Bill Pauly, a Jesuit who worked on the Pine Ridge reservation for nearly twenty years before dying of a heart attack at the age of fifty-nine. A few years before he died, Bill visited the Jesuit house at Loyola where Patrick was a scholastic. Patrick said he was sitting at his computer one night "working on some obscure paper with my shoulders tensed up when Bill knocked on my door. Pushing his bald head through the doorway, he asked, 'Can I read you a poem?'"

He sat down and began reading from Mary Oliver's "The Summer Day:" "I don't know exactly what a prayer is," he recited. "I do know how to pay attention, how to fall down / into the grass." Patrick remembers Bill's voice trembling a little as he asked Ms. Oliver's lovely question: "Doesn't everything die at last, and too soon?"

That night when he went to bed, Patrick asked himself: "Who is this man who stopped by my room just to read poetry? How can I become someone who does things like that?" Men like Bill, he wrote, have "ushered me into this family's tradition…. They carry me along with them in my weaker moments, buoy me up with their own quiet, whimsical, poetic lives."

* * * *

Like any family, every Jesuit community has its quirks, inside jokes, and singular ways of doing things, like the "Unclean" sign the Jesuits at Pine Ridge hang on the dishwasher when it's full of dirty dishes. But at their best, Jesuit communities also are places where men care about each other and take care of each other.

Patrick tells the story of a Jesuit at Red Cloud who developed multiple sclerosis and eventually lost his ability to get around. To make sure he could get to church, Brother Mike built a wheelchair ramp for him, and an elevator was installed in the house so he could navigate his wheelchair from his first-floor room to the second-floor kitchen. But after a while, even with the elevator, getting to the kitchen turned out to be a drawn-out affair, so the president of the Red Cloud mission began bringing the priest a thermos of coffee every morning. He would leave it outside his door so it would be there when he woke up.

One time when Patrick was down with a bad flu, a Jesuit brother who lived in the room next door made sure he had a steady supply of soup and Kleenex. And when his good friend Eric Sundrup had surgery for a torn ligament in his leg, Patrick was the one who drove him to the hospital and stayed with him. Later, when Eric was back at the Berkeley house, Patrick and the other Jesuits took turns getting up every two hours for several nights in a row to check on him and give him his medicine. They helped him take showers with the clumsy cast. It is such small kindnesses that remind Patrick he is not just a single guy fending for himself. He is part of the long, black line of the Society made up of men who inspire him and support each other.

I once spotted Patrick and a Jesuit brother taking turns shaving the backs of each other's necks, and I have seen him hug a brother who was having a bad day. Most Jesuits have to learn to ask for and grow comfortable with this kind of ordinary intimacy. "Guys aren't great at that," Patrick observed, "but when you're able to ask, that's when community is built."

Building a community also sometimes requires an infusion of dart guns and a little golf in the hallways.

When he first arrived at Loyola, Patrick was impressed with the view of the lake but much less taken with the rest of the house. While the residence was in many ways luxurious, it felt to him like "a big, dark building with dark hallways and rooms that were just boxes. And the guys who filled it mirrored that space; all their energies went outside. At home they were drab and dank and boring and boxy. And we didn't take care of each other; other people took care of us."

Because there were upwards of fifty men living in the house, the Jesuits employed a staff to cook, clean, and take care of the laundry and the grounds. Everything was regimented: Mass was at 5:15 p.m., followed by drinks at 5:50 and dinner at 6:15, after which most of the men returned to their rooms.

This was hard for the handful of young men like Patrick who had just come out of the novitiate where they had become accustomed to a kind of emotional intimacy and faith sharing that was unfamiliar to the older Jesuits, who had been trained in a more austere tradition. The young men watched the others return to their rooms and asked, "What the hell am I supposed to do now? Is this all there is?" It was, Patrick said, "like living in an emotional desert." It was just a bunch of men sharing living quarters.

A year later, there was an influx of young Jesuits into the house and things began to change. Someone set up a practice putting green in the hallway, and Patrick's friend Eric ordered a dozen Nerf blow dart guns. Suddenly, pitched battles were breaking out in rooms up and down the halls. "There were sneak attacks all the time," Patrick said. "You'd be sitting at your desk in your room working and you'd hear a sound—like poof—and you'd duck immediately." The newcomers formed Ultimate Frisbee, flag football, and soccer teams and began playing Loyola students in heated intramural competitions.

They arranged excursions for dinner, music, and movies. By the time Patrick left Loyola, he said it felt like a real community.

* * * *

The longer my son is a Jesuit, the easier community life seems to become for him. This is in part because he has had more practice applying the late Jesuit historian John O'Malley's astute advice to members of the order: "Remember, first you're not God. Second, this isn't heaven. Third, don't be an ass." But it's also because "by the time you've been in the Society for seven or eight years, most people have gone through their vocational crises, so they're more stable," Patrick said. "Plus, most of the crazy people have left." These, he said, have included a novice who threw a punch at one of his brothers and another young Jesuit who had to be removed from his job when he completely lost it with his co-workers.

Then there are the men who seem to have entered the order seeking mainly incense and Latin chants and others who are depressed or can't seem to focus on anything and don't know what they want. Some need to be woken up emotionally or are still struggling with their sexuality.

While it's generally accepted that some Catholic priests are gay and have, perhaps, chosen their profession as a way of sidestepping this fact, getting numbers is notoriously difficult. For example, one of the questions in a 2020 survey of American Catholic priests by the Austin Institute asked respondents to disclose their sexual orientation. Of the 1,036 priests who answered the survey, a little over half said they were heterosexual, but just sixty-seven said they were homosexual and 271 avoided the question. Neither is there any way of knowing for certain whether there are more or fewer gay priests today than in the past.

In their book *Passionate Uncertainty: Inside the American Jesuits*, Peter McDonough and Eugene C. Bianchi make the case that there are several subcultures within the Jesuits. The main ones are age (old and young), ideological position (conservative and liberal), and sexual orientation (straight and gay).

Jesuits are undoubtedly getting older. Counterintuitively, the older ones are often the most liberal. They came of age during a time of social and religious upheaval, and they believe strongly in the church's responsibility to the poor and disenfranchised. But many of the older Jesuits McDonough and Bianchi interviewed expressed discomfort with what they call "a gay ethos" they believe exists within many Jesuit communities. This doesn't necessarily mean men are hooking up (something Patrick says he has never seen happen between housemates), but it does mean that gay members may feel less compelled to hide their sexual orientation than they once did.

All these differences—age, political beliefs, and sexual orientation—can create subtle and not-so-subtle divisions and add to the already volatile stew of community life.

Patrick belongs to a generation that shrugs off most of these distinctions. He says he's sick to death of older Jesuits trying to nail down his political persuasions and he doesn't care if a guy is straight or gay as long as he has a healthy acceptance of who he is and isn't just trying to avoid dealing with it—and as long as he's the kind of guy who will make a good priest.

Successfully living in a community, Patrick says, isn't much different than success in ministry. You have to be able to ask for and accept help when you need it, and you need to be unselfish and available to other people.

It seems to me that community living helps with all these things. I doubt there's a better reminder that you're not the center of the universe than sharing quarters with a bunch of guys. It may, in fact, be the best possible test of one's resolve to be a good, patient, and kind person. Just sit down to watch a ball game with the guy who yells "Wow!" every time *anything* happens on the field, even it's the most pedestrian of plays or only a time out. Try not to snap at the otherwise lovely man who makes weird robot noises in lieu of saying hello when you run into each other in the hall. Practice patience while one of your housemates tells another long, boring story at dinner and you feel every last bit of energy slowly leaking out of your body.

Patrick deals with the more unpleasant aspects of community life mostly through active avoidance (and keeping in mind there is the barest possibility that he himself has once or twice been irritating or boring). But if something—or someone—gets obnoxious enough, the matter may be taken to the house superior. Every Jesuit community has a man, usually an older, experienced Jesuit, who lives there and is ostensibly in charge. It's his job to oversee the house budget, organize meetings to discuss house rules, and suggest certain changes in behavior when it's called for. It hardly needs pointing out that this is not a job to which most men aspire.

Despite the vagaries of community life, Patrick says that if Jesuits didn't live, work, and pray together, they would lack the consolation and support they need to do the work they're called to do. "I would not be able to be a Jesuit on my own. I depend on my brothers to care about me, to actually be my companions," he said. "They are not my first priority, and I am not theirs, but a vital and vibrant companionship is essential for the health of my vocation."

I was interested to read in Norris's book *Cloister Walk* that the Catholic order of Benedictines puts even more emphasis on community life than Jesuits do. The monastic tradition is built around close proximity to others in work, prayer, and daily living in the belief that this is how you learn to put the needs of others before your own and find God in everyone around you. As Norris, who has spent months living and praying in Benedictine monasteries observing the monks' way of life, writes: "The God one finds there chooses to be revealed in other people: people we love and people we can't stand; people who are hard on us, who just might love us enough to demolish our complacency."

One monk told Norris, "This life is like being in a rock tumbler, which is really great if you want to come out good and polished." It seems to me that if you can flourish in that kind of environment, you can survive almost anywhere.

When I listen to my son tell stories about community life, I am reassured that he has so many caring people around him, but I always find it jarring when he describes them as his family, as he often does. I know the Jesuits haven't displaced Gary and me and his sisters—not entirely, anyway. And I'm well aware that children grow up and join—or create—their own families. But I'm also conscious that Patrick's Jesuit family is an exclusive one of which I will never be a part. In many ways, I am a spectator, an outsider, an onlooker to his life.

I get only an occasional glimpse of his Jesuit family. Patrick's brothers are constantly moving in and out of various communities, and I often have trouble keeping their names straight. Yet, like members of the military who have been trained and tested together, they are bound by ties that can never be entirely undone. I have noticed, for instance, the number of books written by former Jesuits—often about the Jesuits—who have left the order but still seem utterly Jesuit in heart and mind. Even if they spent only a year or two in religious life, they are somehow indelibly marked. They are, as Norris's monk said, "good and polished" for life.

*   *   *   *

While living in a Jesuit community can be, as Patrick put it, "wonderful and ridiculous at the same time," it is not the primary concern for most Jesuits. It isn't the place where they spend most of their time, and it isn't even the place where many form their most lasting friendships.

Patrick relies heavily on friends from all walks of life for both fun and emotional support. They are, in a real sense, his extended family. Many are college friends or lay people he has worked with on one of his assignments. He attends their weddings, holds their babies, and shares their backyard barbecues. Others are fellow Jesuits, but more often than not, they do not include the men with whom he happens to be living at the time.

His closest friendships within the Society tend to be long-distance, sustained by a preponderance of social media, occasional in-person visits, and the rare but memorable vacation excursion. While he was a scholastic, Patrick and four of his closest Jesuit friends who were scattered around the country reunited for a two-week road trip through the Southwest, eating junk food pretty much nonstop, blasting music in the car, and stopping whenever they felt like it. Like any group of guys, they took great care to avoid any parental homes that happened to be on their route—avoiding Phoenix, for example where my husband and I live, while managing to make it to the Grand Canyon, an omission I'm trying my best not to hold against them.

McDonough and Bianchi, whose interviews with more than 400 Jesuits form the backbone of their book, report that many Jesuits have similar experiences with friendships. Their closest relationships are often not with the people with whom they live but with men they knew as young novices or have met outside the Society. And many of those external friends are women. In one interview, a sixty-four-year-old Jesuit said, "I think a lifetime in an all-male community is a prescription for stultification or workaholism.... I miss that different kind of give-and-take that you get with women. I have a lot of women friends, without whom I wouldn't have made it."

This is certainly true for my son, who seems to have as many female as male friends. They are incredibly supportive of him, making him part of their families and bolstering him with their generosity and warmth. He needs this. Like anyone who spends a large portion of his time focused on other people and their struggles, he needs resting places—time out with people who put no demands on him except that he be himself, people who know him as a person, not solely as a priest.

The other reason so many Jesuits' important friendships lie outside their residential communities is that they change communities so often. It can be easier to keep people at arm's length than to grow so close that saying goodbye is painful. Jesuit life is most transitory during the ten to twelve years of formation and tends to become less so as men settle into their careers. But Patrick's experience to this point has been one of almost constant change. If he doesn't move, someone with whom he has grown close moves, sometimes to an assignment halfway around the world.

The point of all this uprooting, at least in the early years, has to do with the concept of molding, or forming, a Jesuit. "You need lots of experiences that stretch you in a lot of different ways," Patrick said. "And people need different kinds of stretching. Some guys need to be stretched emotionally, others intellectually or psychologically. Some need to learn what it means to do hard work."

My son has been stretched in just about every way imaginable since joining the order. He is no longer the safe, middle-class young man he was when he entered. Since leaving the novitiate, he has been sent into one of the nation's worst public housing projects, to a remote parish on the edge of a jungle in the far corner of northeast India, and to a women's prison outside of San Francisco. In these places and others, he has learned a great deal about himself and tested the limits of what he can—and cannot—do.

During his scholastic studies in Chicago, Patrick joined up with The Brothers and Sisters of Love, a lay Catholic group that works with street gangs in the city's projects. Once a week he would make the rounds of one of Chicago's housing projects like Dearborn or the infamous Cabrini-Green on the city's Near North side. Before it was demolished in 2011, the project was the size of a small city with 15,000 people living in more than 3,000 high-rise units. It was known for guns, gangs, drugs, graffiti, boarded-up windows, burned-out buildings, rats, and roaches, among other things. It looked and felt like a war zone.

I was not happy about Patrick going into Cabrini-Green under any circumstances, but what I found particularly baffling was that he was going with no other purpose than to "be present." Being present, as you may recall, is something in which Jesuits put great stock. They try to enter into people's lives as those lives are lived. There's more listening than proselytizing. The significance is in the fact that they are there at all.

My son's partner in these ventures was Brother Jim Fogarty, a person so colorful that I thought Patrick was exaggerating when he first described him. A few years later, I walked into a room of almost 300 people and spotted Jim almost immediately. He was the six-foot-tall man wearing a floor-length robe made entirely of pieces of jeans. Brother Jim, as he is known, told me it took him six months to stitch the garment out of hundreds of patches cut from cast-off jeans.

When I asked him why he wears such an outlandish outfit, he stated the obvious: It makes him stand out, which is a good thing if standing out keeps you from being shot at by gang members or hassled by the police. Jim was so instantly recognizable that the police who patrolled Cabrini and the people who lived there either got to know him or left him alone.

Jim had been taking Jesuit novitiates into the projects for years, and Patrick assured me he knew what he was doing. The two of them would stroll between the looming concrete buildings, past the walkways where drugs were being dealt, and the shout would go out: "Preachers coming! Preachers coming!" That was the signal to stash the drugs and guns.

Many of the gang members knew Jim and would come out to talk for a few minutes. Jim would admire a new pair of shoes, ask after a sick relative, or listen to a new rap song. He told me how he once stopped a shoot-out by stepping into the middle of it and refusing to leave until the guns were put away. Patrick says Jim has done this dozens of times.

After the projects were torn down, Jim continued to walk the streets of the nearby neighborhoods where Cabrini residents were relocated. He still wore his denim habit and took with him young Jesuits (whose mothers were no doubt just as nervous as I was). The lesson they learned, as Patrick did, was that sometimes the best you can do is just be there. Sometimes it's even enough.

* * * *

There were many more lessons to be learned in India where Patrick was assigned one summer to a church in the village of Maweit (which literally means "shit stone") in the jungles north of Bangladesh and south of the Himalayan mountains. For more than a month, he slept on a matt in the corner of a tiny room behind the Catholic church, assisted local Jesuits with Masses, and tried to teach a group of nuns English, a project that picked up steam when they discovered they all knew the words to John Denver's "Country Road."

Each Sunday, he, another local Jesuit, and several nuns would grab their machetes and head off in a new direction through the jungle to celebrate Mass somewhere even more remote than Maweit. In one village, the children ran out to greet them and danced them all the way down a dirt road to the church. In another, a family slaughtered and cooked one of their few chickens to commemorate the visit.

Patrick lived without running water and electricity, but he got to pat an elephant, drink tea from a cup that had been carved from bamboo just minutes before, and take what proved to be amazingly refreshing baths by pouring large cups of water over his body. He says these experiences taught him to trust more and to be less afraid of trying things he knows nothing about. They taught him that friendships do not require having very much in common and that gifts should be accepted when they are offered. He learned that, very often, he doesn't have the answers.

These were the lessons he tried to keep in mind when he found himself at the Federal Correctional Institute in Dublin, California, a few years later while studying theology in Berkeley.

Almost all Jesuits are trained in spiritual direction. Like a therapist or counselor, a spiritual director listens, offers support, and guides other people. The difference is that a spiritual director works through the prism of religion, focusing on the relationship between the person and God. (This seems to me more a matter of approach

than substance: As Carl Jung once said, every psychological problem is ultimately a matter of religion.)

Patrick and some of the other theology students at Berkeley were
assigned to work at the low security women's prison about thirty
miles southeast of Oakland. Twice a week, Patrick would check
out a car and head to the prison to keep appointments with several
female prisoners who had asked to meet with him. In some ways, the
prison, with its green lawns and outdoor garden area, appears to be
more pleasant than Cabrini-Green, at least from a visitor's point of
view. But it holds an equal measure of despair.

The women Patrick visited had been convicted of various felony
charges that typically involved drugs. They had made bad decisions
in bad circumstances that involved messy upbringings and a short-
age of resources. They were angry and hurt and looking for answers.
Patrick would pray with them if that was what they wanted, but
mostly he listened to their stories and asked questions. He would
try, he said, to help them pay attention to what was going on in their
lives, to what God might be trying to say to them, and how they
might respond.

Speaking to these women each week—seeing them move from
anger to sadness to small slivers of hope—lifted him in unexpected
ways. After a while, he said, "They actually start to sit differently.
They don't wear their tension in the same way. If you've ever doubted
whether God exists, this is proof."

Unexpectedly, his experience with prisoners convinced Patrick
of the fundamental goodness of people—or at least of their desire
to be good, even against great odds. It also helped him recognize
how privileged was his own upbringing and how much he has to be
thankful for.

Although I would be more comfortable if Patrick didn't venture
into housing projects or jungles or prisons, I find this part of my
son's vocation the easiest to embrace. He and his brothers do the
kind of work I could never do, in places I would never want to go,

with people I would prefer to keep at a distance. I'm astonished and grateful they do it.

More than their insistence on community living, their pursuit of advanced degrees, or attention to prayerful rituals and religious orthodoxy, I think it's their belief in living out their faith in the world, in being "contemplatives in action," that defines them. It's what makes them Jesuits.

CHAPTER 13

CONSOLATIONS AND DESOLATIONS

"For we do not have a high priest who is unable
to sympathize with our weaknesses, but one
who has been tempted in all things as we are
yet is without sin."
HEBREWS 4:15

I have learned from bitter experience that you should never show up for a Jesuit ceremony hungry. You could stay that way for a very long time. So, even though we were running late to Patrick's deaconate ordination ceremony in October of 2012, I insisted that we make a quick breakfast stop at Starbucks.

My daughters and I were still slurping lattes and slugging down instant oatmeal when Gary pulled the car into the parking lot of the Mission church at Santa Clara University shortly before 10 a.m. There was no mistaking that this was the right place. It was literally spilling over with priests. Dozens and dozens of them clustered outside the open doors of the church, their white robes blending with the white adobe walls and lit up by a fierce California sun. The effect was blinding, as if we had stumbled onto a white sand beach at noon on a cloudless day.

We made our way through the throng and into the long, deep interior of the church, which began as a Spanish mission founded by the Franciscan order in 1777. It is as ornate on the inside as it is simple on the outside, all pink and blue and gold with a sky painted on the ceiling, the saints and angels floating unhinged among the clouds and stars.

We found our seats about halfway up the center aisle in a row of chairs the church uses in lieu of pews. Patrick had marked the place with a sign, "Reserved for Immediate Family of Paddy Gilger, SJ," so we would be positioned where we would have a good view of his investiture, during which a stole, a piece of cloth that looks like a closely woven scarf and symbolizes the clergy, was to be draped over his shoulder. Afterward, we would be near the start of the line where he would hand out communion, placing the consecrated wafers in our hands for the first time.

Eleven men, including Patrick, were to be ordained as transitional deacons on this day. It would be the second-to-last step in their long journey toward priesthood. In a few months, after finishing their theological studies, each would be ordained again, this time as priests.

Not all deacons become priests. For some, being a deacon is the end of the road as far as ecclesiastical titles are concerned. These "permanent deacons" can preach, assist at Masses, and perform baptisms, marriages, and the rite of Christian burial, but for various reasons they do not become fully ordained priests. Most have day jobs and are married. (The married ones are required to have their wife's permission to join up, and, if their wives die, they are expected to take a vow of celibacy.)

The permanent diaconate, as it is called, is making something of a comeback in the Roman Catholic Church. Deacons were part of the early church, dating back to the time of the apostles, but largely disappeared until the 1960s when the permanent diaconate was reinstated as one of the many changes brought about by the Second Vatican Council. There are now more than 13,000 permanent deacons in the US, according to the US Conference of Catholic Bishops. They help, at least in a small way, to make up for the declining number of men willing to become priests.

In Santa Clara, we watched as Patrick and the other transitional deacons filed two by two into the church, making a slow procession down the long aisle to their seats near the front. Looming above them were nearly 100 other men, also dressed in white, standing shoulder to shoulder and filling every inch of space around the altar. I had never seen so many priests in one place. In fact, if I added up all the priests I have ever seen in my life, I don't think it would come to this number. On the right side of the sanctuary sat the bishop of San Jose, an imposing figure made even more imposing by a gold-trimmed hat called a mitre that rose from the front and back of his head to form what looked like a colossal cone.

Twice during the ceremony, Patrick and the other candidates rose from their seats to kneel before the bishop. He took their folded hands into his own while they promised obedience. He handed them a book of the Gospels while intoning the words: "Receive the Gospel of Christ whose herald you have become. Believe what you read, teach what you believe, practice what you teach." Then, in an ancient ritual called the Laying on of Hands, he placed his hands on their bowed heads, signifying the conferral of the Holy Spirit through him to them.

There were songs sung in English and Latin, incense and psalms, and more incantations, and it seemed to me that every movement, every word, was pitch perfect, the result of centuries and centuries of practice. When I thought it couldn't get any more ... medieval was the word that came to mind ... it did. Acting on some unseen cue, Patrick and the other candidates spread out into the church, spacing themselves a body length apart in the aisles and, in one synchronized motion, they dropped to the floor, arms spread above their heads, their faces stamped into the cold brick.

As they lay prostrate, the entire congregation, nearly 500 strong, began singing the Litany of the Saints, one of the oldest prayers in the Catholic Church, dating back to at least the sixth century. It's more chant than song, a long, haunting recitation of names—Mary and Joseph, Michael and all the angels, Saint Benedict, Saint Bernard,

Saint Dominic, Saint Agnes, Saint Cecilia, Saint Catherine, Saint Clare. The list went on and on—virgins and widows, martyrs and doctors, bishops, patriarchs, apostles, angels, and prophets.

"Pray for us," the congregation chanted after each name. "All you holy men and women, pray for us."

I felt like the song was sinking into my bones and, for a moment, I wanted it to stop and for Patrick to get up off that floor. Then the applause began, and I looked around at hundreds of people lit up with praise and conviction and anticipation. I had no idea whether they knew my son or not; I suspected it didn't matter. There was love here, and there was hope.

When the chant finally ended, Patrick rose from the floor, wiped tears from his eyes, and threw us a ridiculous grin. I don't think he stopped smiling the rest of the day. Outside the church after the ceremony, he hugged everyone and posed for dozens of photos. When a friend offered to take a picture of our family, he dropped to his knees in front of his very pregnant sister, placed both hands on her belly and gave the baby inside her a great big kiss.

* * * *

The next morning, Patrick assisted with Mass at a small chapel a few blocks from the Jesuit house in Berkeley. He genuflected in the right places, passed the wine without spilling it, and generally seemed comfortable in front of the two dozen or so friends and family members who had gotten up early to witness another milestone in his path to the priesthood.

The day's Gospel reading recounted the story of the apostles James and John who came to Jesus with an audacious request: "Teacher, we want you to do for us whatever we ask of you," they began. When Jesus asked them what that might be, they replied that they wanted to sit "one at your right and one at your left" in heaven. Jesus replied, "You do not know what you are asking" and proceeded to give them a lesson in humility along these lines: Those who are worthy don't lord it over others; instead, they make themselves servants.

Jesus, Patrick said from the pulpit, must have been at least a little annoyed when James and John spoke to him in this way, but instead of reprimanding them, "He gathers the disciples together and for the one millionth time explains to them what He's about, the way He wants this community to behave." It's the kind of patience mothers and fathers have, Patrick said. Inordinately patient. Heroically patient. "Like my parents, who would be more than happy to tell any of you stories about the many, many times they've managed—just barely—to restrain from rolling their eyes and saying, 'You don't know what you're talking about, Patrick.'"

I laughed out loud. It's true: There are still times when I think Patrick doesn't know what he's talking about. But it was Jesus' initial response to James and John that I kept coming back to in my mind. The words perfectly captured what I have felt so often during the ten years that led to this moment: You do not know what you are asking.

*　*　*　*

For the first few years after Patrick joined the Jesuits, I did my best to be patient. What other option did I have unless I wanted to be like the mother of Saint Thomas Aquinas, who has gone down in history as the woman who locked her son in a tower to prevent him from becoming a priest? With no tower available, I relied on time. I thought perhaps this whole religious thing was something Patrick just needed to get out of his system and one day he would grow out of it. It would be like a love affair that he would look back on with a certain amount of nostalgia but little real regret.

He has not often talked with us about his doubts, but almost from the beginning they were there. In a poem he wrote near the end of his two years in the novitiate, just after he and his brother novices had been accepted to take First Vows, he described what they were doing as a slender hope.

There are nine of us now.
Nine attempting
A sort of consecration of our lives
Attempting to at least walk straight
Walk a thin line in the same direction each day.
A slender hope holds us,
An anorexic hope for our anorexic age.

There were times when I thought the hope had grown so thin that Patrick would give up, and there was one time in particular when I hoped fervently that he would. It was when he was nearing the end of his assignment on the reservation in South Dakota, and he had to decide whether to apply to continue to theological studies. If he was ever going to leave, this would be the time. I knew the years on the reservation had been difficult for him, but I didn't know how difficult until I read the application letter he had written to his provincial.

His first years in the Jesuits were a time of confirmation, he wrote, but at Red Cloud, a place he had not wanted to go, he fell deeply in love, and it divided his heart. Part of him wanted to be a priest and part longed "to daily share myself with one person" and to experience "the spark of joy that only children give me. It was only a combination of patience and stubbornness," he wrote, "that kept me from fleeing from darkness by fleeing the Society for the vocation of marriage."

There was something else that prompted him to continue as a Jesuit, he said. He had come to believe that suffering opened a path to God, that the experience of desolation, with all its associations with emptiness and the absence of God, was a kind of grace. This grace, he wrote, "acts as a chisel, cutting away my falsity, leaving a truth. My work (on the reservation) has taught me this as well. Both with the volunteers and my Lakota students, it strikes me that the most important thing I have learned to do is to remain with them in their suffering; not to leave when darkness falls; to trust that joy will find us even in the dark.... I name all this as consolation. I write with an increasing sense of being reconciled to my divided self."

Gary handed me the letter one night shortly after I arrived home from work. "Read this," he told me, his face solemn and set. "It's Patrick's letter explaining why he wants to stay with the Jesuits." I skimmed the letter standing at the kitchen counter and then sat down to read it a second time. I wanted to be certain I understood.

"This is all about suffering," I finally said to my husband, who had been waiting for me to finish. "He's saying that he's miserable, but since suffering is good for him, he'll just go ahead and keep doing it." Patrick had, in fact, used the word "suffers" or "suffering" eleven times in three and a half pages. He used the word "darkness" six times.

Gary nodded. "I think we should call him," he said. But first he made a list on the back of an envelope. It was filled with underlines and question marks. "Should consolation be necessary if this is what you really want to do? After three years in Pine Ridge, you're finally *reconciled*? Acceptance of division in yourself? Grace of suffering?? Are you doing anything for <u>you</u>?" All good questions, I thought. We made the call.

Gary, who had never to my knowledge had a serious conversation with Patrick about his vocation, did most of the talking. "I just don't understand," he told him. "If you're not happy, why are you staying? It seems like you want to suffer, that you somehow think that suffering is good for you. That doesn't make sense. Why do you want to do something that makes you so unhappy?"

"We just want you to be happy, Patrick," I echoed when it was my turn to talk. "If being a Jesuit is making you miserable, if this is all about suffering, then you should leave."

We had never been so blunt before. We had never told him how we really felt about his decision to become a Catholic priest. In truth, I, at least, had always felt somewhat ambiguous. I was proud of my son and thought he could do some good in a world that could certainly use more unselfishness. Unselfishness, however, was one thing; masochism was something else entirely.

"Mom," he protested. "This does make me happy. But happiness isn't really the point; happiness is overrated, and suffering isn't as bad as you're making it out to be. Besides, we can't avoid it. Everyone suffers. Americans are so allergic to suffering! The question is what you choose to do with it, what you learn from it, not whether you experience it."

He said he hadn't expected such a strong reaction from us, and our daughters were almost as perplexed. Patrick had sent them copies of his letter, too, and, while they paid attention, they weren't upset. "Did we read the same letter?" Dana said on the phone later that night. "It just sounded to me like he had gone through a painful time and made a difficult decision, but I knew that already. I think he's doing what he wants to do, and it will make him happy." Lauren sent Dana a text: "Why are mom and dad going ballistic?"

The next day after Gary had calmed down, he wrote Patrick an email with the subject line "More than you asked for?" "I hope we didn't freak you out last night. Both mom and I are with you whatever you choose to do. We love you and are very proud of all you've done and will do. Dad."

Patrick replied that it was hard to listen to what we had to say, but "I don't get chances to hear you unfiltered very often. I'm actually grateful for your and mom's honesty. It makes me happier to know how you guys are really reacting and to know that you're still with me even though the letter didn't make sense and left you with bad feelings. I'm going to take your reactions ... and my own feelings in response to you ... into prayer and see what comes of them. I love you a lot, dad." He signed it "Inscrutable Son."

Our one serious attempt at protest was over; it was clear to us that Patrick had made his choice.

Months later, just after his ordination as a deacon, the now-infamous letter came up in a conversation around the family dinner table. Patrick said again how surprised he was that we were so upset when we read it. Dana, who had started thinking like a mother now that she was about to become one, said she thought she understood. "As a parent," she said, "you don't want your kid to suffer."

Patrick nodded agreement. "Your suffering is my suffering. That's true for all of us. But suffering is not the enemy. The best parents are the ones who know that—and let their children learn from suffering."

Easy to say, I thought. Much harder to do when it's your child who is feeling pain.

* * * *

Stubbornness certainly played a role in Patrick's refusal to give up the Jesuits. With the exception of golf, once he starts something, he's usually in it for the long haul. But I think he also felt a strong sense of obligation, of being needed, especially when so many of his brothers began to leave, especially in the early years of formation.

He came to dread the letters announcing yet another Jesuit brother was quitting. The names varied, but the words were almost always the same: "I've fallen in love, and I hope you can be happy for us. I've prayed about this a lot, and I believe this is what God wants for me." Jim Keane, a friend of Patrick's who left the Jesuits after more than a decade, used to joke that instead of writing a letter, he'd just send an email to everyone saying: "I'm leaving. You all know why."

Patrick tried to understand, and sometimes he almost managed it. The departing Jesuit gave it a fair shot, he would tell himself. It just wasn't the right life for him. And even more to the point, it wasn't like the guy was deserting before his term of duty was up and he should be court-martialed. He was always able to leave any time he wanted.

But often the letters left him depressed and angry. When a young man who had entered the novitiate with him announced he was leaving to marry a woman he had met just five months earlier,

Patrick was livid. He learned about it during his time on the reservation when he was struggling with his own decision about whether to leave, and he didn't think five months was enough time to figure out anything, much less the will of God.

When I asked how much time it should take, Patrick practically spewed his answer. "If you're married for a few years and then you meet someone else and five months later you split to marry this new person, what the fuck is that? Where's the respect in that? I don't buy it because I know exactly what it's like to have someone you want to spend the rest of your life with. I know exactly what that's like. Don't tell me I didn't feel that. My love was just as real.

"If you leave because you just can't do it anymore, because it's too hard, and you say, 'I'm sorry if it hurts, but I'm going to be with God in another way,' I'm fine with that. I've seen that happen, and I'm much less angry with those guys. I can be a little angry, then a little sad, and then get over it and support them as best I can. But it takes time to discern the will of God, and when you're depressed or anxious or whatever is not the time to do it. There was no respect in what he did. He was just making a choice."

This outburst was followed by a few moments of silence. "Too fucking many have left," he said finally. His voice had dropped to almost a whisper, and he sounded more resigned than angry. "I'm tired of it. It hurts every time."

Jeff Sullivan, the college friend who helped introduce Patrick to Catholicism and later followed him into the Jesuits, said it's difficult for everyone when fellow Jesuits leave, but he thinks Patrick takes it harder than most. "Sometimes I think he feels a little bit of obligation to stay in because so many people are leaving the Jesuits," he said, "and we need good men to carry on these missions."

The Jesuits still comprise the largest contingent of priests and brothers in the Catholic Church, but the number of men entering has plunged since the 1960s, just as it has for most religious orders. The number of Jesuits peaked worldwide in 1965 at 36,038.

There are now, according to the Center for Applied Research in the Apostolate at Georgetown University, fewer than half that number.

The drop has been steepest in the US and other developed countries. There are only about 2,000 Jesuits left in the US, and their average age is over sixty-five. Patrick says membership is expected to continue a steady decline until it stabilizes at a little more than 1,000. He tries to keep these numbers in perspective. The Jesuit order has always been relatively small. It is, in fact, not much smaller now than it was in the early twentieth century. The 1950s and early 1960s when huge numbers of men joined were the aberrations. And even if the downward trend continues, even if the Jesuits were to die out altogether, "It wouldn't be catastrophic," Patrick said. "Would the world be worse off? Maybe. Does that mean that God would abandon the world? Impossible. God will find another way. God will never be tired of trying to be in a relationship with us."

Still, there's a part of him that worries there won't be enough Jesuits to do the work and he'll be one of those left holding the rope. There are times when he feels overwhelmed by everything he's asked to do, and, when he looks around, he sees only how much more there is that needs to be done.

Some days he feels like giving up and becoming a stockbroker and driving a Maserati. "I could be successful," he has told me more than once. "I could make money out there, but who cares? It wouldn't mean a thing."

*   *   *   *

Two years after the dustup over the letter, Patrick wrote again to his provincial, this time asking to be approved for full ordination into the priesthood. He was finishing his master's degree in theology, and the letter marked another one of those seemingly endless junctures at which Jesuits are asked to take stock of whether they want to continue in the order and when the order evaluates whether they should stay.

This letter sounded almost nothing like the earlier one that had so upset my husband and me. "In contrast with the relative uncertainty with which I wrote petitioning for advancement to theology, I write this letter with joy in the Divine Majesty, with a sense of calm conviction. Writing in such consolation I want to state, quite simply, that I very much want to be a priest."

He talked about his weaknesses, "the darkness" of his time on the reservation, and how conflicted he still felt about some of the church's teachings. But those things, he said, were overshadowed by love. "I want to echo Flannery O'Connor, James Joyce, and Saint Augustine by identifying myself fully with a Pilgrim Church into which all, holy and unholy alike, are welcomed. It is from deep within our Roman Catholic Church that I want to serve the world as a priest."

And it was this fact—that confidence and joy fairly burst from these pages—that finally began to put my mind at ease.

* * * *

We prepared for Patrick's ordination in June 2013 in much the same way we would for a family wedding. There were travel arrangements to make, hotels to book, flowers to order, clothes to pick out, a reception to plan. Lauren designed the invitations, and Patrick sent out more than 250 of them to people in California, South Dakota, Kansas, Iowa, Nebraska, Missouri, Oregon, Louisiana, Florida, New York, Texas, and God knows where else. He had, it seemed, grown a very large family for a single guy with no kids.

We were told that the ceremony would include Patrick and one other Jesuit, Jayme Stayer, who also would be ordained, and that it would take place at the Madonna Della Strada Chapel at Loyola University in Chicago, where Patrick studied for his degree in philosophy. I knew the church. It was white and light and full of soaring arches, Italian marble, and bright gold frescoes. The waters of Lake Michigan lap at its front door.

Gary and I would help "vest" him, draping a stole across his shoulder and settling it around his neck, signifying his official membership in the clergy. Dana and Lauren would help bear the gifts of bread and wine to the front of the church just before communion.

We were all looking forward to it, but no one was more excited than Patrick. He marked the days to ordination on Facebook, posting a photo of himself with a very large clock around his neck, taking a page, he said, from the rapper Flavor Fav's playbook. In a Facebook video countdown, he posted video links to some of his favorite songs—Bob Dylan's "The Man in Me" and The Cowboy Junkies' "Sweet Jane" among them. He could hardly wait; he was almost giddy with anticipation.

"I'm nervous, but I'm ready," he assured me. "I wish I was a priest already!"

There were some serious preparations to be made as well. Patrick would say his first Mass the day after his ordination, a Sunday. He would be the one to bless the congregation, lead the prayers, and consecrate the wine and host. He very much wanted it to be perfect.

"I've been going to different parishes," he said, "and I find myself looking at all these people with amazement and thinking, 'Why are you here? Why do you work so hard to get the kids up and dress them and fight with them to be here, and you're distracted half the Mass, and sometimes it feels like nothing that happens here connects with your life? Why do you come?

"I do not take that for granted. I feel like I owe these people—owe them not just something, but everything. I want to give them everything I can of God. So often, Mass is dry or rote or we preach about stuff that doesn't move hearts. I want to help people be present, help God be present, and then get out of the way so they can be together. That's what people want. Hell, it's what I want!

"There's nothing better I could do," he said. "There's no better job in the world than this."

CHAPTER 14

A TICKET TO HEAVEN

"A vocation comes from the heart of God but
goes through the heart of the mother."
POPE PIUS X

*B*eing the mother of a priest pretty much guarantees
me a ticket to heaven and a comfortable lounge chair
when I get there. At least that's what I tell people. It's a
good way to get a laugh and overcome the awkwardness that usually
ensues when someone learns what my son does for a living. There
might even be a kernel of truth in it.

Dating back to the earliest days of the church, it has been mothers who have gotten most of the credit when their sons have gone
into the church business. I don't know why this is, or why fathers,
dating back to poor, inconspicuous Joseph, have been mostly
ignored. But in this case, the attention has been on women, and, for
once, in a good way.

I'm sure many of these mothers were overjoyed when their sons
became priests. Various Catholic websites eulogize one particular mother, Eliza Vaughan, who lived in England in the mid-nine-
teenth century and is said to have prayed for an hour every day for
a large family and many children who would grow up to be priests
and nuns. Her prayers were answered on both counts. She had nine
sons and six of them became priests—among them were a bishop, an

archbishop, and a cardinal. Of her five daughters, four took vows as nuns. (I expect that Eliza has an entire suite in heaven.)

But even Eliza pales in comparison to the mothers of the tiny town of Lu in northern Italy. In 1881, the mothers of Lu began praying for vocations in this way: "O God, grant that one of my sons becomes a priest. I promise to live as a good Christian woman and will lead my children to all that is good, wherewith I hope to receive the grace to be able to give to Thee, O God, a holy priest. Amen." It worked beyond their wildest imaginings. Within fifty years, according to the Catholic News Agency, 323 young men and women of Lu had joined religious orders.

Other mothers have prayed equally fervently for their sons to enter the church, but not exclusively for reasons of piety. For many years, it was the oldest son in a family who inherited the family farm or other property, a practice that often left the younger sons floundering for something to do. Becoming a priest was a way to get an education and enter a respected profession. In later generations, if you were a son in a large working-class family, you might take a look at the kind of work your father did in a mine or factory and decide the priesthood was a better option.

Besides, if one or two children went off to become a nun or priest, there were always a few more left to carry on the family name and take care of mom and dad when they grew old. As a result, many large Catholic families singled out one of their younger sons from an early age to be the priest in the family. Sometimes this worked out and sometimes it didn't, but it pretty much guaranteed a steady supply of young men entering seminaries.

The mothers of these priests had special bragging rights. They had birthed and raised sons of God. They were officially good mothers, and they could look forward to even more rewards in heaven.

Fast-forward to twenty-first century America. I've met mothers—and fathers—who are thrilled their sons have become priests, but many seem more than a little suspicious of the entire enterprise.

This is in no small part due to the sexual abuse scandal, but it's also because the priesthood is no longer a cushy career choice. In the hierarchy of jobs, it ranks somewhere alongside teachers, military personnel, and other occupations characterized by high stress and low pay.

A few years ago, the question of whether parents would want their sons to become priests drew dozens of comments in a blog written by George Michalopulos, an Orthodox Christian. While some said they would be pleased and proud, a number, including at least one who is himself an Orthodox priest, were adamantly opposed. One man wrote he would rather have his son join the military because "he would know what his mission was and wouldn't be shot from behind, you know?" Parents talked about long hours and vicious parishioners and a church bureaucracy that too often fails to be supportive. "I've seen parish life up close," one father wrote. "It is not for the faint of heart." Another said that if either of his sons decided to become a priest, "I would be sorrowful because I would know they were being put to a terrible test."

The Diocese of Toledo, Ohio, offered another glimpse of how parents react to a son's or daughter's religious calling. For a time, the diocese's Office of Vocations posted a long list of quotes from parents wondering whether their children had made the right decision and if they really understood what they were giving up. These parents worried about loneliness and what kinds of careers their children would have if religious life turned out not to suit them. They fretted over the lack of grandchildren and the upheavals in the church. One parent was quoted as saying, "It scares me that my son could be falsely accused or grouped in with those who have done wrong."

I found none of this surprising. I have felt each and every one of these concerns and a few more besides. What I did find surprising was how shocked so many parents, presumably Catholic themselves, were by their children's decision to become priests. For the most part, they just didn't seem to see it coming.

I had been reading everything I could find about mothers of priests, which wasn't much, so I decided it was time to actually talk to some of them. My first call was to Diane Sundrup, whose oldest son, Eric, is one of Patrick's best friends and served as co-editor of *The Jesuit Post*. Diane's experience was reassuringly much like my own.

Eric made his big announcement one summer day after finishing his sophomore year in college, Diane told me. She and her husband tried to be supportive. "Okay, we're not disagreeing," they kept saying. "But why?"

Eric had been studying biology at Xavier University, a Jesuit college in Cincinnati, Ohio. Like Patrick, it was in college that he got to know the Jesuits for the first time, and, like Patrick, he was impressed. "I want to do what they're doing," he told his parents. "I want to be like them."

Diane and her husband argued that he would be throwing away a full scholarship and should at least finish his studies before making such a big decision. "Get a bachelor's degree first. If it doesn't work out, you'll have something to fall back on," they urged. "We were adamant about it," Diane said. "He wasn't very happy."

By the time Eric did enter the order a couple of years later, Diane was much more comfortable. She could see that her son was happy, and she knew that he still had ten or twelve years in which to make a final decision. Most people take much less time to decide on the vocation of married life, she pointed out, and the Jesuit formation process "is really good. They've got to know they're ready."

Diane is a good Catholic. She was raised Catholic, married a Catholic, and raised all three of her sons Catholic. She and her husband sent their boys to a Catholic high school, and two of them went to Catholic colleges, and yet she had never seriously thought about the possibility that one of her sons would become a priest. Only in retrospect does it make sense to her. She remembers Eric's kindergarten teacher complimenting her on how Eric went out of his way to include a new classmate. "People were always telling me how compassionate and helpful he was," she said. "I didn't think much of it at the time, but now it all fits."

In contrast, Karen Sullivan, the mother of Patrick's good friend Jeff, said she has known her son was destined for the priesthood since he was eight years old. Jeff, however, took a considerably longer time to arrive at that conclusion himself.

Jeff had described his mother to me as an old-fashioned, 1950s-style Catholic, the kind of person who is still a little in awe of the church in general and of priests in particular. Karen, I found, pretty much lived up to that billing. She calls herself and her husband "cradle Catholics," people who were steeped in Catholic tradition and practice from the time they were born. They went to Catholic schools and sent their children to Catholic schools, not just because it was expected of them but because they were convinced it was the right thing to do.

She said she can't explain it, but "I just knew Jeff was going to be a priest. The Holy Spirit or something told me in my heart that this is what he was going to do. It isn't that he was doing anything priestly or religious or anything like that. Just one day I said to myself, 'Oh, he's going to be a priest.'"

She wanted her son to discover his vocation on his own, so she said nothing as Jeff passed through high school, then college, and then several years of toying with various career options—law school, teaching, writing children's books. She remained convinced even when he talked about marrying his longtime girlfriend who had gone with him to Ecuador to work at a Catholic mission. She came back to the states a year later; he stayed for another year.

When he finally returned home, Jeff was more adrift than ever. "He came back to Indianapolis and didn't know what he wanted to do," his mother said. "We weren't getting along very well, and I know now that it's because I was still treating him like a kid." One weekend Jeff packed a bag and headed to Omaha to attend the wedding of some college friends from Creighton. Patrick was attending the same wedding and the two got to talking. The next thing Karen knew, Jeff was in the car with Patrick heading to Pine Ridge. A little more than a year later, he entered the novitiate in St. Paul.

Karen doesn't know why it took Jeff so long to figure things out, but she's glad he finally did, and she's grateful for Patrick's role in it. "It's the right fit for him," she said firmly.

There are things that worried her, at least at the beginning. She didn't know whether she should keep paying Jeff's life insurance, and she wasn't exactly clear about what he could and could not inherit. She thought he might end up going back to Central America or someplace else far too dangerous for her liking. And she would prefer that Jeff stay clear of drinking, which most Jesuits don't seem inclined to do. Her father was an alcoholic, and Jeff gave them a couple of scares when he was in college. But she's more than happy to be the mother of a priest. "It means a lot to me," she said. "I kind of think it means we did something right."

Mary Hendrickson falls somewhere between Diane and Karen on the "who-would-have-thought-my-son-would-become-a-priest?" scale. Like Karen, Mary is a traditional Catholic. Her three boys were expected to go to church every Sunday, serve as altar boys, and attend Catholic schools. Religion was as much a part of their lives as sports are to some families. They thought nothing of saying a rosary to pass the time in the car, and priests were frequent guests for Sunday dinners (although Mary said some used coarser language around her children than she would have liked). No less than five of Mary's cousins became priests and another is a nun. Her brother was a Jesuit for ten years before dropping out to become a theology teacher. Religion, she said, "was kind of a family business." So it made sense to her when her son Daniel decided to enter the Jesuits after attending Marquette University in Milwaukee. Two years later, Daniel's twin brother Scott also decided to become a Jesuit. When I pointed out how unusual it is to have TWO sons—identical twins, no less—who are priests, Mary shrugged.

"People tell me all the time, 'Oh, you must have a very spiritual family," she said. "But I don't know what that means. We always said grace before meals and prayers before bedtime. But it's not like there was a lot of Bible reading in our house. Catholics really don't know their Bible, you know. We just tried to teach our guys: 'Be a good person. Do unto others as you would have done to you.'"

The other thing Mary hears a lot is: "Oh, what a waste!" This is because Daniel and Scott are ... well, rock-star good-looking. We were hosting a dinner for family and some of Patrick's friends at a restaurant in St. Paul the first time I saw them. When Daniel and Scott walked into the restaurant, every head in the place turned in their direction, and I thought my sisters were going to pass out. Suffice it to say that Mary's "guys," as she calls them, are tall, trim, blonde, and blue-eyed and favor turtleneck sweaters under dark sports coats. They could be Robert Redford's younger brothers.

The minute they sat down at our table, my sister Patty got up and moved her chair next to them. "They're priests," I objected in a furious whisper. "Oh, don't get worked up," she shot back. "I just want to look at them."

Mary said her oldest son, Ryan, would have made a good priest as well. But he fell in love while in college, raised a family, and became a professor of political science, an author, and a university administrator. He became very involved in his local Catholic church, and Mary said she was pretty sure he would become a deacon one day.

These women—Diane, Karen, and Mary—all said that having sons who are priests has deepened their faith.

Karen feels a need to "honor Jeff by being a better person." She has become a more observant Catholic, no longer missing Holy Thursday services during Easter week, for instance. And she has thought about starting a club for parents of young men entering the priesthood. The more experienced parents could answer questions—like what to expect when your son is sent on that pilgrimage during his second year in the novitiate. The Jesuits "are so close to each other," she said. "I think it would be nice if the parents were closer, too."

Mary would love this idea. She was so horrified when Daniel was about to embark on a pilgrimage to San Francisco to work with gang members that she drove from Omaha to St. Paul to have a "little chat" with his superiors. Daniel went on the pilgrimage, but only on the condition that he call home every other day.

Diane became a sponsor for people who are interested in joining the Catholic Church, guiding people through the Rite of Christian Initiation of Adults (RCIA), the same program Patrick completed at Creighton before he was confirmed as a Catholic. Initiates take classes and participate in church rituals for nearly a year under the sponsorship of a guide or mentor before deciding whether to convert. The first person who Diane sponsored was her own father.

"We were having lunch one day, and I told him I had decided to be a RCIA sponsor," she said. "I thought it would be a good way to reinforce my faith, especially since my son was studying to be a priest. My dad said, 'Why don't you sponsor me?'"

Diane was well aware that her father was not Catholic, although it had always been pretty hard to tell. In order to marry her very Catholic mother, he had been asked to pledge that any children they had would be raised in the church, and he had kept his word. Four decades later—just two years before he died—he converted under his daughter's tutelage.

Mary said she and her husband attend church every day of the week when they're at their second home in Coronado, California, where they spend half of the year now that they're retired. And she has seen her family grow in unexpected ways, becoming a kind of second mother to a number of her sons' friends in the order. They come to visit on Mother's Day and fill her table at Thanksgiving. "I have inherited a lot of Jesuits," she said.

Talking to these women, I feel a slight unease, a looming sense of obligation. What does it mean to be the mother of a priest? I wonder. Are there special duties involved? What exactly is expected?

I suspect I am already inadequate. I have not started going to church every Sunday, much less every holy day. I cannot imagine mothering a bunch of priests, starting a support group, or mentor-ing would-be Catholics. And I am not the least bit comfortable with Mary Helmueller's admonition that it is "absolutely necessary for a mother to be part of her son's mission to save souls."

Mary, according to the website TheCatholicSpirit.com, is a Maplewood, South Dakota, mother who prayed the rosary every day from the time she was married in the hope that she would have a child who would one day enter religious life. After one of her three sons was ordained, she cast about for something more she could do and decided that what was needed was a support group for mothers of priests, so she started one. I can't tell if the group still exists, but for a while at least, its seventy-some members attended Mass, visited other mothers of priests in nursing homes, and prayed for their sons, for their sons' parishioners, and for other people so their sons would find their way to the priesthood, too.

That's a lot of praying. I, on the other hand, have been to a prayer meeting only once, and that was while visiting Patrick in Berkeley. I thought it was something the mother of a priest should do, a way to get a glimpse of his vocation, just as I might visit my son's classroom or accompany him to an art show if he were a teacher or an artist. I did not find it to be a comfortable experience. In fact, I felt like a fifth grader being forced to watch a sex education video. It made me want to avert my eyes.

There were about fifteen of us—men and women, Jesuits and non-Jesuits—sitting in a classroom contemplating Mary's reac-tion to an angel appearing out of nowhere and asking her to be the mother of God. "Imagine you're a young woman and this happens to you," said George Murphy, the elderly Jesuit who was leading the discussion. "Notice your reaction. What's it like to hear that, and what would it be like to say 'Yes' when you might be tempted to say, 'There's a real nice girl down the street!'"

We were given ten or fifteen minutes to think about this. Patrick sat very still with his eyes closed, while others laid their heads on the table or wandered outside. One young woman sat on a couch in the lobby with her hands over her ears to drown out distractions. When we were all back in our chairs, a nun in the group offered that she had spent the time imagining she was pregnant and no one in the convent would believe it was the work of the Holy Spirit. A young Jesuit priest said he had mixed feelings: It would in some ways be like winning the lottery, he said, "but then you couldn't help but ask, 'Why me?'"

As the former director of spiritual formation for the Jesuit community in Berkeley, Father Murphy, who encouraged us to call him George, has plenty of experience guiding such discussions. He is gentle and accepting, even when someone gets a little carried away, as did one woman who volunteered she had seen Jesus on the cross and He had glittering eyes but didn't want to look at her.

"He said that to you?" George asked.

"Well, no," she replied. "But He asked me if I wanted to be His spouse. He said I looked real pretty."

George did not wince at hearing this. People seemed comfortable saying almost anything around him, and he seemed comfortable hearing whatever it was they had to say. Even his appearance was sympathetic—wispy white hair set off by a well-washed, short-sleeved shirt in a startling shade of pink. I could see a patch of orange skin showing just above his green socks.

George can begin a discussion about the Annunciation, transition without a bump to the feminist pronouncements of Saint Teresa of Avila, throw in a few thoughts about the fine line between appearance and narcissism, and wind up with a discourse on the devil. (It was during the discussion of the devil that I realized I was possibly the only person in the room who had not seriously considered the devil since the fifth grade.)

Sometimes I wish I could be more like George (minus the white hair and orange skin) and not just because he's so masterful at steering a conversation. He seems to have no expectations. He dispenses no judgment. I, on the other hand, am overflowing with judgments—about the woman who is convinced she's going to marry the crucified Jesus, about the young man who shared a story about encountering Christ in the laundry room, and even about Saint Teresa of Avila, a sixteenth-century mystic who spent much of her adult life in "devotions of ecstasy," helped along by a few mortifications of the flesh. In truth, they all seem just a little crazy to me.

I know that if I had more patience, if I could better tolerate excess, these eccentricities could teach me something. And I think I know what Patrick would say. It would be something about how God might appreciate a little more foolishness, a little less resistance, from some of us. I have resolved to think about that, but for now I'm steering clear of prayer groups. I'm going to have to find another way to be the mother of a priest.

* * * *

When I talk to other mothers whose sons have chosen the priesthood, I ask about their views of the Catholic Church, what their experiences were like growing up Catholic, and whether they harbor any fears about the kind of life their children have chosen. But what I'm really interested in is grandchildren. I don't think anyone would call me the grandmotherly type, but I have always made it abundantly clear to my children that I expected them to produce children one day—and preferably lots of them.

Patrick was still a couple of years away from being ordained when I put the grandchildren question to Mary, Karen, and Diane. Mary was happy with three grandchildren, thanks to her sole son who did not join the priesthood, and Karen was about to become a grandmother after a long wait. With Jeff out of the picture, she had only one shot—Jeff's older brother, Dan, who didn't marry until he was thirty-two. Dan and his wife were expecting their first child, and Karen was so thrilled that she talked about moving to Houston to be closer to the baby (and possibly to Dan and his wife).

"It's a boy," she told me excitedly, "and I don't want to miss anything. I plan to go to every sporting event, every recital, and every school function. I always promised myself I would be part of my grandchildren's lives."

Diane, though, had three grown children and not a grandchild in sight. "I have a lot of friends with grandkids, and I have to admit I'm a little jealous," she said. "I would love to have grandkids." I hung up the phone feeling happy for Mary and Karen and hopeful for Diane. I wondered if Mary Helmueller and her support group up in Maplewood, South Dakota, would have room for her in their prayers.

It seems to me that mothers who give up the possibility of grand-children—or more grandchildren—when their sons become priests deserve every special consideration the church has at its disposal.

Karen has her eyes on a pair of white gloves. She heard some-where that mothers of priests have the right to be buried wearing white lace gloves. Neither one of us could verify that a glove ritual has ever existed, but I did find an article by Monsignor Charles Pope, the pastor of a Catholic church in Washington, D.C., who tells of another practice honoring the mothers of priests.

According to the Monsignor, it has long been church tradition to wrap a priest's hands with a *manutergium* (Latin for hand towel) after his hands are anointed with sacred oil during his ordination ceremony. The purpose is partly practical—to prevent excess oil from dripping onto vestments or the floor during the remainder of the service.

Traditionally, the manutergium was given to the priest's mother, who kept it in a safe place until she died, at which point it was placed in her hands as her body lay in the casket. The belief was that when she arrived at the gates of heaven, she would be escorted directly to the Lord. The Lord would say to the woman: "I have given you life; what have you given to me?", and she would hand him the manuter-gium and say, "I have given you my son as a priest." At this, she would be granted entry into paradise.

Given a choice, Karen and I would prefer the gloves. But neither one of us would turn down a ticket to heaven.

CHAPTER 15

THE RETREAT

"The desert will lead you to your heart where I
will speak."
HOSEA 2:16

Every few months I break out in a rash. It starts on my lower back and spreads to my legs, and then my head starts itching and I can't sleep at night. It drives me wild for a couple of weeks and then vanishes, but never for long.

My body has always been a pretty good barometer of what's going on in my life. This may be because I devote very little time to thinking about how I actually feel. I spent the first night of my honeymoon throwing up because there was so much acid built up in my stomach. Was I nervous? the emergency room doctor asked. "I don't think so," I said before throwing up some more. Sometimes I can be walking around with a serious knot in the pit of my stomach, and I won't have any notion why it's there. I have to stop and concentrate on what's bothering me before I can fit the pieces together.

When I finally drove my red, itchy body to the doctor after yet another rash outbreak, he told me, "The important thing is not to scratch it. And it wouldn't hurt to reduce the stress in your life either."

I was doing my best to follow his advice one summer when Patrick arrived home for a few days' respite from theology studies. We had dutifully made the drive to the nearest Jesuit parish, St.

Francis Xavier in central Phoenix, to attend Sunday Mass. At the end
of the service, the priest announced there would be a parish retreat
based on the Spiritual Exercises of Saint Ignatius. It was to be held in
early September at the Redemptorist Renewal Center just north of
Tucson. It would be quiet and peaceful, and all were invited.

I had never been on a religious retreat before. I had never had
the slightest desire to go on a religious retreat before. But this would
be a chance to experience for myself the Jesuit Exercises about which
Patrick had talked so much. It would be research, I told myself, and
a few days away from the everyday stresses of life might be just what
I needed.

When we got home, I checked the church website for more
information. The Redemptorist center at Picture Rocks, so named
for the prehistoric rock art found there, is situated in the Sonoran
Desert at the edge of Saguaro National Park West with a view of the
Santa Catalina Mountains. "Retreatants, surrounded by so much
beauty, can easily enter into a spirit of recollection," I read. "With
amenities like hiking trails, a pool, chapel, prayer spaces, and a labyrinth, the Center encourages retreatants to feel God's Presence in
many ways."

Except for the fact that retreatants could not possibly be a word
and that I couldn't imagine what the labyrinth was for, there was
nothing here I couldn't handle, so I read on: The program would be
highly unstructured. There would be some formal gatherings—Mass
and prayer sessions—but retreatants (that word again) were not
required to attend anything. The food was good, and there would be
as little talking as possible.

A silent retreat appealed to me. At least I wouldn't be asked to
read the Bible out loud or share my feelings with strangers. I wouldn't
have to pretend piety. I could just go on a hike. How bad could it be?

I asked Gary if he would consider going along. "It's a beautiful
place," I said, "and we could spend the weekend together. Besides,
the cost is $160 per person if two people go and $180 per person if
only one person goes." Economic arguments always work best with

him. But he just gave me a funny look. "You're not turning religious on me, are you?" he asked.

When I reassured him that my interest was purely academic, he considered it for possibly one minute, then said, "I don't want to go. We'd both be sitting there, and it would be 'Oh, Jesus' this and 'Oh, God' that. I don't want to do that."

I know how uncomfortable Gary is with overt religiosity—with overt anything, really—so I let the idea drop. But a few minutes later he spoke up again. "I'll do it if you want me to," he said.

"You're such a good husband," I told him.

"It's what you do," he said, "when you have a good marriage."

Later that night, I filled out the form for the retreat—for one person. I knew Gary didn't want to go and maybe this was something I needed to do alone. I love my husband, but I didn't need a skeptic on this trip. I wanted to keep my mind open. I had a few itches to scratch.

*　*　*　*

I was the last person to arrive at the church a few Fridays later and almost missed my ride to the retreat center. A couple of dozen parishioners were sitting around a table in a crowded meeting room eating Subway sandwiches, drinking diet Cokes, and getting their instructions from John Auther, a fifty-something Jesuit priest who looked to me like a slightly frumpy leprechaun.

Father John, as he is known, was the associate pastor of St. Francis Xavier, the church associated with Brophy College Preparatory, the Jesuit high school in Phoenix. He grew up in the city, one of six boys whose father made his money in real estate. Fluent in Spanish, he led parishioners on trips to the US-Mexico border and helped organize efforts to repeal anti-immigration legislation in Arizona. He has worked in barrios, jails, and prisons in San Diego and Phoenix since joining the Jesuits in 1977.

This sounds like the resume of someone with convictions, and

no doubt Father John has them, but he didn't appear to be the proselytizing type. In fact, he seemed to actively avoid calling attention
to himself or making any impression whatsoever. He wore baggy
Dockers and an open-collar shirt and looked like he could use a
shave. He spoke softly and often seemed to be addressing his feet.
You wanted to move chairs out of his way because you were pretty
sure he would stumble over them.

Still, Father John managed to sort us out, making sure everyone had a ride, and we all headed to the parking lot. I was assigned
to ride with Cathie, who was in her mid-seventies and had more
wrinkles than Barbara Bush. The other two passengers were a polite
middle-aged woman who said "excuse me" a lot and a dark-haired,
rangy young man who looked like he was barely out of high school.
I couldn't fathom what he was doing there.

Cathie was spry and talkative and relentlessly cheerful. Before
she even pulled her new Forester out of the church parking lot, she
launched into a resounding "Hail Mary," asking us all to pray along.
She followed that with a prayer I had never heard before, explaining
that she never goes on a road trip without first asking the "Lady of
the Highway" to protect her on her journey. It works, she assured
us as she weaved onto Interstate 10 and joined the chorus of cars
making their way toward Tucson.

Hoping to avoid conversation, I got out the textbook I had
assigned to my freshman history class and started reading about
Benjamin Franklin's early career as a journalist. The book and a few
rounds of Words with Friends on my iPad got me as far as the gates
of the retreat center.

I looked up as we pulled into the parking lot, but it was too dark
to see if the place lived up to its description. At the registration desk
we were given maps, little keychain flashlights, and directions to our
rooms. I have never been able to read a map, so I just rolled my suit-
case in what I thought was the right direction, past the chapel and
the bookstore and several clusters of low buildings with names like
Perpetual Help and Saint John Neumann until I stumbled onto my

room. Number thirty was in the Saint Gerard wing, and, luckily for me, directly across from the Saint Clement building where we had been told to gather for an evening prayer. Not even I could have trouble finding it.

My room was beige, beige, and more beige, from the walls and carpet to the easy chair and cheap bedspread. There was a simple wooden cross above the bed and a sign firmly stating that guests were expected to change their own linens. I sighed and unpacked my laptop. I was pretty sure I wasn't supposed to bring it with me, but I was hoping to get a little bit of work done.

This is exactly the wrong approach for a retreat, I learned a few minutes later after joining the others in another mostly beige room in the Saint Clement building. The plastic chairs were drawn into a semicircle with Father John at the head. He was still wearing his baggy Dockers and rumpled shirt, and he was telling us not to work our way through this retreat, that this was a time to pretend we were free of responsibilities and allow the calm and quiet of nature to slow us down. And when we slow down, he said, "Our hearts naturally turn to God." This is what happens in prisons, he said. It's why so many prisoners discover God.

The reference to prisons did not make me more comfortable, so I distracted myself by looking around the room. My fellow inmates for the weekend, besides the three with whom I had shared a ride, were, unsurprisingly, mostly older women (meaning older than me). They were dressed sensibly in cotton slacks and walking shoes. Two or three grey and balding men who had arrived alone were gazing at the floor.

The only bright spot in the room was a dark-haired woman wearing a purple scarf, tailored black pants, and heels who pulled her chair close to her husband and closed her eyes. The only remarkable sight was a young, enormously overweight young woman who had claimed the room's only easy chair, placed against a wall outside the circle. She was wearing a giant Mickey Mouse T-shirt and appeared to be asleep. This did not, I thought, promise to be a particularly lively group.

Father John, meanwhile, had launched into an explanation of the Examen, an end-of-the-day prayer the Jesuits have been saying for more than 500 years. It is literally an examination of conscience. There are different versions, but Father John said he prefers a contemporary variety that begins with thanking God for all the good things that have happened to you that day. These can be as mundane as a good cup of coffee and as weighty as a successful operation or a promotion at work.

Next, you're supposed to enlist the Holy Spirit to "open your eyes" so that you can look at your life as "a vast project of the grace of God." "We live a lie," Father John told us. "The lie is that our lives are about ourselves and our problems.... God says to let go of that."

The third part calls for you to review your day, thinking about what you said and did and thought about and what God might have been trying to tell you and how He may have been acting through you. Finally, you talk to God directly, thanking Him and saying you're sorry, if that should be necessary. You think ahead to the next day or two, paying attention to anything that concerns you and asking for guidance.

I started at the beginning, trying to remember the good things that had happened to me that day. The list was pretty short, although it did include a cup of really good coffee with a friend that morning. And I *had* managed to find my room at the retreat center without too much bumbling about. How God had figured into my day was easy to pinpoint: I was actually present at a spiritual retreat! And while I thought that fact had more to do with my son than with God, I couldn't dismiss the idea that God might have some interest in the matter.

I could have spent a lot of time thinking about what I did and didn't do that day and how I might have acted differently. There was the small matter of Gary, for instance. He was the reason I almost missed my ride to Tucson: He was supposed to pick me up at work and take me to the church to meet the group, but he had been late—very late—and let's just say I wasn't very nice about it. I could have come up with a half dozen more examples of my lack of patience in a single day alone, but Father John was signaling that our time was almost up. I sent up a quick prayer that I would get through this retreat intact and headed back to my room.

We had been given a schedule for the next day. We were to meet for morning prayers at 7:30, followed by breakfast at 8, another morning prayer at 9, and another Examen before lunch. There was to be an evening prayer at 5:15, followed by Mass. This left a lot of time with nothing to do. But that, I was learning, was exactly the point.

*　*　*　*

I skipped the 7:30 a.m. prayer. I am not at my best early in the morning, and it was all I could do to make it to the cafeteria while there were still oatmeal and scrambled eggs remaining. It was a strange experience to eat in total silence surrounded by dozens of people, some of whom I recognized from the night before and others who appeared to be part of another retreat group. We all spent a lot of time staring intently at our plates.

At 9 a.m. sharp, we were back in our chairs facing Father John and listening to a CD of bad Christian music. Most of the music favored by Catholic churches and featured on Christian radio is unequivocally bad—shrill and sentimental and instantly forgettable, which is particularly unfortunate if you consider the great classical musical tradition of the church. It's as if they're *trying* to drive people away. Blessedly, we were required to listen to just one song before Father John opened the Bible on his lap and began reading from a Gospel. I tried to listen, but I was distracted by his hands. He was actually caressing the pages, touching the words as he read them.

When he had patted the last page, Father John offered

suggestions as to how we might spend our day. We could select a Bible passage from a list he would provide and try to bring the stories to life by placing ourselves in them. If we were reading about the miracle of Jesus walking on water, for instance, (Matthew 14:22-33), we could imagine we are one of the apostles on the boat, trembling in fear as the storm comes upon us, feeling and smelling the waves as they crash into our tiny vessel on the Sea of Galilee. Suddenly, we see Jesus coming toward us over the water. We're astonished and a little afraid; we think it might be a ghost. But Jesus speaks to us and tells us not to be frightened, and when he joins us in the boat, the winds and the storm die down and all is calm.

I already knew from Patrick that the Jesuits favor this kind of inventive participation in Biblical scenes, and I suppose it is not all that different from entering into a character on stage or film. But I suspected that I lacked the necessary acting skills to pull it off, and I was pretty sure I lacked the required imagination.

Father John told us about another kind of reenactment that he was part of during an earlier retreat. Everyone cut holes in bed sheets and walked around all day imagining themselves as companions of Christ. I noted thankfully that there were no sheets in sight.

Another option, he said, was to read the passages, then watch videos he had prepared that explained the readings. This much I thought I could handle, so I took a flash drive with the recordings back to my room, found one of the recommended readings in the Bible that had been conveniently provided, and powered up my computer. There was Father John, sitting in an overstuffed red chair with a bookcase to one side and a Bible in his hands—and he was talking about imagining what it would be like to be on that boat with Jesus.

I decided to take a walk.

The renewal center is a beautiful place and unnervingly quiet. I followed a path past clusters of low-slung buildings, a fountain, a stream, and tiny desert gardens populated with Palo Verde trees, finches, and stone benches. Beyond it all stretched the Sonoran

Desert, which was anything but deserted. It was, in fact, impossibly full. Hundreds of small, round Barrel cacti competed for space with Agave, Prickly Pear, Cholla, Creosote, Mesquite, Bursage, thorns, and all manner of prickly items wedged between towering boulders. There were butterflies, moths, and lizards galore. The only thing that seemed to be missing was sand. I tried for a moment to count the Saguaros, the distinctive cacti that grow forty to fifty feet tall and sprout arms that turn upward like priests in prayer. I lost track after thirty-five.

I wandered a few yards into the desert, sat down against a rock, and pulled out more assigned readings from Father John. These were "contemplations," and they were filled with observations, some of which I had heard before, such as "Love ought to manifest itself more by deeds than words." There were instructions telling me to consider how God dwells in creatures, in plants, and in human beings and to "ponder with deep affection how much God our Lord has done for me." I read the pages over and over, and I tried. I thought about how grateful I am for what I have been given, how lucky I am and, ultimately, how undeserving. But somehow this did not make me feel closer to God.

I looked at my watch. It seemed as if I had been in this particular desert for forty days and there were still hours to kill before dinner, so I wandered over to the bookstore, which could be distinguished from most of the other buildings by a large and disturbing figure of Jesus nailed to the cross near the entrance. Inside, I was surprised to find an entire section of books for women with titles like *Defiant Daughters* and *The Knitting Way*. I passed these by and moved on to what appeared to be the self-help section, featuring such selections as: *There's Nothing Wrong with You; Why God Loves Us No Matter What; How God Changes Your Brain;* and *Jesus 101*.

I passed these by, too, and finally lighted on something I recognized: Thomas Merton's famous autobiography *The Seven Storey Mountain*, one of Patrick's favorite books and one I thought I might like to read. After buying the book and a plain Celtic cross for

Patrick from the impossibly old and slow woman at the cash register, I headed to the cafeteria next door for a cup of coffee. I was fingering my cell phone before I even sat down. I knew this was supposed to be a silent retreat, but I clearly was not getting anywhere, and I wanted to talk to Patrick. Maybe I just wanted him to give me credit for trying.

He picked up on the third ring. This retreat, I told him before he could finish saying hello, is not working. I ran through the agenda— prayer meetings, Bible readings, videos, contemplations, and a little wandering in the desert. I liked the setting and the silence, I said, but I couldn't play-act these little Biblical scenes. "It just makes me feel silly."

"Did you talk to God about that?" he asked.

"I can't do that either."

He seemed unperturbed. "You aren't strange for not being readily able to," he said. "It felt weird to me, too, when I first joined the Jesuits. Just start by trying to be quiet and listen to what God wants to say. Sit down someplace pretty and quiet and focus on your breathing for a while and just notice what comes up. Then see if you can say anything to God about that, even if you're not sure there is a God. Or you can just say, 'I feel stupid.' That's a good place to start. It's okay. God is not mad at you for starting out skeptical.

"It will feel a lot like talking to yourself," he continued in what I think of as his priest voice, which is caring and careful at the same time. "But that's healthy psychology if nothing else. Whether it's our subconscious or God, it's something other than our conscious minds bringing up things."

"What kinds of things?" I asked. I had almost forgotten this was my son I was talking to, so eager was I to know the answer.

"Well, I think part of the reason you work so hard all the time is so you don't have to feel hard feelings. You don't have to think about: Why is my family the way it is? Why does my mother have such a hard life? Why is my son doing something that I can't understand?

"It's in silence that God will talk to you about things that it may be hard for you to think about. But you can't get to that part until you're willing to suspend disbelief for a second. You don't have to believe yet—you just have to not disbelieve. Don't intellectualize too much. There's time for that later. You have to *have* the experience before you can *think* about the experience."

I told him I would try, but I was not at all confident I could pull it off—and I still felt silly. He told me he was just glad I was trying, and then he said the thing I had long suspected but had not wanted to hear.

"God is the most important thing in my life," he said. "The fact that you and dad don't give God the same chance is hard. It's hard all the time. I know that God is not a person to you like He is to me. And what I want to say to that is: 'Not yet.'"

His words felt to me like a blessing and a rebuke. I couldn't give up yet.

*   *   *   *

A little while later, it was time to go see Father John. He had offered to meet individually with those attending the retreat, and I had signed up for an afternoon slot. His room was on the opposite side of the building from where I was housed, and it looked much like mine except it had a small sitting area. Father John gestured me into an armchair and sat down across from me on a flowered sofa. I told him my son was about to be ordained a priest, and I wanted to talk to him about what it's like to be a Jesuit. "It seems like a hard life," I said. "And a lonely one."

He surprised me a little when, after assuring me that he's not a poster child for the Jesuits, he said his life is not very different from anyone else's. "Almost everyone's life is difficult in some ways, and everyone lives with their own loneliness," he said. "I know many people who are alone. They lose their spouses, or they divorce, or they never marry at all."

"That's true," I acknowledged, remembering a friend of Gary's whose wife had recently announced that she wanted a divorce after forty-three years of marriage. (The man insisted he had no idea why, a claim I find highly unlikely.) I thought of my sister who was in her third marriage and more alone than almost anyone I know. Still, these are not people who set out to live solitary lives. They have given companionship a shot, and they have children who might possibly keep them company and look after them one day.

"What will happen to you when you get old?" I asked Father John. "Where will you go? Who will take care of you?"

This made Father John laugh. "Most of us keep working well into our eighties," he said. "And if we can't work anymore, we may go to a Jesuit retirement home like the one in Los Gatos, California." These homes, which are sprinkled across the country, are much nicer than most retirement homes, he assured me, "and we are very well taken care of there."

I later looked up the website of the Sacred Heart Jesuit Center in Los Gatos, and it did look rather nice. It houses somewhere in the neighborhood of ninety men whose average age is eighty. According to the website, the men spend a great deal of time praying, and those who are able assist with Masses at nearby parishes or work in shelters. There are arts and crafts classes, Bible study, lectures, nature outings, swimming, weightlifting, and Pilates. There was, unsurprisingly, no mention of women.

Being a priest has other advantages, Father John said. He ticked them off: interesting and challenging work; job security; a comfortable place to live; a sense of being needed and appreciated; spiritual fulfillment; time to pray.

"I think of my brother trying to sell real estate. My father did it and hated it," he told me. "I really don't feel like I've given up a lot. In fact, the older I get, the more I feel how little I've given up." I nodded my head as he talked and jotted down notes. I was in full reporter mode, about to ask another question, when he stopped me with one of his own. "Is it just because of your son that you came here?"

I suddenly felt the fundamental weirdness of the situation. I was not even a member of his church. I was, in fact, a perfect stranger who was asking rather personal questions that have little to do with the reasons most people go on retreats or ask to meet with a priest.

In a rush, I told him I was raised Catholic but left the church long ago because I could not reconcile the church's stands on social issues with my own beliefs. I told him I was no longer certain what I believed about God or Catholicism or a good deal else. I told him I was trying to figure it out. Father John didn't seem the least bit surprised to be confronted by a potential agnostic on a religious retreat. He just asked if I was enjoying the weekend.

"I'm having trouble with the Bible readings," I told him. "I think I lack the necessary imagination."

"One of the things that separate us from animals is the ability to create images in our minds and project ourselves into situations," he said. "That's where ideas, inventions, and creations come from. People think of the Jesuits as being intellectuals, but the Exercises are all about—or mostly about—feelings."

Still, an intellectual approach isn't a bad thing, he assured me. We talked for a few minutes about contemporary philosophy and intelligent design, and I was writing down the titles of a few books he suggested when I noticed his next appointee hovering near the door.

I felt calmer as I stepped outside. Being a priest might not be so bad, I thought. And who knows how many paths there are to God?

＊　＊　＊　＊

It was time to try again.

I found a little wooden gazebo with a comfortable chair and sat facing the desert. Next to me was the briefcase-sized purse I had been lugging around with me everywhere, but this time I didn't reach for my iPad or phone or the folded pages of Bible passages and instructions on contemplation.

I just sat there quietly and tried to clear my mind. This was much harder than I had expected. Every time my mind wandered—which was often—to the phone calls I hadn't returned, the emails I hadn't answered, and the pleasures to be had in a cup of strong coffee, I pushed aside the thought. I asked myself, "How do I feel?" I had been too long in control to surrender entirely, but I tried to let go just a bit.

I concentrated on the "hard feelings" Patrick suspects I suppress, running through the list in my mind. It's true that I grew up in what can politely be described as a dysfunctional family and pretty much had to make it on my own. It's true that most of my brothers and sisters never fully escaped that scarred upbringing. They have endured so much death and disease and disappointment that I sometimes marvel that they're still standing at all. And it's also true that my mother, never close, was becoming more distant with every passing year. Just thinking about her life made me want to weep.

But these are old hurts, and I have learned to live with them. I have put my energy into creating the life I wanted instead of the one I was given, and I felt light and grateful when I thought about what my life could have been—and what it is.

The quest that brought me to this retreat in the desert felt right, too. I was caught with a sense that I was doing what I was supposed to be doing, and I felt overwhelmingly thankful for the surprise that has been my son, for the bewildering gift he has given me that has moved me beyond myself and forced me to ask questions I would never have otherwise asked. And if it's God, I thought, who is truly behind all of this, then I am indebted to God, too.

I doubted that I would ever feel the certainty Patrick feels, and I was almost positive I would never be able to count God as my best friend, but these things no longer bothered me as much as they did before. I was on alert; more aware. From now on, I told myself, I'll be watching.

This ceasefire lasted all through evening Mass. I stopped arguing with myself, at least for a while, and I tried to be quiet—peaceful even—although there was one bad moment involving a large spider.

Mass was to be said that night around an outdoor altar, a piece of granite slab facing a half a dozen stone benches set in a patch of gravel at the edge of the desert. To get there, we walked single file along a dirt path through absolute blackness. A few of us thought to get out our little flashlight key chains, and just as I flicked mine on, I saw something very big and black and hairy shoot off the path in front of me. The others saw it, too, and several of us screamed and scurried in the opposite direction, making an awful lot of commotion for what was supposed to be a silent retreat.

"Don't worry; it's a tarantula, but it's gone now," said one stalwart woman at the front of the line. "We scared it off." Still, I gave the tarantula crossing a wide berth, and when I found a seat on one of the stone benches a few yards up the path, I was careful to keep my purse as far from the ground as I could manage. I did not want to take a tarantula home with me.

We were facing the altar, lit by only the moon and a ridge of tiny votive lights flickering in the breeze. Father John moved one of the candles close to the pages of his Bible and began to read, slowly and haltingly. For the first time, he looked the part of a priest. The Dockers were hidden by a long white robe tied with a green sash, garments he had forgotten to bring with him and had to have sent overnight from Phoenix.

Someone had brought the ingredients for communion in a Walgreens sack. The wafers came out of the bag, along with a bottle of red wine that Father John unscrewed and began tipping into a cup that also had been produced from the bag. As I joined the line for communion, I heard a horse whinnying in the distance, followed by a single howl from a dog or a coyote, I couldn't tell which. Father John smiled and pressed the host into my hand.

It was the simplest service I had ever attended and also the most beautiful. There was no singing, no sermon, or mumbled prayers. Instead, there were stars and long silences. For a while, I almost forgot about the tarantula.

*   *   *   *

After morning prayers, we were given forms and asked to evaluate the retreat. I gave it high ratings and checked the box indicating I might be interested in doing another one. A few days of quiet and reflection each year might not, I thought, be a bad thing.

I climbed back into Cathie's green Forester along with the colorless, middle-aged woman whose name I learned was Margaret and the gangly boy named David. This time, I paid attention.

Margaret, it turned out, was a public health nurse and had worked for years with Doctors Without Borders, an international medical humanitarian organization. She spoke French, Italian, Spanish, and Portuguese and had cared for the poor and sick in almost a dozen countries in Latin America and Africa. She, Cathie and David all volunteered their time on the US-Mexico border, distributing care kits, helping out at a Jesuit-run aid center for deportees, and depositing water jugs at desert stations where thirsty migrants might find them.

They are none of the things I have judged them to be. It's true they are the kind of people who would be unembarrassed to walk around in sheets all day pretending to be companions of Christ. But I no longer think this makes them dull or insipid or unsophisticated.

I am almost envious of them. They seem so good—and so certain.

CHAPTER 16

A WOMAN'S PLACE

"Let the beauty we love be what we do
There are hundreds of ways to kneel and kiss
the ground."
RUMI

*W*henever *I* feel myself getting closer to the faith in which I was born, I think about the virgin martyrs. Catholic history is rife with stories about these young women who chose the most awful of deaths rather than give up their beliefs and their virginity (not necessarily in that order). For me, they are a reminder of what I still find most objectionable about the Catholic Church.

Generally, these virgin martyrs appear during the first couple of centuries after the time of Christ when the Romans were intent on wiping out the new and dangerous insurgency called Christianity. Many of the virgin martyrs were just children—twelve or thirteen years old—whose fathers were intent on marrying them off to pagans. These fathers were, to put it mildly, not very nice people. Saint Barbara, who is thought to have lived in the third century in what is now Turkey, was particularly unlucky in this regard.

Barbara's father reportedly locked her up in a tower until a suitable husband could be found for her. After she secretly converted to Christianity, her father had her tortured, but each night her wounds were miraculously healed. Finally, her father stepped in and finished her off with his own sword. On the way home, in a most gratifying turn of events, he was struck by lightning and consumed by fire, and Barbara went on to become the patron saint of artillery-men, armourers, gunsmiths, miners, tunnelers, and anyone else who comes into contact with explosives.

Saint Wilgefortis, or Saint Uncumber as she is sometimes known for reasons that will shortly become clear, was another virgin martyr whose father insisted on marrying her to a pagan. A teenage noblewoman who had become Christian and took a vow of virginity, Wilgefortis prayed to become so repulsive no man would want to marry her. Her prayers were answered in the form of facial hair. The impressive beard she grew overnight ended the engagement and so enraged her father that he had her crucified. Wilgefortis became the patron saint of difficult marriages and those who wished to be unencumbered of men altogether. Here is a saint who many modern women could appreciate.

Interestingly enough, there are at least two other female saints who are said to have grown beards, although the reasons for this are not entirely clear. Neither is it clear how precisely true some of the stories of the virgin martyrs are. The Catholic Church, in some cases unable to sort myth from fact, has distanced itself from no small number of these early saints, relegating them to the category of legend or wishful thinking.

No matter. The early virgins still have something important to tell us. They have become archetypes of the relationship between the Catholic Church and women, a relationship that hasn't changed all that much in more than 2,000 years and can be pretty much summed up in one word: Sex. Yes, it has always been about sex.

The early virgin martyrs were glorified as much because of their refusal to have sex as their unwillingness to disavow their religion. The message, according to Norris in *Cloister Walk*, is that "to be holy you have to be a virgin and preferably a martyr. Married Christian women, then, and those who do not suffer enough would seem doomed to be imperfect models of Christian faith."

I would add that the more gruesome the suffering the better. The virgin martyrs met their deaths in astonishingly inventive ways. They were set on fire, their heads chopped off, their tongues torn out, and their breasts removed. They were fed to lions, trampled by wild horses, stretched on racks, pierced with iron hooks, fed to wild dogs, tied to spiked wheels, smothered with snakes, shot with arrows, thrown into furnaces, and rolled naked upon bits of broken pottery, among other ingenious methods of torture. There was frequently some nudity involved.

Saint Agnes serves as an example. In one version of her story, she proclaimed herself a Christian and was promptly stripped naked and sent to the fire pit. However, she managed to preserve her modesty by covering herself with her long hair. In another more colorful telling, she was taken to a brothel where her tormentors planned to rape her, but her virginity was preserved when her hair grew to cover her body. Therefore, according to Saint Ambrose, who wrote about her some years later, Agnes suffered a double martyrdom—the first of modesty, the second of faith. I don't think it's insignificant that he listed modesty first.

In researching the virgin martyrs, I was surprised to come across both Irene and Christina, the saints for whom my mother was named. In a story that will by now sound familiar, Irene, who is recognized by the Eastern Orthodox Church, had a pagan and highly overprotective father who locked her in a tower from the time she was six. Irene refused to marry any of the suitors her father brought to her, and to make matters worse, she smashed her father's collection of idol statues. This led to her being tied up and thrown beneath the hooves of wild horses. Instead of trampling her, however, the horses turned on her father, who found the whole episode convincing enough that he was baptized and went to live in the tower he had built for his daughter, repenting for the rest of his life. Irene proceeded to convert thousands of fellow Persians, until the king decided to have her beheaded.

Christina of Bolsena, too, was born into a wealthy family and grew to be very beautiful. Her father wanted her to become a pagan priestess, but Christina declared herself a bride of Christ. Her father tried everything he could think of to kill her, including tying her to a millstone and throwing her into the water, but nothing worked. She outlived her father, whose cause of death is not recorded, only to finally die at the hands of his successor, who presumably came up with a more effective method of execution. Christina is one of those early saints, like Saint Christopher, who have been demoted by the church. She is no longer listed in the official Roman Catholic Calendar of Saints, although that has done little to discourage her admirers.

While it's a little incongruous that my mother, who bore eight children, carries the name of two virgin saints, in another way it makes perfect sense. Irene and Christina, like the other virgin martyrs, were nonconformists. These were not shy, retiring women who did what society expected of them. Irene, for one, openly defied authorities by becoming a sort of itinerant preacher. She traveled around talking back to men and performing miracles. At one point, legend has it that she confronted a Persian king and his entire army, demanding they stop persecuting Christians. When the king refused, Irene uttered a prayer that blinded the whole lot of them.

Catherine of Alexandria, who once declared she would never marry because Jesus Christ was her spouse, could mount such persuasive arguments that she is said to have converted fifty philosophers who were sent to explain to her the error of her ways. Once considered the most important of the virgin martyrs, her existence is now severely questioned, at least in the West. Elsewhere, she is still the patron saint of young women, philosophers—and virgins.

I like to think of Irene standing in front of that army and Catherine talking circles around a bunch of philosophers. I like to think of them as women who refused to be silenced, who insisted on control over their own bodies in the face of crushing male authority. You get only a glimpse of this subversive side of them, however, in the way these stories have been told over the centuries. In church literature, these women are virgins first and martyrs for their faith second. The fact that they were mounting a series of small revolutions against established authority is almost never mentioned.

This should perhaps come as no surprise in a church whose number one saint, the mother of Jesus, has the word virgin attached to her name. It has never made sense to me why it's such a big deal whether Mary was a virgin, but it most certainly has been a big deal throughout the history of the church. There have been entire schisms over it.

We no longer spend a lot of time arguing about virginity. In some ways, our society no longer even places a particular value on virginity, at least not in the way it once did. But it seems to me that the impulse that caused the church to glorify the virginity of the virgin martyrs is the same one that underscores the current battles going on in the church over birth control, abortion, same-sex marriage, and even the question of whether priests should marry. It defines the church's relationship with women and strikes at the heart of why it's so difficult to be a woman in the Catholic Church today.

* * * *

I have always admired Anna Quindlen. In truth, I have always wanted to *be* Anna Quindlen and, while I suspect she doesn't know it, we have a lot in common. We both come from big Irish-Catholic families and are about the same age. We married young, raised three children apiece, and made our careers in journalism.

After that, I must admit, the similarities begin to fade. Quindlen worked for *The New York Times*, where she was deputy metro editor at a time when female editors were rare. She pioneered a column that was a striking departure from the usual somber *Times'* pronouncements on public life. She believed that the real meaning of politics is its effect on people, and so she dared to be personal, writing about herself, her family, friends, neighbors, and people she met on the streets.

Predictably, her approach to the news came in for much scorn, mostly from men. One male critic called her (and other women writers like her) "monsters of empathy" who "self-subjugate and domesticate and assimilate every distant tragedy." He called it "The Quindlen Effect."

Regardless, in 1992, her columns won a Pulitzer Prize and then, when Quindlen was at the top of her game, just when it seemed she was poised to rise even higher in the all-male *Times'* newsroom hierarchy—higher than any woman before her—she quit and began to write novels and memoirs and publish collections of her columns. These, too, have been a success. Of her ten novels, several were turned into movies and (this really makes me jealous) one was made into a feature film starring Meryl Streep.

Besides all the obvious attractions, what has really interested me about Quindlen over the years is her Catholicism. Here was a smart, successful, *thinking* woman who acknowledged being Catholic, publicly and without apology. Even while admitting to ignoring the church's teaching on birth control and disagreeing with its stand on abortion, even while calling the resistance to the ordination of women as priests nothing less than misogyny, she remained Catholic, having her children baptized, taking them to church on Sundays, and answering "Catholic" when anyone inquired of her religion. She was born Catholic, she once wrote, and she expected to die one.

I had come to think of Quindlen as a rare sort of being—a woman who had figured out how to be Catholic, liberal, and a feminist all at the same time. What was it she knew that I didn't? I wondered. How did she make it work?

When I read that Quindlen had changed her mind, that she, like so many others, had quit the church, I felt a shock of recognition, even though I understood her reasons—the sex abuse scandals and the Catholic hierarchy's initial abysmal response, the church's refusal to admit women as priests, and its constant "obsession with gynecology," as she put it.

"Enough," she said in one interview. "Every time I sit in the pew, I ratify this behavior, and I'm not going to ratify it anymore." She told another reporter, "The Catholic hierarchy has been disinviting people like me, and especially women like me, for so many years that I finally took the hint."

This should have been a Gloria Steinem moment. I should have been pumping my fists in the air and yelling "Right on! Say it like it is!" But instead, I felt let down and a little sad. If Anna Quindlen can't find a place in the church, can any uppity woman? Can I?

*   *   *   *

For some time now, I have been keeping a file of newspaper clippings, magazine articles, and printouts about the tribulations of the Catholic Church. It has grown quite fat. In it are nearly a dozen articles about the priest sex-abuse scandal in the US and elsewhere and nearly as many about the Vatican's jaw-dropping reprimand of American nuns for failing to toe the church line and "promoting radical feminist themes."

There is a report on a teacher who was fired from her Catholic school after she became pregnant through artificial insemination and another on an Irish priest who said he was threatened with excommunication for publicly endorsing the ordination of women. An American nun wrote a book arguing for a new sexual ethic based on justice and equality that ran afoul of church censors for failing to adhere to Catholic teachings. The church put up a big fight against former President Barack Obama's plan to require institutions—Catholic or otherwise—to include birth control in their health insurance plans. And the Vatican was repeatedly embarrassed by revelations of shady dealings at the Vatican bank involving possible money laundering.

The not-inconsiderable bank embarrassment was quickly over-shadowed by an even more improbable scandal involving the arrest of Pope Benedict XVI's butler, who was leaking documents to Italian journalists describing in detail power struggles, political intrigue, and corruption at the highest levels of the church. "If you wrote this in fiction, you wouldn't believe it," Carl Anderson, a member of the board of the Vatican bank, was quoted as saying in several articles. "No editor would let you put it in a novel."

I have to make myself read some of these articles, especially the ones about pedophile priests. I knew the Franciscan order had shut down a boarding school in Santa Barbara, California, where priests had been preying on young boys for years, but the enormity of these assaults didn't hit me until *The Associated Press* and the *Los Angeles Times* published excerpts from a slew of internal documents and sworn testimony regarding the case.

It seems that a Franciscan, the Rev. Robert Van Handel, formed a boys' choir at the school for the express purpose of grooming vic-tims, and for the next eight years he proceeded to choose boys from its ranks. One of the documents contained a note he wrote to a therapist in which he recalled one victim, a boy of about nine years, whom he described as tan and effeminate. "Now that I think back on it, he was probably the most beautiful child that I molested," Van Handel wrote. He served four years in prison.

Van Handel was not a lone actor. A 1993 church-appointed board of inquiry found that eleven priests had abused thirty-four students at St. Anthony's from the 1960s to 1987. They allegedly fondled, masturbated, or had oral sex with children. At least one checked teenaged boys for hernias as an excuse to grope them. Van Handel liked to coax the boys to pose for nude photos.

For many years, the church did little to stop such priests, and even protected them. One of the articles I saved relates the story of Philadelphia's Cardinal Anthony Bevilacqua, who ordered that a fifteen-page list that named priests in his jurisdiction along with the sex acts they had allegedly performed be destroyed. The list was found years later in a long-abandoned safe at the archdiocese, along with Bevilacqua's orders to shred it. It was too late to be used against Bevilacqua—he was dead—but it came in handy during the trial of a monsignor who had helped compile the list and then said he couldn't find it. In 2012, former Monsignor William Lynn was convicted of felony child endangerment for failing to stop the coverup. He was the first US church official punished by a court for his handling of priest-abuse complaints.

A beautiful nine-year-old choir boy. A list of pedophiles hidden in a safe. These are the kinds of details that bring me to my knees.

I feel a different kind of anger about the church's treatment of nuns. Like many people who attended Catholic schools in the 1950s and 1960s, I have had a complicated relationship with nuns, and I don't immediately buy the portrayal of all nuns as religious good guys (or, in this case, gals). I guffawed when I read *The New York Times'* columnist Nicholas Kristof's description of them as "among the bravest, toughest and most admirable people in the world." I'll allow that some of them are indeed brave, tough, admirable, and many more laudable adjectives besides, but I also have known too many bitter, repressed, and angry nuns to accept the description as universal.

Still, I'll agree with Kristof that it's not a good idea to mess with nuns. In what could pass as a modern-day inquisition, the Vatican in 2012 launched an investigation into the organization that represents about eighty percent of American nuns and concluded they were promoting "radical feminist themes." Several American bishops were charged with making sure the good sisters saw the error of their ways, which seemed to largely involve purging their literature and programs of anything that smacked of favoritism toward birth control, abortion, homosexual relationships, and the ordination of female priests.

This crackdown was followed by predictable outrage in the media (the liberal media, as church authorities would undoubtedly say) and among a fair number of churchgoers and church watchers, including my daughters. As my daughter Lauren put it, "You mean they did nothing for years and years about pedophile priests and now they're going after *nuns?*"

Having inherited the imbroglio from his predecessor, Benedict XVI, Pope Francis first reaffirmed the report condemning the nuns and, in the process, managed to further insult them by calling them "spinsters," which could have been an unhappy accident of translation but did nothing to improve matters. Eventually, peace was declared, with the nuns agreeing to some oversight of their publications and conference speakers, but for the most part, happy to be left alone.

When the controversy erupted over the sisters, *The New York Times* opinion columnist Maureen Dowd called it a "Shut up and sit down, sisters" moment, which I thought summed it up pretty nicely—except it wasn't just one moment. It has been almost every moment since the church elevated the first virgin to martyrdom almost 2,000 years ago.

For most of the twentieth century, women tended to ignore the Red Hat Society in Rome that was so consistently, so insistently, hostile toward them. They went about their business, attending church on Sundays, teaching their children the Hail Mary, running catechism classes, arranging flowers for Mass, and polishing the pews. For centuries, they even entered religious orders in far greater numbers than men.

But the axiom that women are more religious than men is changing. Several studies have concluded that American women are leaving organized religion, Catholicism included, in greater numbers than men, reversing decades-long trends. Many women, in other words, are fed up. They're the ones who put up billboards proclaiming, "Quit the church. Put Women's Rights over Bishops' Wrongs" and placed full page ads in *The New York Times* urging Catholic women to wake up. "If you think you can change the church from within—get it to lighten up on birth control, gay rights, marriage equality, embryonic stem-cell research—you're deluding yourself," one such ad read. "By remaining a 'good Catholic', you are doing 'bad' to women's rights. You are an enabler. And it's got to stop."

Part of me nods in agreement with such sentiments. They aren't all that different from my own reasons for leaving the church decades ago. But that was before my son decided to become a priest. That was before things got complicated.

When I point out to Patrick the all-too-obvious flaws in the church, he is quick to agree with me. The church is sinful, he says. It's a human institution, so how could it not be? The church needs to change, he says, and if people leave—if women leave—how will it ever change?

But why bother? I press. Why not start over with something else? Why not just do the best you can on your own?

This kind of reasoning drives Patrick crazy. Americans (like me, apparently) always think the answer is individualism. We think we can just ditch institutions and replace them with our own moral codes, and everything will be fine. Millions of Americans have done just that, he says, with the result that we have become a society focused on satiating ourselves. We live to fulfill our own needs, and when those needs are satisfied, we create more. This is the definition of a consumer society, and it *is* our moral code. But it isn't a satisfying one.

"People want a destiny," Patrick insists. "They want to be called to something. Are we just going to do whatever we want as individuals? The answer has to be no."

He believes that the church, with all its failings, still offers the best alternative: a moral code built on living in as close an approximation to the way Jesus lived as one can possibly manage and a way of living that has meaning beyond comfort and self-indulgence. Moreover, the church provides both a scaffolding and a community to help us get there.

The scaffolding is made up of theology and tradition and the rituals and symbols that tie us to history and each other. In *Cloister Walk*, Norris explains this beautifully. "I was raised to believe that rituals were meaningless in the modern world, meant to be out-grown, like superstitions. I was educated to mistrust the rich ambiguity of symbols." Yet in church, she writes, she found "ritual and symbol that has meaning.... (They) are as necessary to human beings as air and water. They mark us as human and give us identity."

In her book *Radical Reinvention*, Kaya Oakes, a self-described punk-rock, shaved-head, tattooed atheist, describes how she found her way back to Catholicism. She was drawn by the comfortable Catholic rituals of her childhood and the sense that she was praying in the same way generations of her family had prayed before her. But what has kept her in the pews is community. In church, she says, she has found "spiritual soulmates," mostly women like herself who spend a lot of time bitching about the church and then go serve meatloaf in soup kitchens.

To her surprise, Oakes said she discovered, "You can be Catholic and feminist. You can be Catholic and lesbian. You can be Catholic and a straight female and not have kids. You can be Catholic and have children but wonder if they should be Catholic. You can be Catholic and believe in better access to birth control." You can be Catholic and be anyone.

Oakes seems to be saying that it's the people in the pews, not the dogma and the rules, that make the church, and while this appeals to me, given there are no small number of rules I could do without, I'm not entirely comfortable with being a cafeteria Catholic either. There's something fundamentally unfair about saying you're Catholic and then proceeding to pick and choose what aspects of Catholicism you'll accept and which you won't. It's cheating.

When I raise this with Patrick, I realize almost immediately that I'm in over my head. ("Does he just think about this stuff all day?" I asked him once. "Actually, yes, I do," he replied.) But the gist of it, I think, is that Catholicism is not an either/or religion. People matter, but dogma does, too. "After all," he says, "what would it even mean to say, 'You can be Catholic and not believe in the Incarnation'—that God became flesh in the person of Christ?"

Dogma, he says, shapes us, but it's we human beings who, with God, have shaped dogma in the first place. "It's mutual," he says. "But I also know that I need to be open to being changed by what the church teaches in order to have a deeper relationship with God and people."

To define the church as the sum of its members leaves out too much, he argues. It leaves out truth and the transformative power of God. "You can be Catholic and start as anyone—as yourself, in other words," he told me. "But you can't end up there." I think Anne Lamott put this best when she wrote: "I do not at all understand the mystery of grace—only that it meets us where we are but does not leave us where it found us."

Finally, I think, I've put my finger on it. Patrick believes in the people and the institution of the Catholic Church, despite all the obvious flaws, because he believes in mystery and grace. Because he believes in God.

I'm more skeptical than he is about people in general and the Catholic Church in particular, and I'm still not sure what I think about God. I resist mystery. I want to count things and have them explained. But I have seen grace. I have seen the way Patrick and his brother Jesuits lift the people around them and give them hope and how they are lifted in return. I have experienced the favor of loved ones and witnessed the efforts of strangers who do things, who give love and mercy and unmerited favor, that would be inexplicable in a world without divine influence.

I still find it hard to be Catholic, but I have discovered it's easier to reject the church when I can hold it at a distance. Close up, the flaws are much harder to see.

CHAPTER 17

CLAIM TO FAITH

"My father was very sure about certain matters
pertaining to the universe. To him, all good
things – trout as well as eternal salvation—
come by grace and grace comes by art and art
does not come easily."
NORMAN MACLEAN, *A River Runs Through It*

hile neither of my daughters were raised Catholic, it seems to me they have a claim to the faith, a claim rooted in their family's history—and in their brother.

Patrick's "Jesuit-ness" doesn't seem nearly as strange to them as it does to my husband and me. Granted, as teenagers they thought it was a little weird that their brother had decided to become a priest. Dana says she could never adequately explain it to her friends, some of whom just wanted to date him. But they are united in their support of Patrick, and they don't question his choice, which they readily admit profoundly influenced their own choices.

I think Lauren, most especially, has been shaped by her brother's life. "I was thirteen when he called and said he wanted to be a Jesuit," she told me. "So many of my decisions—from going to Fordham (University) to deciding what I want to do with my life—have been affected by him. Having your brother devote himself to something so crazy changes your perspective. It's so foreign and so big that you have to rethink everything."

Patrick's vocation as a priest drove home for her the idea that devoting oneself to an ideal —a belief—is an option. It made her realize the possibility of a faith so great it overshadows the things to which most of us devote our lives—careers and possessions and even our relationships with others. It made her resolve that whatever she does, it must be for good. It must mean something.

At Fordham University, a Jesuit college in the Bronx, Lauren majored in French and visual arts and earned a certificate in Catholic Studies. When she was invited to apply for the prestigious Catholic Studies program, which carried with it a small scholarship, she called home, unsure what to do. "I can't see how this would work," she protested. "I'm not even a Catholic!"

I told her I didn't think formal religious membership mattered much to the Jesuits; they were more interested in the best students, the ones with leadership potential. The program would place her in an elite group taught by the smartest, most influential people at the university. She would be challenged and make good connections. She should do it.

One of her favorite teachers in the program turned out to be a nun, Sister Elizabeth Johnson, a theology professor and author of a well-regarded book, *She Who Is: The Mystery of God in Feminist Theological Discourse,* about feminine images of God in the Bible. As a young nun in 1968, Sister Johnson defied her superior's order and joined a march against the war in Vietnam. It was, she told her students, a matter of conscience. Her picture ended up in *Newsweek* magazine and she was almost thrown out of the order for insubordination and disobedience. In the end, her religious chapter passed a resolution stating that a sister may follow her conscience politically even if it clashes with the church's prescribed rules.

Through Sister Johnson and others like her, Lauren managed to find a connection between Catholicism and feminism. She wrote papers about how nuns were treated in the church and how women were written out of the Bible, relegated, as in the case of Phoebe, a deacon in the early church, to a single line. She joined thousands of others, including Patrick and a large contingent of Jesuits, at the annual protest against US foreign policy at the School of Americas in Georgia, riding a bus for twenty hours from the Bronx to get there. She discovered, as she put it, "that faith and social justice are inextricably connected."

Lauren can get very excited talking about faith and justice, and, like Patrick, those things are a big part of what made her, too, decide to become Catholic. But that doesn't keep her from objecting—often loudly—to the church's treatment of women. When she brings this up with her brother, I can close my eyes and hear myself saying the same words in the same no-take-prisoners tone. There's simply no arguing with her (although Patrick tries).

She can almost persuade herself that she has no business being part of a religion that has treated and continues to treat women so poorly, but she also has great respect for the Jesuits, who "used their Jedi mind tricks" on her to great effect in college. "It's totally true," she says of the mind tricks. "People think I'm kidding and I'm not. They outsmarted me."

The Jesuits taught her that God isn't a metaphor or some remote symbol of goodness. He's real and present in the world, and it's this presence that gives life meaning. This analogical way of thinking feels true to Lauren. "I don't want to live in a world where you can't find God, a world where God isn't in this with us," she told me.

A lover of tradition and pageantry of all kinds, she's also drawn to the 2,000-year-old traditions of the Catholic Church. "There's something romantic and beautiful about repeating the same symbols and gestures and prayers that people have used for thousands of years," she said. "Those things have weight. They mean something."

While Lauren came to terms with her faith largely through argument and study and analysis, Dana's path was much more direct. She simply followed her heart. She agrees with her sister that the church is weighed down with the anti-female detritus of centuries, but she doesn't let it bother her much. She isn't very interested in theological or political debates. Aside from Patrick, she is the most unabashedly religious member of our family. She goes to Mass—and sometimes gets her husband to go with her—not because she agrees with official pronouncements or doctrine but because it feels right. It makes her feel close to God.

Her religion is reinforced every day in her work as an assistant principal at—you guessed it—a Jesuit high school. She sees her job as making sure students are prepared for college, but, more importantly, that they become the kind of people who live not just for themselves but for God and for others. The kind of people who do good in the world.

Her work brings her into contact with a lot of young people who are both scarred and scared. Often, the high school students who end up in her office are dealing with all the worries of adolescence and a good bit more besides. Their parents are getting divorced; they can't eat or sleep; they're failing their classes; they can't afford to go to college; they don't think they're good enough. She does what she can.

After one of her students killed himself, she earned a certificate in suicide prevention so she can teach faculty and staff how to spot a kid in trouble, what words to use, how to help. It's interesting to me that she chose a career that is so *helpful*. And it occurs to me that in some fundamental way, what she and Patrick do is not all that different.

Dana married a man who is a lot like her father. Brandon and Gary have the same oddball sense of humor, which is to say that most of their jokes are bad, a fact that never seems to bother either of them. They are both steady and loyal and kind.

Dana says she and her sister know what they deserve from a relationship because they saw in their father what men are supposed to be like. "I wasn't looking for a macho guy to sweep me off my feet; I was looking for a partnership," Dana told me during a family conversation that had us all sitting around the dining room table until well past midnight. "With Brandon I was able to just be me. He has that kind of non-judgmental, love-you-for-what-you-are attitude. He has never asked me to change. It was the true dedication dad has always shown to you. I have never felt a wavering of love for me."

Lauren shook her head in disbelief at this: "You and mom," she said in disgust, "got the last two good men left in America."

Dana, who was pregnant at the time with her first child, told us she had been spending a lot of time thinking about what kind of parents she and Brandon would be. Based on their experience with a very beloved dog, she figured she would be the one to set the rules and mete out the discipline; Brandon would be the playful one, the pushover. That was fine with her. She just wanted them both to be fully engaged in this business of raising a child. She wanted them to be in it together.

She would like to bring up her child, she said, the way she was brought up. When I asked her to describe what that was like, she surprised me. "You had very high expectations for us, but you didn't try to control us too much," she said. "We had a free and easy house. We knew where the boundaries were, but as long as we stayed within those boundaries, we were pretty free. You let me dress the way I wanted. You let dad carry a purse."

I had almost forgotten about that purse (a man's purse) that Gary carried for several years. My brothers still talk about how he had the nerve to show up in Nebraska carrying it. But more to the point, I had never thought of myself as a free and easygoing person. I was the kind of mother who insisted on meeting every one of my children's friends, who was not above listening in on their phone calls, and who once tracked Dana down in the middle of the night in Florence, Italy, calling every hostel in the city until I found her because she had failed to check in with me as promised. I did not, however, think this was the right moment to remind her of any of these things.

"We moved a lot, but it didn't feel like it broke things up," she went on. "Our lives moved in a predictable way; there was a rhythm to it. It was hard when we left behind best friends, but we had each other, and you always had only one best friend."

"Dad?" I asked.

"Dad," she said.

There was a pause around the table before Dana continued. "It's funny because dad isn't particularly religious, but Patrick looks at dad's life and sees God in it."

"Everywhere. All the time," Patrick chimed in. "I think it's a big part of the reason I can be a priest—because I see service as being part of being a man. A man can be somebody who just goes and does the dishes."

Gary, who had been characteristically quiet up to this point, piped up: "Well, someone has to do the dishes!"

"Dad is such a good person and raised such good people," Lauren said thoughtfully when the laughter died down. "Dad looks at his life and he just says, 'I did what I had to do, what I thought was right.'"

"That's God working within him," Patrick said. "There's a Jesuit prayer I love: 'Lord, teach me to be generous. Teach me to serve you as you deserve, to give and not to count the cost, to fight and not to heed the wounds, to toil and not to seek for rest, to labor and not to ask for reward ...' That's dad right there."

I wouldn't go so far as to call Gary a saint, but almost everyone else we know ends up joking that he comes close. My brothers and sisters are even more explicit. They call Gary a saint for being married to *me*. And my mother was not kidding in the least when she repeatedly told anyone who would listen: "Gary did such a good job with those kids!" (Part of me took this as a compliment, but at the same time, it's hard to ignore the fact that she left out any role I might have played.)

The truth is: He did do a good job. *We* did a good job. Our children have grown into accomplished, caring individuals who are working hard to make a difference in the world. We like to spend time with them, and, gratefully, they like to spend time with us.

Patrick points out that this is not something any of us should take for granted. He says it wasn't until he joined the Society that he began to realize how ruinous so many childhoods are. (As a priest, or priest-in-training, you apparently spend a lot of time listening to people talk about their screwed-up childhoods. Granted, it may be a skewed sample of humanity.)

He often thanks us for giving him such a happy childhood and for loving him unconditionally, even when we questioned his decisions. Like the one to become a Jesuit.

*   *   *   *

Gary and I have been slower than our children to return to the church of our childhoods. But we, too, now identify as Catholic, if only by default. I realized this a few years ago when filling out a form that asked for my religion. "Catholic," I wrote, almost without thinking. What other choice did I have?

But it's also true that it has become easier in recent years for me and other tenuous Catholics to realign ourselves with the church. This is in large part due to Pope Francis, who, instead of engaging in the same old polemics that have divided us for so long, simply asked: "Who am I to judge?" and spoke instead of crushing poverty, social inequality, and the idolatry of money. He championed migrants, stood up for the Ukraine, and demanded action to stem climate change. And while he arguably didn't go far enough to punish and prevent sexual predators in the church or to fully elevate women and LBTQ+ Catholics, there was indisputably progress. It remains to be seen what Pope Leo XIV will do, but the early signs are promising. "Never again war!" he cried out during his first Sunday appearance as pope. The next day he made it clear to the cardinals that he intends to carry on Francis' legacy of serving "the least and the rejected."

Some, of course, would not call any of this progress. They would gladly return to the days of Latin Masses and exclusionary doctrine. Patrick is not one of them. Everything about him these past few years has seemed more charged, more energized, and more hopeful. Pope Francis, I think, had something to do with that. And Patrick's newfound certainty about being a priest is surely a big part of it. But I also like to believe he is buoyed by us, his family, and our own inexorable, if uneven, movement toward the church he loves so much.

I sometimes think about all the families that have lost a loved one to death or distance, disagreement or dogma. Too often, they have no choice but to let go. But if there is a choice, if there is a way, these mothers and fathers and brothers and sisters would do whatever they could to hold on, even if it means going places they never meant to go and considering possibilities they would never otherwise have considered. That's what we did. We went with Patrick, haltingly and stumbling at times, but we went with him. We're still going with him.

When I consider the journey that has brought us to this point, I shake my head in disbelief. Much of it still makes no sense to me. I can't follow closely enough the trail of evidence, the how and why of one thing leading to the next thing and then the next and how it ended here, back where I started. But I know what Patrick would say.

He would tell me that none of this is an accident. He would say that God influences the course of our lives in the most ordinary ways and through the most unlikely people. If the way we raised him led him to be open to a different kind of life, led him in some way to God, and if that somehow influenced his sisters and us in our faith, why would I assume it was all chance?

"You can see it, mom," I can hear him saying. "You just need to pay attention."

CHAPTER 18

DAYS OF AWE

"Religion for many is becoming a lived and
constantly shifting experience rather than a
series of handed-down gestures and prayers."
KAYA OAKES, at ReligionDispatches.org

It did not require a miracle to bring me back to the Catholic
Church, but it did take just about every sacrament the church
has to offer.

The seven sacraments of the Catholic Church are rituals or ceremonies that follow the faithful through their lifetimes, beginning
with birth and ending with death. Some sacraments, like receiving
the Eucharist during Sunday Mass or Reconciliation to seek forgiveness for sins, may take place hundreds or even thousands of times
over the lifetime of a Catholic.

Other sacraments are meant to happen just once. Babies are
baptized, young people are confirmed as they pass from childhood
to adulthood, couples are married, men are ordained to the priesthood, and those who are about to die are anointed for the journey
ahead.

It makes sense to me that people feel an urge for God at such
critical passages in their lives. I have certainly felt that way. These are
the times when I am most in need of reassurance that everything will
be all right—that the child will be protected, that the relationship

will last, that a loved one will not be lost forever. These are the times when the need for hope overshadows the habit of doubt.

The final sacrament a Catholic can expect to receive is the Anointing of the Sick, during which a priest recites a prayer and anoints the person's forehead with holy oil. The sacrament may be given to the elderly and people living with a long or chronic illness or facing serious surgery. Those who are dying may receive Last Rites, which includes not just the Anointing of the Sick but also confession and communion when possible.

My dad was administered the sacrament three times—once just before he died in 2011 and twice during his hospitalization about ten years earlier when he was expected to die but (much to everyone's surprise, including his own) did not. My mother also survived well past her first encounter with this last sacrament but, in retrospect, I don't think there's anything very surprising about that. I don't believe she had the least intention of dying.

At my dad's funeral, my mother was wooden and stiff, impervious to emotion. I did my best to understand, to remind myself that there is no one right way to mourn. But after the family had dispersed and she was alone in the trailer she and my dad had shared for years, she began slipping slowly into depression. She stopped doing her beloved crossword puzzles and gave up driving and going to church. She turned down invitations to baptisms and missed family weddings. She skipped the funerals of her closest friends. She couldn't do it, she said, her bones hurt too much.

Eventually, her doctor prescribed anti-depressants, a stupendously bad idea, I thought, given her history of addiction. My mother, though, got exactly what I think she wanted. The drugs exaggerated her indifference. They helped her disappear.

* * * *

While my mother was arguably self-absorbed (most of my siblings would say indisputably, colossally self-absorbed), she was never materialistic. She never owned anything expensive in her life and seemed perfectly happy with second-hand couches and cast-off clothes. One Christmas my sisters and I gave her a gift certificate for a spa package, which clearly offended her. "I don't want that," she sniffed. "Whatever made you think I would go to a spa?"

Despite her seeming indifference, I sent her small gifts now and then—a fuzzy robe, a set of nail polishes, boxes of something sweet. Giving presents is one of the ways I show I care (just ask my children, who would point out that I go overboard every Christmas even though I keep promising not to).

My mother acknowledged these gifts only if I asked her about them. She often didn't seem to remember what her children gave her for her birthday or Christmas—or whether they gave her anything at all. Mother's Day, though, was different. She was proud of being the mother of eight children, and this was the one day she expected to be remembered.

On Mother's Day a year or so after my dad died, I realized I had forgotten flowers until it was too late to order them, but I knew she would at least expect a call. The phone rang a half a dozen times before she finally picked up. "What?" she said, the single word surfacing like forced air. "What do you want?" "It's Kris," I told her. "I'm calling to say happy Mother's Day." She hung up.

I called back, and when no one answered I called again, and then again. The third time, she picked up the receiver and, without saying a word, dropped it. By this time, I was seriously worried. As far as I knew, she hadn't started drinking again, but I recognized that wobbly voice on the phone, and it promised nothing good.

I started calling my sisters and brothers to see if anyone else had talked to her or seen her that morning. No one except my brother Creighton had yet tried. He said he had driven over to her trailer, but she was still in bed and refused to get up. She kept telling him to leave, so, after about half an hour of arguing with her, that's what he did. He had grown up seeing her drunk or drugged or both. He thought she just needed to sleep it off. But now the alarm had been sounded. One of my sisters headed to the house and found our mother in bed, unresponsive. She called an ambulance.

A week later, my mother was still in the hospital, and we still didn't have a clear explanation of what had happened. She had likely overdosed but on what the doctors could not say with any certainty. They did tell us she was weak and uncommunicative, badly dehydrated, and underweight. She almost certainly would not be able to live alone again.

Like most people nearing the age of eighty, my mom took a lot of pills, and she sometimes lost track of exactly how many she had taken and when. It's possible that she simply got confused and took too many, which is the version of events most of my family has elected to believe. But the more I thought about it, the less convinced I became. My mother lived alone and rarely left the house. Days would often pass without anyone in the family checking on her. Could it be a coincidence that she overdosed on Mother's Day—the one day she knew she would be getting calls, the one day she knew someone would come to visit?

Patrick, who was serving as assistant pastor of St. John's Parish at Creighton University at the time, went to the hospital to see her. He asked if she would like the Anointing of the Sick, but she refused to talk to him. She wouldn't even look at him. A few days later, he returned and asked the question again: "Grandma, do you want me to anoint you?" She didn't answer directly, and she still wouldn't make eye contact, although Patrick caught her looking at him when she didn't think he would notice. He felt she was aware, and she wasn't resisting, so he went ahead, making the sign of the cross on her forehead with the oil and saying, "Through this holy anointing, may the Lord in his love and mercy help you with the grace of the Holy Spirit." He then anointed her hands, saying, "May the Lord who frees you from sin save you and raise you up."

My mother did not rise up, but neither did she die. Instead, she was admitted to a nursing home outside of Omaha where she would spend the final six years of her life.

Her first roommate was a woman who seemed to have no family and rarely spoke. At night my mother could hear her weeping from the other side of the thin curtain that separated their beds. When I visited, I felt like weeping, too. "Don't let me end up in a place like that," I told my husband afterward. "Just shoot me." "Ditto," he said.

My mother, though, insisted she was just fine. The food was decent, and she almost always won at Bingo. She made new friends, and the old guys in wheelchairs told her she was pretty. The crying didn't bother her as much as it once did.

She spent a lot of time thinking about my dad and the life they had together. "He loved me so much," she told her children over and over. "I wish I had been nicer to him. I wish I had been a better wife."

We hushed her when she said these things. We told her dad wasn't the easiest person to live with, and we reassured her that he knew she loved him. But she knew the truth, and we knew it, too. My dad spent more than half a century seeking her approval. He was like a puppy—a big, slobbery puppy—who vied for attention in all the wrong ways. He would have been happy with an occasional pet. She gave him indifference.

Looking back, I think perhaps we should have let her speak freely about what she wished she had done differently. Regret, it seems to me, was the one clear, true thing in her life. She had a right to it.

* * * *

Repentance has long gone out of fashion. Even the word is seldom used any longer outside of a church or synagogue. But Catholics are still asked to repent their sins during the Sacrament of Reconciliation, which I knew as confession when I was a child. This usually consists of reciting your sins before a priest and asking for forgiveness.

Patrick says it's his favorite of all the sacraments because he believes that when people enter the confessional, they're anonymous and honest in ways they rarely are in ordinary life. They have no pretenses; they know exactly who they are. These people tell Patrick the most extraordinary things, the details of which he will not divulge even in a general way, even to his mother—even though I've asked. He is, he reminded me, bound by what the church calls the "seal of confession," an inviolable obligation to secrecy.

I'm sure Patrick helps many people who come to him for confession, and he's exactly the kind of priest I would want to tell my sins to if I were inclined to tell my sins to anyone. But, at least growing up, the whole thing had the feeling of an assembly line to me: You lined up to enter the forbidding box and, if you were lucky, you could be in and out in five minutes. If you took longer, you were apt to get curious looks from the people waiting behind you.

When it comes to repentance, I'm much more drawn to the Jewish Days of Awe, in part, I must admit, because Days of Awe may be the most awesome title ever given to any observance, religious or otherwise. The Days of Awe are also known as the Days of Repentance, which is not nearly as catchy a title but is perhaps more to the point. According to the Jewish Virtual Library, they are the ten days that start with the Jewish holiday of Rosh Hashanah and end with Yom Kippur, during which the faithful are to reflect on all the sins they have committed in the previous year.

The observance is based on the idea that God has books in which he has written our names and recorded what will happen to us in the coming year—who will live and who will die, who will do good and who will not. God writes all this down on Rosh Hashanah, the Day of Judgment, but the books are not sealed for ten days, leaving a small window in which to alter the outcome. There's still time to repent and pray and perform good deeds. There's still a chance to set things right with people you have wronged and, in so doing, persuade God to look upon you more favorably.

I love the idea of a God so personal he writes down our names in a book, a God so omniscient he knows exactly what is going to happen, and yet a God so generous he gives us all a second chance.

Patrick said something in one of his homilies that I think captures the essence of both the Catholic sacrament of Reconciliation and the Jewish Days of Awe. "It is explicitly because we trust in God's goodness and not our own that we have the outrageous courage to expose ourselves—individually and communally," he said. "Because we are ourselves both loved and sinners and because our church is both holy and broken ..."

Loved and sinners. Holy and broken. These are words that might comfort my mother. I know they comfort me.

Patrick would be happy if his message consoles, but I also know that he wants more than that. He has never been satisfied with mere comfort. He has, in fact, embraced discomfort as a way of life and likes nothing better than to ask unsettling questions designed to get others to think about things they might prefer not to think about— like what it means to expose ourselves to God and others and how much courage that takes. Outrageous courage, much like the kind of courage I think that it took for him to become a priest.

I am slowly building up my own courage, and the sacraments help. There have been a lot of them over these years—baptisms and confirmations, weddings and funerals, and Patrick's ordination, of course. Each one has eased me closer to the church. Each time I leave feeling a little more comfortable being Catholic.

I still chafe at the church's treatment of women and LGBTQ+ people and the excruciatingly slow pace of change. I still don't agree with a whole litany of teachings that seem to me both pigheaded and provincial. And I don't think I'll ever become reconciled to the music.

When I'm feeling discouraged, I repeat Patrick's words like a mantra: "Loved and sinners. Holy and broken." Yes, I tell myself, we could all do better, and we all need something to hold us together.

Sometimes necessity is what keeps you from flying apart. You have children to raise and work to do. You have enough crises to deal with every day without creating existential ones. You don't have time to ask questions and, anyway, you're pretty sure you already know the answers. But then something happens that makes you question everything and forces you to recognize the spaces in your life. I'm lucky that something was my son.

The old English translation of the word sacrament is "holy mystery," and that's the way I now think about religion in general and Catholicism in particular. It seems appropriate, given that for millennia religious leaders have had such a hard time explaining exactly what a sacrament is or what it means.

The Catholic Church bases its explanation on Saint Augustine's description of sacraments as "signs of the divine." Taking a cue from Augustine, the Council of Trent in the sixteenth century described them somewhat obliquely as "a visible sign of invisible grace." For a long time, Catholics and some Protestants insisted that sacraments are a means by which God bestows blessings, while other Protestants argued that they are simply a profession of faith by those who already have been granted God's grace. (These are the kinds of arguments that must have made people in the Middle Ages long for the Romans to return.)

I think it's safe to say that some things defy explanation, or at least defy explanations that satisfy everyone, that leave no room for doubt. God is one of them; our choice of religion is another.

Recognizing the presence of God, becoming Catholic again, has added mystery and wonder to my life. I've given up trying to know everything, and I'm beginning to accept what I can't possibly know, yet deeply feel. These are, without a doubt, my days of awe.

CHAPTER 19

CHANGING THE ENDING

"Yield up what scares you. Yield up what makes
you want to scream and cry. Enter into that
quiet. It's a cathedral. It's an empty football
stadium with all the lights on."
MARY KARR, *Lit*

A couple of days after the big news about Pope Benedict's decision to resign, I got an email from Lauren. It was Ash Wednesday, she wrote, and did I want to go with her to the 7 p.m. Mass?

I ignored the message and purposefully didn't pick up the phone when she called a little while later. I was hungry and tired and wanted to go home after a long day at work. Besides, it had been years since I had observed Ash Wednesday, which marks the start of forty days of Lent, the traditional Catholic season of fasting and penance that leads up to Easter.

Ash Wednesday is literally about ashes. You go to church with a perfectly clean forehead and walk out with a smudge of ashes in the shape of a cross on your brow. When we were children, we were taught the ashes signified that the season of Lenten mourning was about to begin, a season that would end with the crucifixion, death, and resurrection of Jesus. Furthermore, the ashes were to remind us of what the Bible told us we ourselves would become one day.

"Remember that you are dust, and to dust you shall return," the priest would intone as he traced a cross onto our brows.

Our ash crosses were applied during the morning children's Mass and were supposed to remain intact until bedtime. This presented the considerable challenge of getting through an entire day without once thoughtlessly resting your hand on your forehead, wiping your brow, or overzealously combing your bangs. Few of us managed to get past dinner with anything remaining but a big black smudge.

Ash Wednesday, with all its hazards, was an appropriate introduction to the even more serious business of Lent. All good Catholics, most especially children, were expected to give up something for Lent—and the harder it was to give it up, the better. My friends and I would debate for weeks about whether to sacrifice candy, soda, television, or dessert. All were excruciatingly hard to live without.

One year when I was nine or ten, I decided I would do something for Lent rather than do without something. I vowed to go to Mass every single day for forty days—forty-one counting Easter Sunday. This wasn't as difficult as it sounds, given that I already went to church six days a week—with my family on Sundays and with my classmates every morning before classes began at my Catholic elementary school. But it did mean adding Saturdays to the schedule.

I talked a couple of classmates and my sister Sandy into joining me, and we would set off every Saturday, walking the ten or twelve blocks to church to catch a morning Mass. Returning home one week, I was walking a little ahead of the rest of the group when I crossed a road, glanced up the street to my left, and saw a man standing next to his car in the middle of the road. He was wearing a dress. He looked straight at me, lifted the dress and began to pee. I did not necessarily take this as a sign from God, but the next year I decided I could live without candy after all.

Catholics are still encouraged to give up something for Lent, but the sacrifices demanded of the faithful seem less exacting than they used to be. Giving up your daily latte or turning off your cell phone for a day (imagine, an entire day!) appear to be perfectly acceptable options.

In a search for the unconventional, one Catholic website asked teens to share their ideas for "cool stuff they've done" for Lent. Teens, you'll be interested to know, have given up their beds, their shoes, forks and spoons, social media, and warm showers (although presumably not showers altogether). No one who has ever met a teenager will have any doubt as to which of the options on that list is the most difficult for them to live without.

The Episcopal Church, in which my children were raised, also observed the Lenten season, but it seemed to me a kinder, gentler form of Lent, aimed at encouraging children to say their prayers or refrain from sassing their parents. One year when Dana was in middle school, Gary and I convinced her to give up a single word for Lent. "So?" had become her favorite response to almost anything we said to her, and she could pack more disdain into that one syllable than most people can muster in a lengthy diatribe. "It's time for bed," I would tell her. "So-o-o-o?" she would retort. "You didn't eat your vegetables," Gary would observe. "So-o-o-o-o-o?" she would say.

When she was small, Lauren, who seemed to have no bad habits to give up for Lent, would forgo meat instead, but I took this more as a sign of social than religious consciousness. Now here she was, twenty-six years old and pestering me about going to Ash Wednesday services. I had avoided actually talking to her, but I knew she would be at St. Paul's, the Catholic church near our home in Phoenix, and after work that night, I found myself in the church parking lot.

I was late and the service was well under way when I edged my way into the church. I had thought it would be an easy matter to find Lauren, but the place was packed, and I didn't see her anywhere. I stood against the wall as hundreds of people lined up to be touched with ashes. "Well, I'm here," I thought. "I may as well join them."

Afterward, my forehead daubed with a thick black cross, I was thinking of slipping out before the rest of the crowd when I finally spotted Lauren. She made room on the seat beside her. "I'm glad you came," she said. I squeezed her hand and told her I was glad, too.

As we were leaving the church a little later, I asked her: "Why did you want to go to Ash Wednesday service?" She said she had made herself a promise to attend Mass during Lent. She was starting out with Ash Wednesday and planned to go each Sunday through Easter. I sighed, thinking this could only mean more Masses in my future.

But Lent still wasn't done with me. The next day, I was in a meeting when I saw Patrick's name flash across my phone. My daughters call me often, but Patrick's calls are much rarer, so I stepped out of the room to answer. "What's up?" I asked.

"I was at church and got ashes on my alb," he said. "Any idea how to get them out?"

An alb, I was pretty sure, is something priests wear, which undoubtedly means it is long and white and easily stained. I had no idea how to clean one, but I knew who probably did. "Take it to the dry cleaners," I told him.

"That will take too long," he objected. "Isn't there anything else I can do?"

I was standing in the middle of a reception area where several people were working and milling about. "Hey," I called out. "Anyone know how to get an ash stain out of clothes?"

Our office manager suggested the dry cleaners or, as an alternative, a bit of baking soda and water. "Baking soda; great idea," I said, and passed this information along to Patrick, who agreed to give it a try. Crisis averted, I told Patrick I had ordered a couple of books by Garry Wills. Had he seen *The New York Times* article about Wills' book *Why Priests? A Failed Tradition*?

Patrick hadn't, but he had seen Wills on Comedy Central's "The Colbert Report" on the same day Pope Benedict announced his resignation. Wills had argued that Catholics don't need priests.

Worse, Patrick said, his voice rising, Wills said he doesn't believe in transubstantiation.

"Transub-what?" I asked.

"Transubstantiation. You know—when the bread and wine in communion are turned into the body and blood of Christ. Wills actually said eating the Eucharist is like eating Jesus' arm. Can you believe that crap?"

Patrick was pretty worked up by this time, but I couldn't resist asking why this transubstantiation thing was such a big deal. Why couldn't communion be just as valid as a metaphor, a way to remember and reenact what Christ taught?

"There are lots of ways to understand how Christ is present in the Eucharistic," Patrick replied, "but Wills isn't interested in having a conversation about that. He's just being an intellectual bully. He's going on national TV and breaking apart people's faith without offering anything in return."

This clearly required a longer conversation, but I had to get back to my meeting, so I told Patrick to let me know if the baking soda worked and promised to call him later. As I put away my phone, I couldn't help but laugh: Who else gets a call in the middle of a workday asking how to remove ashes from a priestly garment and ends up in a discussion about transubstantiation?

It had been a week unusually filled with things Catholic—the pope's resignation, Ash Wednesday, Lenten promises, and stains on albs among them. But then, my life, in a reversal of the usual parent-child roles, seems to have been moving steadily in this direction for a long time.

Whenever I think I have left the church behind, my children are there to pull me back. They are Catholic—and religious—in ways that seem permanent and inextricably part of who they are. I have only to look at their tattoos to remember this fact. Despite my strong objections, Patrick had a rather substantial Celtic cross—exactly like the one he had given his grandpa in the hospital—tattooed between his shoulder blades. Dana has a tiny cross etched on her hip, and Lauren has a trio of bird wings nestled on her rib cage. She says they are the ancient female representation of God.

It was for my children and for Patrick, in particular, that I started writing this book. Since the day I left him at the novitiate in St. Paul, worrying vaguely that he had entered some kind of cult, I have struggled to understand what he so clearly accepts as truth. I have been forced to question my own truths because I knew that if I didn't, I would be the one left behind.

I do not mean this in an end-of-the-world-bodies-rising-into-heaven sense; I was simply a mother worried about losing her son. The signs were clear. With each passing year, Patrick was becoming more and more Catholic, more and more *Jesuit*, and we had less and less to say to one another. He would talk about how he felt when he prayed, about how close it made him feel to God, and Gary and I could barely refrain from rolling our eyes. Patrick began talking less about the things that matter most to him.

Gary and I are not the kind of people who bring up God in conversation. I have trouble bringing up God even when convention calls for it. "We're thinking of you," I'll write on a sympathy card to a friend or relative when someone more devout (or less self-conscious) would write: "We're praying for you."

When my father was hospitalized for the last time, my mother suggested we all say a rosary for him. There were ten or so of us gathered in his hospital room—my brothers and sisters, some of their spouses, and a spattering of their children. As my mother bent her head and started the first "Our Father," two of my sisters and one of their husbands moved to her side and began to pray with her. The rest, me included, hung back, silent and a little embarrassed, as if someone had just asked us to take off our clothes in public. Even then, I knew I couldn't hang back forever. If Patrick had been there, he would have been leading the prayer. I had to decide: Was I in or was I out?

I was comfortable being out. It had been a long time since I had thought of myself as Catholic, years since I had thought seriously about religion. But Patrick had changed that, and he wanted more from me than some kind of neutral blessing. He wanted a relationship that wasn't possible unless I also made room for God—or at least the possibility of God. The alternative, it seemed to me, was one of increasing distance: We would become the kind of family for whom the only safe topics are what teams have the best chance of making the World Series and what we should have for dinner.

I had to change the ending.

This book began as a kind of internal monologue, an argument with myself that eventually turned into a conversation with my son. Make that many conversations. We have spent hours discussing how much damage the Catholic Church has inflicted and whether it can ever recover, the illogic of letting children decide for themselves what religion they will follow without first giving them any kind of religious grounding, and whether people are intrinsically good or bad.

In these discussions, Patrick is almost invariably the absolutist, and I am the relativist. When I question whether a belief in God is necessary to live a good life, he tells me that either Nietzsche is right, or Jesus is right. Either life means nothing, or it means everything. "There is no in between," he says. "Nothing else makes sense."

When I tell him I wish I could be as certain as he is, he says certainty isn't what's important. Doubt is not the problem. This comes as quite a surprise. I had thought the whole point of what we had been talking about was to dispel uncertainty, to clear away the doubt.

"A lot of people think that believing is about being certain about God and the church, and it's really not," Patrick says. "There are things a lot more important than certainty."

"Like what?" I ask.

"Like being willing to enter into a relationship with God."

I know he is waiting for my response, and I don't want to hurt him. But I also know that I owe him the truth, so I say as gently as I can, "I'm not sure God will ever seem like a person to me."

"But you're asking the right questions," he says brightly, not ready to give up on me or God. "You just have to be open to the unexpected answers."

I look at him and smile. That, I tell him, is something I can do.

EPILOGUE

hen my mother first told me she was writing a book about me, the whole project struck me as exceptionally weird.[1] What kind of mother, after all, finds her son's journal from high school and not only reads it but takes passages and puts them into a book years later? Was there any way, I found myself wondering, for me to stop this?

It turns out that there was not. And now it seems that all that weirdness-*in-potentia* has come screaming into the present.[2]

Fortunately, my worries were, mostly, unfounded. And the reason for this is because, as you now know as well as I do, this is not actually a book about me, but a book about us. It took a lot of talking and writing and thinking (for her), and a lot of reading and editing and talking (for me), to realize this. But we did, and it's true. It's a book about us. And that has been a great gift.

Which does not mean that there weren't times when it was awkward or jarring to see myself through my mother's eyes. She has me saying things I swear I don't say—at least anymore—and, of course, I

---

[1] Lauren and Dana teased me pretty much nonstop about the fact that mom was writing a book "about me" and not one about them. "Sibling rivalry!!!"

[2] I would be tempted to label this book a 2014 version of Augustine's "Confessions" written by Saint Monica, only neither my mom nor I are saints, and it doesn't have nearly enough Christian neo-Platonic undertones (or guilt over peach thievery) for the analogy to really hold.

wanted to "correct" them.[3] As I read, I had to keep reminding myself that it's okay not to have been born already completed and that I need not pretend that I am perfect. I think this is a sign of growth, an indication that the years and years of Jesuit formation have begun their work on me.

Still, there are some things that no amount of time could have prepared me for. I mean, what am I supposed to say about having been baptized on a day when the clouds were so thick that the sun seems to have broken through only once? And the rays of sunshine fell onto me? Just as the priest poured the water? What can you say about a story like that?

Some of my mother's stories felt to me like poems: My grandpa twirling my grandma around the sticky kitchen floor; my dad's Jesus-hair and the frayed jean jacket he wore when my parents first met. I'd stop for a second and let those scenes coat my heart like a good Scotch.[4] Other stories surprised me; there were just so many things I didn't know. My rational, too-intense, always-another-question, journalist mother, had once wanted to be a saint? She had stared at the statue of the Virgin, pleading: "Blink!"?

And there were things I knew but didn't fully understand. Like my mom making the terrible, life-saving choice to move out of her family's house, to leave her brothers and sisters behind in the detritus and go to college. Imagining her, all of eighteen years old, hugging them goodbye and climbing into her car and not coming back for a year—a year—hurt. It just hurt. And it hurt even more when I realized that it's because of what she did that I have never been asked to make such a choice.

Other times, her words would make me feel uncomfortable or sad,

---

[3] When my mom describes our conversations, she often concludes with a question that I've asked her. I hope the tone of those questions doesn't make me sound like a pedantic jackass. I really don't mean them that way. Speaking of tone and being a jackass, who says things like "sit with" or "aspiring to benefices" anyway? Jesuits, that's who. Ugh, it's so annoying to become a stereotype of yourself.

[4] I'm a Jesuit; we get to make Scotch analogies.

as when she described her experience of the prayer class we attended by saying that she "felt like a fifth grader being forced to watch a sex education video; it made me want to avert my eyes." I let go of a breath after reading that sentence and did my best to do the same with my desire to do something to correct her impression *this minute*.

And, yes, there are a few issues on which I would like to set the record straight. First among those is this: I do not think being a Jesuit or a priest is harder than being married, or holier. It's not, and for a priest or a religious to say otherwise only reveals a lack of understanding of how hard real relationships are—and how fragile our own vocations can be. And I don't think that something has to be hard or painful to be good, just that the things that are most good in this world are often only experienced on the other side of sacrifice.

Speaking of sacrifice, I have to admit that it's ... well, irreplaceable what this choice to live celibately has taken from me—namely a family and the daily intimacy within which family life is lived. But I love my students, and on my desk I have pictures of my beautiful niece and nephews. The other night I went to a minor league baseball game with two college friends and played with their combined seven kids. I once launched a fake Twitter war with former Pope Francis to see who could kiss more babies (I lost approximately 340,620 to 17).

It is not all darkness. There is light. And, in addition to the reality of human intimacy that surrounds me in forms other than family, that light comes primarily through the fierce and persistent love of Jesus, who just will not let me go. He will not leave me alone. And I could not be more grateful.

And, yes, yes, the Catholic Church is a flawed institution, as are all institutions, religious or otherwise. The question is not whether the flaws are real but whether any of them are worth the investment we put into them—and not in a cost/benefit financial analysis kind of way. Instead, I think we ought to ask ourselves what is, ultimately and finally, true? Even more, how can we align ourselves with that truth, not just mentally and not just emotionally, but habitually, all the way, through and through? That's the big thing. And it's what I think the church really is —not an institution but a way of trying, together, to live the truth in love. It's something like this that I hear as I read my mom's words: "I have discovered it's easier to reject the church when I can hold it at a distance. Close up, the flaws are much harder to see." I hear her making inside her heart a space for those other people who compose the body of Christ.

But the most beautiful part of the book, by my lights, comes near the end. As both her son and a priest, I wanted my mom to close this book differently than she began it, i.e., not with lines about me but with a statement about her own relationship to God. That was *my* goal—that this book you hold would end up being not about me (or even about *us*, me and her) but that it would be about her and God. And as you know by now, having read her last words, that's not what happens, at least not exactly.

What does happen, so deeply that I almost missed it, is that she has written this entire book because she was utterly unwilling to allow our relationship—hers and mine, I mean—to wither. These pages exist because God existed only at the edges of her life but at the center of mine. Which meant that as I centered more and more of my life on God, that center drifted to the edge of hers. I didn't intend for this drift to happen. Mine wasn't an intentional choice. But hers was.

How archetypically motherly is it to do whatever it takes to love one's child in all their choices? Even when what it takes is to change again and again?[5] There is ferociousness in such a radical and ascetical willingness to change. My own life more or less comes down to a response to having been loved like that—by her, by others, by God. I hope you have felt love like that, too. It's what I want my whole life to be about. It's why I am a priest today, why I want more than anything (more than having a family, more than having a polished persona) to be a conduit of that immense and merciful love that

[5] "Again" because isn't that what she has been doing my entire life? Being willing to become the version of herself that could be a good mother to me at four years old, and when I turned twelve, and then at twenty, and again now?

precedes us and follows us on our way. This is what Saint Augustine called the *vera religione*, the true religion, the kind that Jesus talked about over and over again in His own life. True religion is the communal structuring of love given not out of obligation but because it is the only adequate response to our having been loved first. This is what my mother has done for me and in me. It's what I know how to do because of the "us" she helped create.

Still, there is an unwritten question to which this book is the beginning of an answer: Exactly who is included in that "us"? Certainly, it includes the two of us, certainly my sisters and her siblings, and my dad, and her parents. But Jesus? God? Is God included? Are my Jesuit brothers? Who is us? At heart, this book is about that question and the effort she has made—and is still making—to answer it.

When she broke the rules and called me from her desert retreat, she writes that I ended the conversation by talking about how God is the most important thing in my life, how badly I wanted her to be open to her own version of what I have experienced. In response, she wrote: "His words feel to me like a blessing and a rebuke. I can't give up yet."

This is enough. Even though I always want more, it is enough.

In writing this book, my mom has offered me the chance to have the kinds of discussions I crave like an addict—discussions about the meaning of life, about what prayer is, about who God is, and why the church might be relevant. We have learned to love each other better and more fully. Our lives have been brought into tighter orbit. What a perfectly motherly gift.

It is also perfectly motherly to allow another to have the last words. I want to use them to say thank you. So, thanks, mom. Thanks for saying "yes" as much as you can. Thanks for being open to God in order to be a little more open to me. Thanks for "us" not being done yet.

Patrick Gilger, SJ

ACKNOWLEDGMENTS

Because this book covers a period of more than two decades, people are often described as they were years ago when the events and conversations I relate took place. But, of course, people are rarely frozen in time, which calls for a few updates.

First, my family. Lauren did find one of the "last good men in America," and he decided to convert to Catholicism in the long runup to the wedding. Together, the two of them completed the Rite of Christian Initiation of Adults, better known as RCIA, which means they are both now officially Catholics. And, happily, Patrick was ordained in time to perform their wedding. Lauren and Jesse now have three beautiful little boys.

Dana, who was pregnant with her first child when I started writing this book, had a wonderful baby girl, followed a few years later by an equally wonderful boy, all of which makes me the very happy grandmother of five grandchildren (and pretty much lets Patrick off the hook).

Karen Sullivan and Diane Sundrup also got their wish for grandchildren. Karen has five now and Diane has two, incontrovertible proof, in my eyes at least, that God is good.

A number of the priests who appear in these pages have gone on to other duties. Patrick's best friend, Jeff Sullivan, was ordained in 2020 at the height of the COVID-19 pandemic and is now assistant director of campus ministry at Creighton University, where he and

Patrick met and first got interested in the Jesuits. Only a few dozen people, Patrick among them, were allowed to attend the ordination. I tried to make up for my absence by sending Jeff the best present I could think of—two tickets to a Nebraska football game.

Patrick's other good friends, Fathers Sam Sawyer and Eric Sundrup, both served stints as editor of *The Jesuit Post,* which continues to flourish. Sam went on to be editor-in-chief of *America Media,* and Sundrup is associate vice president of mission and ministry at Xavier University in Cincinnati, where he grew up. Eric and Patrick produce a video series called *Jesuit Autocomplete* in which they answer questions like: Why does God allow natural disasters? And why does the Catholic Church have so many rules? It is exactly up their alley.

Father John Auther, who so gracefully led the spiritual retreat I was part of, has left the desert to join the pastoral staff of the Jesuit Retreat Center in Los Altos, California. And Father Warren Sazama, who my husband still holds responsible for recruiting Patrick to the Jesuits, retired after fifty years from full-time ministry, although he doesn't seem to have slowed down a bit. For one thing, he's superior (i.e. the house boss) of a Jesuit community in Minneapolis.

Bob Brave Heart, who was superintendent of Red Cloud Indian School during the years Patrick spent at Pine Ridge, continues to serve as a senior vice president. In 2021, the school was awarded the $1 million Opus Laureate prize in recognition of the work that Brave Heart and his colleague, Peter Klink, SJ, have done to address poverty and injustice.

Brother Bill Foster, who for so many years kept the school running in different but equally important ways, left the reservation in 2013 to live at the St. Camillus Jesuit retirement community in Wauwatosa, Wisconsin. He died four years later. Patrick still has the rosary that Brother Bill prayed every night. He carries it with him on days when he feels he needs some special support. Brother Mike Zimmerman remains at Red Cloud, where there is always work to be done and prayers that need to be said.

Patrick's rebel hero, Father Daniel Berrigan, lived and worked in New York City until he died in 2016 at the age of ninety-five. Patrick concelebrated his funeral Mass at St. Francis Xavier Parish in Chelsea. And Lauren's hero, Sister Elizabeth Johnson, is now Distinguished Professor Emerita of Theology at Fordham University. I can only hope that she's still asking uncomfortable questions.

Father George Murphy carries on as a teacher and spiritual director at the Jesuit School of Theology at Santa Clara University. And as far as I can tell, Jim Fogarty—he of the floor-length robe made entirely out of pieces of jeans who introduced Patrick to one of Chicago's most notorious housing projects—still walks unafraid among the city's gangs.

I retired from the Walter Cronkite School of Journalism and Mass Communication at Arizona State University in 2023 after sixteen years in various roles, including associate dean and interim dean. Working with college students for so long was a great gift; spending time with my grandchildren is an even greater one. Lauren's three little boys are with us nearly every day, at the end of which I am almost always assured of finding rocks in my pockets. They don't weigh me down in the slightest.

I owe all of the people named in this book and many others associated with the Catholic Church gratitude for sharing a small part of their lives and their faith with me. I owe my husband, especially, and my entire family—the one I came from and the one I helped create—infinitely more. Thank you.

MORE READING

In preparing to write this book, I read everything I could find about the Society of Jesus and a good deal more that dealt with spirituality in general and the Catholic Church in particular. My son contributed additional suggestions for those who are interested in knowing more.

Barry, William A., SJ, and Doherty, Robert G., SJ, *Contemplatives in Action: The Jesuit Way* (Paulist Press, 2002).

Augustine, Saint; *The Confessions of Saint Augustine* (Harper, 2022). (Project Gutenberg also has made this available online.)

Brackley, Dean, *The Call to Discernment in Troubled Times: New Perspectives on the Transformative Wisdom of Ignatius Loyola* (Crossroad Publishing, 2004).

Burke, Kevin F., *Pedro Arrupe: Essential Writings* (Orbis Books, 2004).

Cahill, Thomas, *Desire of the Everlasting Hills: The World Before and After Jesus* (Anchor, 2001).

Collins, David J., *The Jesuits in the United States: A Concise History* (Georgetown University Press, 2023).

Doyle, Brian, *A Book of Common Prayer, 100 Celebrations of the Miracle and Muddle of the Ordinary* (Sorin Books, 2022).

Farley, Margaret A., *Just Love: A Framework for Christian Sexual Ethics* (Continuum, 2008).

Friedrich, Markus, *The Jesuits: A History* (Princeton University Press, 2022).

Gilger, Patrick, SJ, (ed.), *The Jesuit Post* (Orbis Books, 2014).

Harter Michael, SJ, (ed.), *Hearts on Fire: Praying with Jesuits* (Loyola Press, 1993).

Hendra, Tony, *Father Joe: The Man Who Saved My Soul* (Random House, 2005).

Hsia, R. Po-chia, *A Jesuit in the Forbidden City: Matteo Ricci, 1552-1610* (Oxford University Press, 2012).

Idigoras, Jose Ignacio Tellechea, trans. Cornelius Michael Buckley, SJ, *Ignatius of Loyola: The Pilgrim Saint* (Loyola Press, 1994).

Johnson, Elizabeth A., *She Who Is: The Mystery of God in Feminist Theological Discourse* (Crossroad Publishing, 2002).

Karr, Mary, *Lit: A Memoir* (Harper Perennial, 2010).

Kunkel, Thomas, *Enormous Prayers: A Journey into the Priesthood* (Westview Press, 1998).

Lamott, Anne, *Traveling Mercies: Some Thoughts on Faith* (Anchor, 2000).

Manney, Jim (ed.), *Charged with Grandeur: A Book of Ignatian Inspiration* (Loyola Press, 2011).

Martin, James, SJ, *In Good Company: The Fast Track from the Corporate World to Poverty, Chastity and Obedience* (Sheed & Ward, 2010).

Martin, James, SJ, *My Life with the Saints: Tenth Anniversary Edition* (Loyola Press, 2016).

Martin, James, SJ, *The Jesuit Guide to (Almost) Everything: A Spirituality for Real Life* (HarperOne, 2012).

Martin, Malachi, *The Jesuits: The Society of Jesus and the Betrayal of the Roman Catholic Church* (Simon & Schuster, 1988).

McGreevy, John T., *American Jesuits and the World: How an Embattled Religious Order Made Modern Catholicism Global* (Princeton University Press, 2018).

McDonough, Peter, and Bianchi, Eugene C., *Passionate Uncertainty: Inside the American Jesuits* (University of California Press, 2002).

Merton, Thomas, *Life and Holiness* (Image, 1969).

Merton, Thomas, *The Seven Storey Mountain: An Autobiography of Faith* (HarperOne, 1999).

Moore, Thomas, *Care of the Soul: A Guide for Cultivating Depth and Sacredness in Everyday Life* (Harper Perennial, 1994).

Norris, Kathleen, *The Cloister Walk* (Riverhead Books, 1997).

Oakes, Kaya, *Radical Reinvention: An Unlikely Return to the Catholic Church* (Counterpoint, 2012).

O'Malley, John W., *The First Jesuits* (Harvard University Press, 1993).

O'Malley, John W., *The Jesuits: A History from Ignatius to the Present* (Roman & Littlefield, 2017).

O'Malley, William J., *The Fifth Week: Second Edition* (Loyola Press, 1998).

Rizzi, Michael T., *Jesuit Colleges and Universities in the United States: A History* (Catholic University of America Press, 2022).

Rohr, Richard, *Falling Upward, Revised and Updated: A Spirituality for the Two Halves of Life* (Jossey-Bass, 2023).

Rolheiser, Ronald, *The Holy Longing: The Search for a Christian Spirituality* (Image Books, 2009).

Russell, Mary Doria, *The Sparrow* (Ballantine Books, 1997).

Silf, Margaret, *Just Call Me Lopez: Getting to the Heart of Ignatius Loyola* (Loyola Press, 2012).

Silf, Margaret, *Simple Faith: Moving Beyond Religion as You Know It to Grow in Your Relationship with God* (Loyola Press, 2012).

Steinfels, Peter, *A People Adrift: The Crisis of the Roman Catholic Church in America* (Simon & Schuster, 2004).

Swarns, Rachel L., *The 272: The Families Who Were Enslaved and Sold to Build the American Catholic Church* (Random House, 2024).

Traub, George W., *A Jesuit Education Reader: Contemporary Writings on the Jesuit Mission in Education, Principles, the Issue of Catholic Identity, Practical Applications of the Ignatian Way, and More* (Loyola Press, 2008).

Wills, Garry, *Why I Am a Catholic* (Mariner Books, 2003).
Wills, Garry, *Why Priests? A Failed Tradition* (Penguin, 2014).

www.ingramcontent.com/pod-product-compliance
Lightning Source LLC
Jackson TN
JSHW021512061225
94221JS00001B/1